Books by the Author

FICTION

Full Snow Moon

Something's Lost and Must be Found: Seven Short Tails on a Long Leash

When We Fostered Furley (A Collar and a Dream Book)

NON-FICTION

Dog's Best Friend: Will Judy, Founder of National Dog Week and Dog World Publisher

Around the World in 1909

Around the World in 1909

Harriet White Fisher and Her Locomobile

Lisa Begin-Kruysman

Copyright © 2014 Lisa Begin-Kruysman

All rights reserved. No part of this book may be transmitted in any form by any means electronic, mechanical or otherwise using devices now existing or yet to be invented without prior written permission from the publisher and copyright holder.

American History Press

Staunton, Virginia

(888) 521-1789

Visit us on the Internet at:

www.Americanhistorypress.com

ISBN 13: 978-1-939995-07-0

Library of Congress Control Number: 2014957369

Manufactured in the United States of America on acid-free paper. This book meets all ANSI standards for archival quality.

TABLE OF CONTENTS

Foreword	ix
Preface	xi
Dedication	xv
Acknowledgements	xvii
Prologue	xix
Ewing, New Jersey, August 2013	1
Tea and Cake with the Anvil Queen	5
The Rise of the Lady Iron Master	9
The Travels of a Royal Personage	13
Heading Into the Sun	17
Car Meets Devil's Bridge	23
The Hospitality of the Italians	27
"Honk Honk Must Not Be Forgotten!"	31
"I shall be very pleased to send you a card from Calcutta"	35
Wild Nights in the Jungle	41
A Royal Reception at the Gwalior State	49
On to Delhi	53
The Gracious Hospitality of Judge Motilal Nehru	57
His Highness of Benares and the Burning Ghats	69
A Rough River Crossing and a Brush with Brigands	75
On the Road to Calcutta	83
Bidding Namaste to India	87
Sir Thomas Lipton and Billikins the Monkey	93
A Guarded Tour of Shanghai	99
"I fear, Mrs. Fisher, you do not know what you are up against."	105
Honkie meets Billikins	109
Touring with the Emperor's Blessings	117
Crossing the Raging Rapids	123
"The Female Napoleon"	131
"The Talk of Tokyo"	137

Sailing Homeward	147
A Farewell to the Royal Family	151
Officer Ketchum and the Corruption in Cleveland	169
The Extra Lap	175
Epilogue	187
Bibliography	201
Index	205
About the Author	211

FOREWORD

From the time I was a little girl, the story of *Around the World in 1909: Harriet White Fisher and Her Locomobile* has been a part of my family's story, especially since we lived with many of the artifacts from the trip in our home. I remember family members speaking with pride about the excitement and dangers of this miraculous journey around the world at the beginning of the automobile industry in the early 1900s. And, of course, in the middle of the entire story was always my grandfather, Harold Fisher Brooks. This marvelous narrative you are about to read brings this incredible tale to life with all the great adventures and pitfalls the travelers faced on a thirteen-month journey across four continents.

Harold Fisher Brooks, my grandfather, served in the position as the chauffeur for this world tour. He also took about 250 photographs, hunted for pheasant and pigeon, arranged for the shipping of all gasoline and oil, figured out how to get across all waterways, and generally served as the fix-it guy for anything that went wrong. I remember him as a tall, six-foot-two, distinguished-looking gray-haired gentleman. He always wore a suit and tie, and never came to the dinner table without his suit jacket on. This did not harmonize with the description of him always getting dirty with oil and grease, but I did notice he always did the driving for our family.

Unfortunately, I wasn't ever able to talk to him about the trip since he died when I was eight years old. But in my early teens, I was able to visit the house that Harriet once lived in since it was close by in Ewing Township, New Jersey. Although relatives of Harriet's second husband lived there at the time I visited, it was still Harriet's house to me. My siblings and I had a name for a room off the main corridor since it held so many of the treasures that Harriet brought back from her trip. The "Throne Room" contained a huge, massive chair on a pedestal in the middle of the room, and it was surrounded by huge vases, tapestries, and large tropical plants. The house was a great mansion, but the Throne Room was the magical space of another time for us.

Foreword

My mom, who was one of Harold's daughters, inherited one of the horns that had been kept at the front of the car. My siblings and I often blew it since it sounded like a duck and caused our dog to begin howling. In our front hallway, holding our mail, we always kept the huge Chinese bowl Harriet had purchased as one of her many souvenirs of the trip. By my early teens my mother had begun to print and duplicate the photos that my grandfather took. I still have my favorite pictures from his trip hanging on my walls. This was the time when I really grew completely interested in all aspects of the journey.

For the last four decades I have researched, catalogued, discovered, and written about this unique excursion by four people, a dog, and a monkey. There was a time when I was hoping that my generation of the grandchildren and also the following generation of great-grandchildren of Harold Brooks would try to duplicate the trip around the world on the one-hundredth anniversary of the trip. We would travel to all of the same locations and try to take photographs of the same spots exactly one hundred years later to compare the differences. Sadly that date has passed, and yet I still find I am excited with each new discovery I make. So, instead of taking my own world tour, I will be happy to assist others in discovering this wonderful story.

Lisa Begin-Kruysman reached out to me after an article appeared in our local newspaper. I had initiated a story about the one-hundred-year anniversary of Harriet Fisher returning to Trenton, New Jersey at the end of her journey. Since then she and I have searched the files at the Trentoniana Room of the Trenton Library to locate new information about Harriet and Harold. As each of us discovers new sources on the Internet or from living people, we have shared and discussed our findings. It has been a pleasure for me to have a new friend who is as driven as I am to find the truth.

In these pages Lisa Begin-Kruysman has brought to life the wonderful adventures of *Around the World in 1909: Harriet White Fisher and Her Locomobile*. Harriet Fisher was clearly ahead of her time; her boldness and bravery were unusual for 1909. Yet my grandfather's skill and resourcefulness made her trip possible. As in all great stories, the characters drive the narrative and the forward motion of the narrative. And in this amazing story, both Harriet and Harold actually *drove a car all the way around the world!*

Rebecca Urban
Granddaughter of Harold Fisher Brooks

PREFACE

When I started writing this book I intended it for a middle-grade readership, but I should have known I was on the wrong track (no pun intended) when a fifth grader, disappointed with a synopsis of the book, stated, "I thought you were going to tell us a *real* story!"

The young readers thought this account of a woman driving her car through jungles over a century ago had to be fiction. I became aware that my audience and focus needed to change because Harriet White Fisher's accomplishment was too complex for most youngsters to really appreciate and understand.

When adults heard that I was writing the story of Trenton, New Jersey's very own Harriet White Fisher and her revolutionary world-wide automobile voyage, I often received wary questions: *How* was it that *I* came to learn about this intrepid woman, *what* made *me* worthy to tell her story, and (asked mostly by males) *how* did Harriet obtain a consistent supply of gasoline and motor oil in the most remote regions of the world, even by today's standards, in which she, and her entourage, traveled in 1909?

It all came about with a chance viewing of an episode of *Antiques Road Show* while channel-surfing. I was intrigued by a photograph of a group of women standing by a very old automobile as the announcer relayed that these women were the first to have traversed the continental United States in an automobile. The travelers were identified as Alice Huyler Ramsey, one of her close friends, and Alice's two sisters-in-law.

I was surprised when I learned that Alice and I had both grown up in the city of Hackensack, New Jersey, and we both had graduated from that city's high school, even if several decades apart.

A book about Alice had already been written for elementary school readers, so I set about writing one for adults. Soon, I found myself taking another detour as the name of Harriet White Fisher kept popping up during my research, a woman about whom no book had *ever* been written by anyone but Harriet herself, over one hundred years earlier.

At a Highlight's Foundation Founder's Workshop on writing children's literature I was encouraged by an editor to pursue Harriet's story. I realized that any book I might produce would be meant for a mature audience, readers interested in women's and automotive history, and those who just wished to be inspired by this intriguing tale. I christened the project *eat, pray, drive*, inspired by another New Jersey-based author and adventurous world-traveler, Elizabeth Gilbert, and got to work.

Soon after that writer's workshop, a fellow-attendee sent me an article from the *Trentonian* newspaper about Harriet's trip, and also reporting that Harriet's beloved farm, Bella Vista, had just been demolished, a terrible loss as far as many were concerned. I contacted the reporter and he graciously put me in touch with Becky Urban, the granddaughter of Harold Brooks, the young man who served as Harriet's loyal driver, mechanic, and jack-of-all trades during her 20,000 mile plus "Joy Ride."

When I told Becky that I was writing a book length account of the world-wide auto trip, she was eager to help. She soon became a valued partner in my research and a good friend.

What a thrill it was to arrive at her home in Ewing, New Jersey one warm summer day, to find a roomful of the wonderful artifacts brought back from that historic trek: camping gear, a tea pot, boots, and even the horn and American flag proudly displayed on the front of Locomobile. With Becky's help and encouragement, I finally felt that my project was on the right path.

On a personal level, I could relate to Harriet's and Alice's respective quests for a memorable road trip. In 1973, when I was thirteen, my parents informed myself and my siblings to begin packing for a journey to Boulder, Colorado, since my father had been granted a one-year academic sabbatical at the University of Colorado. And, like Harriet, we would be traveling with our own canine mascot, a hyperactive and gassy toy poodle named Cocoa Puff.

Ah, but there were differences in our trip. While it took Harriet and her crew over a month to drive from Colorado to the East Coast, our family made the trip in three days. On the American portion of her trip, Harriet was surprised that she often had to camp under the stars or stay at some dirty, run down poor excuse for accommodations serving bad food. My family, on the other hand, had the advantage of comfortable, clean hotel

Preface

rooms, complete with pools and decent restaurants. We had detailed travel plans from AAA with maps (GPS had not yet been invented), while Harriet had to rely on sketchy directions offered by a "Blue Book" or obtained from locals, some of whom did not wish her well.

Besides living vicariously through Harriet's exotic travels during the writing process, I came to bond with this unlikely, but intrepid, team of travelers. A British butler, an Italian maid, two translators, and of course the handsome and talented Harold Brooks, who never got over the wonder of this trip of a lifetime.

As a dog-centric author and blogger, I was glad to learn that Harriet loved pets. They were a constant joy to her, and she considered them a priority no matter where her travels led. And as far as the inquiry about obtaining gas and motor oil along the way, Harriet and Harold were pretty clever. Their ingenuity gave me some interesting moments to include in my narrative.

Harriet White Fisher's travels, and those of my family, may have been initiated for different reasons, and experienced under decidedly diverse conditions, but both journeys were taken in the same spirit of adventure, and both brought new appreciation for taking the road less traveled.

For my parents, Jack and Cindy Begin
Who instilled in me the belief that anything is possible

ACKNOWLEDGEMENTS

This story could not have been told with such vibrant detail and imagery without the diligence and generosity of Becky Urban, the dedicated granddaughter of Harold Brooks. For many years Becky had desired to have the tale of this remarkable trip shared with the world. Her generous contributions of the photos contained in this book make the journey come alive. Becky wishes to credit her siblings and cousins, who are also custodians of this photographic collection. They are, alphabetically, Chris Avallone, David Brooks, Gordon Brooks, Gregory Brooks, John Burton, Pamela Burton, Richard Burton, Donna Culbertson, Debora Markovitz, Carol Thomas, Phil Urban, and Ginger Whitehead. A note of thanks is also extended to Jack Koeppel, Photographer and Historical Preservationist, whose skills perfected the photographs taken by Harold Brooks during his worldwide trek by transferring the images from glass-plate negatives.

Much appreciation is also extended to Robert Sands, Past Director of The Trenton Museum at Ellarslie, Richard Willinger, President of the Board of Trustees, Trenton Museum at Ellarslie, and Karl Flesch, Board of Trustees, Trenton Museum at Ellarslie, for their hard work and dedication on the museum exhibit "Trenton Entourage Motors Around the World in 1909" presented during the summer of 2013, and to the American Automobile Association (AAA) for their contribution to the exhibit. With the guidance and creativity of Becky Urban, the display was a terrific success!

A note of appreciation is also offered to Ellie Calcagno, Site Manager at the Benjamin Temple House, Ewing Township Historical Preservation Society, and Fred Andrew for their insightful input.

I would also like to thank historian Don Lynch of the Titanic Historical Society, co-author of the book *Titanic: An Illustrated History* with Ken Marschall, and co-author of *Ghosts of the Abyss*, for sharing his personal knowledge of *Titanic* survivor Edwina Troutt.

Acknowledgements

My appreciation is also given to auto writer and automotive industry specialist Tara Baukus Mello, who shared her research, and personal experiences of her 3,500 mile automobile trip that retraced the historic cross-country route taken by Alice Huyler Ramsey in 1909. I am also thankful to the faculty at the Highlights Foundation for their grant to participate in their Art of Biography Workshop.

I am grateful to David Kane of American History Press for recognizing the relevance of this project and to my editor, Paula Tupper, for her input.

And last, but not least, I thank my husband, Rich, who listened patiently to my countless stories of the "world-wide trip" and for coming to appreciate the outstanding qualities of Harold Brooks and the enduring legacy of Harriet White Fisher.

PROLOGUE

May 14, 1910

The Locomobile idled on the banks of the Fujikawa River, its carload of passengers awed by the powerful Fuji Rapids whirling just yards ahead. The weary travelers had experienced their share of unique challenges in the remote and uncharted regions of India, Ceylon and Japan since having left the paved city streets of Trenton, New Jersey, but they were astonished at what they beheld.

Harriet White Fisher, her driver Harold Fisher Brooks, and her loyal servants had dined in royal Indian palaces, toured the magnificent gardens of the Japanese emperor, camped in tents nestled among untamed jungles and had even been chased by wild animals and crazed bandits. However, nothing in their ten-month journey had prepared them for this new challenge of crossing the violent Japanese waterway that churned before them.

"I have made 'never turn back' a motto for my life," Harriet declared, glaring defiantly at the angry torrent.

Inspired by his boss's words, the quick-thinking Harold came up with a solution. With the help of hired laborers called coolies, he constructed a makeshift floating raft on which the Locomobile and its occupants might safely cross the river.

The coolies, assisted by local policemen, circled and guided the raft in their own watercraft that was attached to the Locomobile by ropes. Some of them then used long poles to push the raft away from the rocky shore.

"This won't work," Harriet cried. "The current is too strong!" She tightened her grip on the little dog and monkey that she was carrying in her arms. "Hold on everyone."

The raft broke free from the grips of its rescuers. The Locomobile and its frightened passengers spun helplessly out of control in the rough water.

Along the side of the river a crowd of locals had gathered. Many of them had never seen people from another land, much less an automobile.

Prologue

They gasped in disbelief and horror as this curious contraption and its odd passengers hurtled toward almost certain doom.

"…but it may be that I have a story to tell which will engage the interest of folk who care for the unusual, the romantic, the practical and the adventurous."

Harriet Fisher White, *A Woman's World-Tour in a Motor*, 1911

CHAPTER ONE

Ewing, New Jersey, August 1913

I approached the address on Ewingville Road with a mixture of trepidation and excitement. Bella Vista Farm, my destination, was the country estate of the illustrious Mrs. Harriet Fisher Andrew, the woman who two years earlier had completed a remarkable tour around the world in a motorcar.

A brilliant industrialist, Harriet was also the head of her late husband's company, the Fisher & Norris Anvil Works, and was sometimes variously referred to as the *Anvil Queen, Lady Iron Master, The Female Napoleon, The Talk of Tokyo,* and *A Lady of Great Consequence.*

An anvil is a solid block of metal or iron, the cornerstone of all metal working. It allows objects like horseshoes or railroad ties to be struck and formed quickly against a strong and resilient surface. I had come to learn that Harriet's spirit was similar to those anvils her company produced; unyielding, resilient, and enduring.

I was a bit early for my appointment so I tried to delay my appearance at her front door, stalling every few steps to look about the hundred and thirty-five acre farm she and her new husband, the noted Argentine businessman Alfredo Silvano Andrew, had purchased the winter of last year.

I didn't think Harriet would mind my early arrival. After all, I had met her briefly last January at a meeting of efficiency experts held in New York City where she had been a special guest speaker.

At that gathering of great minds, Harriet had attracted her share of attention. Not only did she oversee the largest production of anvils in the nation, if not the world, but she was the first female to have been honored by the Automobile Association of America. I imagined that Harriet had probably spent more time in the seat of an automobile than that entire association's male membership combined.

At the efficiency event in New York I had listened in awe as she spoke of how she had her own method of taming rebellious employees, and had been successfully bossing (her own words) the men at her iron foundry for fourteen years. She spoke of how she came to manage the plant through circumstance but had remained by choice, explaining that she liked her work and learned something new each day.

At the end of that meeting I had introduced myself. I told her that I was a reporter for a newspaper covering stories in the Trenton area and asked if I might interview her for an article. When she learned of my home's proximity to hers, she had invited me to call on her once she and her husband had settled into life at Bella Vista.

That moment had arrived, and I had reached the entrance of the imposing home. I paused once more. The ribbon that held my bonnet tightly to my head dug into my chin. It was a very warm morning and beads of sweat had gathered on my brow. I would have removed my hat, but it made me feel tall and sophisticated. It reminded me of the one Harriet had worn when she had posed for a photograph in her Locomobile. The picture had been taken outside her residence at 125 East Hanover Street in Trenton on July 19, 1909, the day she had departed on her historic trek. The expression on her face told the world that nothing, and no one, would stand in her way.

I loosened the ribbon a bit, and retrieved a handkerchief from my purse, dabbing at my brow. I did not want to appear weak or frail in the presence of a woman who had, after all, endured extreme heat and harsh conditions.

There were so many questions I wanted to ask Harriet, a person who seemed to have made up her life as she went along. How old was she, really? I had discovered contradictory dates of birth in my research. Where was she really born? Most accounts noted her birthplace as western Pennsylvania, yet she once referred to the state of Ohio as her place of birth. I took into account that in rural places, borders often changed over time, and only Harriet could set the record straight.

I had only recently learned of Harriet's previous marriage to the renowned engineer, Gustav Lindenthal, the man who had once served as Commissioner of Bridges for New York. In an article that had appeared in the *New York Times* in April of 1906, it was reported that Harriet, while staying at her mansion in Flushing, New York, had been out for a ride in her motorcar when her chauffer had struck an Italian day laborer. The man had jumped into the path of the car and had been critically injured. His chances for recovery were reported to be slim. The article ended with the simple statement that Harriet and Lindenthal's marriage had ended in divorce.

Apparently this incident had not soured her on automobile travel.

And then there was the sad episode surrounding her husband Silvano's younger brother, Edgar Samuel Andrew. He had been crossing the Atlantic to be present at his brother's wedding, when his life had been taken in the sinking of the *Titanic*.

These sobering recollections brought me back to the present. I took a deep breath and stood up straight. In the unlikely event that the handsome Harold Brooks should suddenly appear, I wanted to look presentable.

Dashing blonde Harold had served as the driver who had transported Harriet and her entourage on their trip around the world. Many called him a genius, a gifted mechanic and talented photographer. Harold's quick wit and hard work had been a blessing, and a life-saver, on many an occasion during their record-making tour.

It occurred to me that Harold and I were both in our early twenties, yet I had never even been for a ride in an automobile, and had only traveled out of state once by rail. I may have been lacking in travel experience, but I hoped I would come away more educated about the world beyond New Jersey by spending some time in the presence of Harriet Andrew.

In my reverie the front door of the house flew open and caught me off guard. A small monkey charged straight toward me, letting out a series of little shrieks as it circled me twice before running off. As I turned to watch him, I stumbled backward, nearly losing my balance. My hat became unhinged and fell into the dirt.

As I reached down to retrieve it, I heard the voice of a woman calling out behind me. "Billikins! You naughty monkey."

I turned around to find Harriet Andrew standing in front of me. In this setting, she seemed taller than I remembered. She was of stocky appearance, immovable you might say. In the sunlight, her face was wider, both handsome and homely at once, and her eyes were filled with curiosity, amusement, intelligence and kindness as she appeared to size me up.

"I am sorry for that unprofessional greeting," she said, extending her hand. I stopped fiddling with my hat and accepted her welcoming gesture, receiving a firm and confident handshake in return.

"Thank you for your invitation. So pleased to meet you again, Mrs. Andrew," I managed.

"Please call me Harriet," she said. "I apologize for my monkey's behavior. Billikins has gone out looking for his dog friends. I think he believes he is one of them."

"Billikins, of course," I said, regaining my composure. "If I recall correctly, you acquired him on the grounds of the Lipton Tea Company in Ceylon."

"Yes, Billikins is one of the many treasures I brought back from my automobile trip. He's adjusted well to the woods of New Jersey," Harriet replied. "Speaking of tea, please join me inside. I will have Albert prepare a pot for us."

"Albert!" His name involuntarily escaped from me in my excitement.

"Yes. Albert. He is my butler. Surely if you've read my book, you know Albert toured with me."

Read it? I had devoured every word of *A Woman's World Tour in a Motor,* the book she had written about her trip while spending time in Cuba. I had heard rumors that she had met her third husband, Silvano, on her return trip home from Cuba. I knew that Albert had acquired his skills in service while working as a butler and valet on the steamships embarking from London. Harriet had described him as someone who could cook a good dinner *and* write a proper business letter.

Billikins had now returned with his two dog friends in tow.

"Meet Honk Honk and Jappy," Harriet said. "Honkie, as we call him, was given to me at the start of my trip as my mascot by the Locomobile Company to accompany me around the world. Jappy, the fluffy little black and white dog, was a gift from the Japanese Press. He was acquired just before I made my journey home."

The little dogs sat calmly. Their pink tongues hung out of their mouths as they panted in unison and kept their eyes on me. Billikins stood quietly at my side, his little hand extended now in a more proper greeting. Although he appeared to be as sweet as Harriet's book portrayed him, I accepted his hand with caution.

Worried that I might be appearing overwhelmed, I struggled to push stray wisps of my hair under my hat, and tried to regain my composure.

"Oh, please stop fussing with your hat, and feel free to remove it. Perhaps I should have Albert bring us something a little stronger than tea," she suggested, shaking her head and laughing. "Even at 10:15 in the morning."

She disappeared into the house, motioning for me to follow. Her skirt rustled as she went. There was nothing slow about this woman, and I was challenged to keep up with her. Billikins held my hand as we followed closely behind.

"Albert," she called out. "Albert, we have a visitor. Please bring some sherry, a pot of tea, and some of those little cakes I adore."

CHAPTER TWO

Tea and Cake with the Anvil Queen

Once inside the spacious home, Honkie and Jappy rushed past me, perhaps afraid that I would eat their biscuits or cakes. Billikins soon released my hand and followed them in a loping manner. I found them all, plus their mistress, in a small parlor down a long hallway. This room was packed with furnishings and decorative elements unlike any I had ever seen.

These items must have been the ones described in accounts of Harriet's exotic shopping trips! Area rugs of brilliant hues were scattered about the room to compliment the rich wall coverings. Decorative vases, intricately carved figurines and a myriad of bric-a-brac were scattered about the surfaces of small decorative tables. An immense bunch of American Beauty roses filled a vase, infusing the parlor with a sweet aroma.

Harriet motioned for me to take a seat in a finely upholstered sitting chair located in front of a stately writing desk. I accepted her invitation. Once I had settled in, Billikins climbed onto my lap while the dogs made themselves comfortable on a small settee nearby. Obviously Harriet, an animal-lover, allowed her pets free rein inside and outside of her home.

"Will you please excuse me for a moment?" Harriet said, rising out of her chair. She always seemed to be in motion. "Albert! Maria!" she called out as she exited the room.

I found myself alone with the animals.

I ventured an educated guess that this was the same Maria who had served as Harriet's personal maid during the globe-trotting voyage. Not only had Maria and Albert remained in Harriet's service after the excursion, they had become husband and wife soon after returning to America.

I noticed that the walls and desks of the room were lined with photos that featured Harriet in exotic locales posing with mysterious, important-looking persons. My curiosity aroused, I stood and went over to study them. There was Harriet in a sari standing beside a woman who looked like an Indian princess; there she was perched on top of an elephant draped in bejeweled layers. In another photo she was carried by servants on a type of bed called a litter, high off the ground.

"As you can see, this home is a veritable museum of my world-wide trip," Harriet announced, returning to the parlor. She stood beside me while I admired an unusual grouping of figures displayed on a table. "Sometimes I have to look hard at these souvenirs in order to realize the whole thing was not a dream," she said. "Those figurines are among my favorite items brought back from the trip," she added.

She told me that the sturdy figures had been presented to her at a dinner in Calcutta and represented all of the servants of an Indian household and the trades of the nation's people. Made of native clay, Harriet explained that they were perfectly natural in their pose and draped in realistic styles of that region.

I turned to the wall filled with the photographs of her posing with what looked like members of royalty and remarked, "I see that you spent time with some notable people."

"Young lady," she said. "I need you to understand my motives for my travels. Please don't paint me as some rich spoiled female adventurer who flittered about squandering money all over the world."

"So how would you like your journey to be portrayed?" I inquired.

"I suppose you can sum up my journey by saying that my trip was not a succession of narrow escapes, but rather one continuous and splendid reception, intermingled with amusing incidents from the time I crossed the Turkish border until I left the shores of Japan."

She made it clear, however, that she wished for her activities to be viewed as notable, if not regal, adding, "I would say it was more the tour of a royal personage than that of a single American woman traveling for her health."

As she spoke, her eyes came to rest on a photo of a dark-haired young man. It was one of the several framed images grouped on the wall. A shadow of sadness passed over her face. "Poor Edgar," she said. "Edgar was Silvano's younger brother. He was a on his way to America to work for us at the Anvil factory. You may have heard he was a passenger on the *Titanic*."

"Yes," I said, acknowledging that I had heard of her sad news. "I am so sorry to hear of your loss." Not wishing to dwell on this sensitive topic, I moved our conversation along. "Please be assured that I will not portray you, or your travels, in an unflattering light," I promised.

She nodded approvingly and then said the words I had waited to hear for so long. "Well, get your notebook and writing instruments ready, young lady. Let's get started. We have so much to cover!"

But we weren't quite ready to begin. A man of small stature entered the room and set a large silver tray on a table near Harriet's desk. On it rested an exquisitely-painted teapot, two matching cups and saucers, a bottle of amber-colored liquid with two small glasses, and a plate of tea cakes with a small jar of jam.

"Thank you, Albert," she said. "That will be all for now. But hold on, if you please. I'm sure this young lady from the newspaper would like to meet you."

Albert flashed an easy smile, his eyes betraying a temperament that was at once both warm and kind. He shook my hand and nodded. "I do hope you have brought enough pencils and paper," he said in a chipper British accent. "Madame loves to talk of her travels."

His total lack of pretension set me at ease at once.

"Come along, Billikins," Albert spoke to the monkey. "It is time for your lunch." The monkey followed him with the two dogs in tow.

"Now, where were we?" Harriet asked, returning to her chair behind her desk. "Well perhaps we should start from the beginning, as they say."

I let her take the lead.

CHAPTER THREE

The Rise of the Lady Ironmaster

"I've always possessed the spirit and heart of an adventurer, a spirit never held back by the expectations of society," Harriet began, as if dictating her life story.

She started by speaking about growing up on a farm in western Pennsylvania, where she was not typical of most girls her age. "I baited fishing hooks with wriggly worms, squirted milk from the udders of dairy cows and scaled the highest of trees. I could do a hundred and one other things that only boys were supposed to do," she said, with pride.

"Even at age fourteen I remained rebellious. After graduating from the Young Ladies' Classical Seminary in Cleveland, Ohio, I was shipped off to Hildesheim, Germany, to further my studies. It was hoped that I would become more proper and ladylike," she said with a sigh.

This course of action apparently failed. She recalled one summer day in particular when she and a friend were out for a walk in Hildesheim when an arrogant German officer came swaggering toward them. The sidewalk was narrow and as was customary, the girls were expected to step aside to let him pass.

"What a surprise that officer received," Harriet said. "When he failed to yield to us I gave him a hard whack with my parasol!"

This account caused Harriet to laugh so hard she had to stop talking. It was contagious and I found myself laughing with her, imagining the expression on the officer's face.

"That will teach him for not respecting a daughter of Uncle Sam!" she said, regaining her composure. She paused to pour tea for us both. "Even the polite education of the smug Victorian Age was unable to stifle my defiant nature."

Her fiery spirit and confidence would come to serve her well.

In July 1889, she married Clark Fisher in a ceremony held in London,

England. "Clark was more than thirty years my senior, an accomplished engineer and the owner of a very successful anvil manufacturing business in Trenton," she explained.

She told of how Clark's father, Mark Fisher, had established the Eagle Anvil Works after the tannery he owned in Maine had been destroyed by a fire. While picking through the ashes of his former tannery, Mark had inadvertently stumbled upon a great opportunity when he discovered a piece of beam that had become fused with a segment of steel in the intense heat of the blaze.

Mark was inspired. He experimented until he came up with a formula for something called flux, a material used in the welding of metals.

"At last," Harriet said, "someone had found a way to join iron and steel in a way that had never been done in America! This formula was protected very carefully. Visitors were not permitted on the grounds of the factory."

Harriet told of how Mark relocated his business to New Jersey, where he received a patent for this procedure, and began to manufacture his special line of Eagle brand anvils. With the financial backing of a silent partner named John Norris, the Fisher and Norris Anvil Works opened on Bloomsbury Street in Trenton in 1853.

Clark was sent to Rensselaer Polytechnic Institute in Troy, New York, to study engineering. Before rejoining the family business, he enlisted in the United States Navy and served during the Civil War, retiring as Chief Engineer. His father died in 1871, and John Norris the following year, leaving Clark the sole owner of the Anvil Works.

"I began my marriage to Clark in typical fashion; content in my role as the wife of a successful business man," Harriet said.

But her life would change within a year of their marriage when Clark became seriously ill, and Harriet was suddenly transformed from traditional society lady and housewife to temporary plant manager. Suddenly there were many pressing business matters that required her immediate attention.

Her first challenge was to handle a payroll crisis. Because she lacked power of attorney, the bank could not give her money to pay the employees at the Anvil Works.

"But this was not a problem," she said. "I used my personal funds to see that our workers were paid on time."

Despite her generous efforts, Harriet relayed how her husband's all-male staff refused to take her authority seriously. On her first supervisory visit to the Anvil Works, Harriet was surprised to find the shop in perfect silence.

"What's going on here?" Harriet demanded.

She was informed that the machinery room was flooded and work had stopped. When she ordered the problem to be fixed, she was told that they didn't "propose to stand for petticoat government."

Harriet handled the situation swiftly and sternly. She warned the impudent workers that if the room wasn't cleaned and dried up immediately they would be dismissed and a new factory superintendent would be appointed.

It was obvious to this reporter that the spirit of the umbrella-wielding girl in Germany had returned with a vengeance.

"Despite the dire predictions of his doctors, Clark recovered and returned to work. But now he fully understood how invaluable my natural business abilities were to the future success of the Anvil Factory. He saw to it that I learned all aspects of the business."

By her own account, it seemed that there was no job she wouldn't do. Dressed in work overalls, and standing shoulder-to-shoulder with her employees near the intense heat of blasting furnaces, Harriet chiseled the faces of anvils, molded vises and produced rail joints.

Things seemed to be getting back to normal, but the couple soon endured another life-changing event. On October 8, 1902, while headed to New York, they were victims of a train wreck in Menlo Park, New Jersey. Clark and Harriet were both seriously injured.

"But there was a business to run," Harriet said. "Despite my own pain and suffering, I announced that I would take full charge of the factory until my husband recovered from his own injuries."

But she was sorely disappointed and surprised by the rude reception she received by the foundry's male employees. "I was disturbed by their behavior," Harriet recalled. "My entrance was met with quizzical looks and mocking smiles. Why, some men paid me no attention at all, looking through me like I was an atom of dust!"

She was obviously agitated by these recollections. She left her chair and paced as she spoke, gesturing excitedly with her hands as she relived these indignities. At times she would stop, and with one hand placed squarely on her hip, point at an imaginary workman as she continued to talk.

After awhile, she ceased her ranting long enough to pour some of the amber liquid into the small glasses for us both. She took a sip and continued.

"I was baffled. After all I had done at the factory, I expected the men to respect my leadership and to admire my abilities."

But Harriet's petticoat remained unruffled. She was determined to prove that she was fully capable of being their supervisor. As a boss, she insisted on performing any task required of her employees.

She told of how one day she came upon some workmen lowering an anvil onto the floor. "Allow me," she said, taking hold of the rope. "But Mrs. Fisher," they warned, "that anvil is very heavy."

"I have always prided myself on being able to handle a pair, and even four horses," she replied, as she held tightly to the rope while lowering the weighty anvil slowly to the ground.

"But even this did not impress the men," said Harriet. "In fact I heard one of them mumble, 'Poor Mr. Fisher'."

Clark never recuperated from his injuries and died that New Year's Eve. "Over time, I gained the respect of the factory workers and in time I even quadrupled business," Harriet reflected. "You could say I found comfort and distraction from my grief and hardship in my role as the so-called Lady Ironmaster."

Harriet settled into a parlor chair, as if all the reminiscing was exhausting her.

"After seven years of hard work, I announced that I was ready to take the trip of a woman who has grown a little weary of the details of a useful but somewhat heavy business," she continued. "All of my high society friends assumed I would take my typical holiday to my *Villa Carlotta*."

I knew that Harriet had taken several excursions to Europe, often staying at her rambling thirty-seven room vacation home nestled in the hills of the picturesque Lake Como region of Northern Italy.

"But no, that would not do," Harriet continued. "I told them that I longed for a more exciting get-away, one not taken in the approved and dull fashion popular among our social circle."

And although she had made history as a female traveler, she made it clear that she did not wish to be portrayed as someone trying to change the world for women. "I will tell you what I told that reporter from the *New York Times* not too long ago. I still believe a woman's place is in the home."

This woman was full of surprises and certainly was not easily categorized.

I had been scribbling furiously to keep up with her, and I had so many questions. At the moment, I was very thankful for having taken a course in something called "Swift Hand" as I had a feeling that it was going to prove to be a wise investment by day's end.

My fingers were holding up, but my mind was reeling, and we hadn't even gotten around to talking about her travels.

CHAPTER FOUR

The Travels of a Royal Personage

"I wanted to explore what lay beyond my familiar European borders," Harriet declared. "I wished to have a great adventure, but not one taken by train." As she spoke, she shuddered as if reliving that fateful train wreck in which she had suffered over a decade ago. "I like to say I left Italy when the peach trees were in blossom, and toured Japan as the petals of cherry blossoms were strewn on our path."

Harriet recalled how she set about throwing all of her time and energy into planning a very special voyage. "I shall not forget the happiness of anticipation nor the joy of preparing for that long trip I had determined to take," she declared. "A trip almost literally around the world in a motorcar, something no woman, and very few men, had ever done."

Harriet's face seemed to brighten as her thoughts returned to this exciting time.

"No. Trains were not for me. I began my search for the safest motorcar money could buy."

In 1908, Harriet purchased a brand-new gray touring car, a stock type 1 Locomobile, the same model as the first American-made car to win the Vanderbilt Cup Race on Long Island in the same year. With its four-cylinder engine, the car was standard for its time, but was uniquely equipped with a larger-than-average gasoline tank mounted under its rear seat. It also had a higher capacity oil tank than other cars. To accommodate rough terrain, its front tires, made of canvas, measured thirty-six inches in diameter by four-and-a-half inches wide, with those in the rear slightly wider by one inch.

"Now that I had found the motorcar, I was in need of a qualified chauffeur and mechanic to keep it running smoothly."

She found the perfect candidate in a young man named Harold Fisher Brooks, an employee at the Anvil Works. A native of Lowell, Massachusetts, Harold had moved with his family to New Jersey at the age of nineteen.

Capable and reliable, he quickly found work at the Standard Motor Construction Company in Elizabeth, and became known as an expert in the installation and tuning of motorboat engines.

Harriet took note of Harold's special talents. "I had purchased a boat I planned to ship to Lake Como and needed a reliable mechanic. I approached Harold and insisted that he leave his job at the Standard Motor Construction Company to come and work at my factory where he could also maintain my motorboat."

But Harold was very close to his parents and siblings and had no desire to leave home. "I thank you for your offer, Mrs. Fisher," he told me. "But I am paid well here and my family relies on me."

"I refused to take no for an answer," Harriet said. "I persisted and told him that if he came to work for me, I would increase his salary several times over and he would have opportunities he could not imagine."

Harold finally gave in. It was an offer the bright and talented young man could not refuse.

True to her word, Harriet took Harold with her to Europe on several occasions before their epic 1909 global journey. Harold was awed by his travels. In London, he visited the National Art Gallery, where he saw classic paintings for the first time, and attended Sunday services at Westminster Abbey.

While in London, Harold noticed the names Brooks and Fisher several times in and about the city. On one such occasion he remarked to his boss that the name of Bishop John Fisher appeared on a tablet in a small chapel.

"I explained to Harold that Bishop Fisher was the man from which "my" Fishers had descended, and that it was because of his execution that my great-great-grandfather had fled England. I also relayed to him that I was a direct descendant of Peregrine White, the "first born" American citizen who came into the world on the *Mayflower*."

On one such overseas trip, Harriet had shipped the Locomobile to Europe and had Harold drive her across France. One year later, Harold learned of Harriet's grand plans for him.

"How would you like to drive the Locomobile around the world?" I'd asked him. "I know that among your other skills you are a very talented photographer. You'll have the chance to take some incredible pictures of places and people most will never see, or meet, in their lifetime."

Understandably, Harold was honored and thrilled.

Harriet knew that despite his lack of formal education, Harold, with his rugged strength and sharp mind, and an appearance that presented well, was more than qualified for the task ahead of him. When dressed in his button-down shirt and pin-striped suit, Harold made the perfect professional associate for Harriet. She knew he would fit right in when they called on royal hosts and dignitaries on several continents.

"Due to the similarity of our last names, many people assumed that we were related. That, and the fact that my mother's maiden name was also Fisher," she said with a laugh. "All the reporters think you are my aunt,' he would tell me. 'To which I would reply 'Well then, let's just let them think we are.' It was easier than just having to explain it all."

Harold quickly became like a son to Harriet. "He called me 'Mrs. Fisher,' but I was aware that he often referred to me as Hattie, or Mrs. F. among his friends and family members."

In April of 1909, Harriet planned a trial run with Harold at the wheel. "It's time to test those tires of my Locomobile on the open road," I announced. "We traveled to Baltimore, the District of Colombia, Pittsburgh, and Youngstown, Ohio with our final destination being Cleveland."

The trip went smoothly until they attempted to cross the Susquehanna River from Perryville, Maryland to Havre de Grace. There, the motorcar was boarded on a ferry powered by a small gasoline-propelled engine. A cold spring wind lashed at the party and the waters grew rough. As the ferry attempted to cross the river, it was pushed farther and farther from the opposite river bank.

"Harold was worried. He confided that he didn't know if we would make it to land."

After several failed attempts, the boatman finally succeeded in tossing a rope to a curious crowd of onlookers that had gathered along the shoreline, who then helped to pull them ashore.

Harriet let out a sigh and said. "Little did we know then that we were actually practicing for those times we would face much more frightening challenges in more remote places."

Although the Locomobile had met with Harriet's standards of perfection, the condition of the local landscape greatly disappointed her.

Seeing this region from the seat of a motorcar for the first time, her eyes had followed the destructive path of portable sawmills that reached in all directions, leaving large piles of sawdust where forests had once stood. "I was grieved to see the magnificent forests of the Alleghany and Laurel Hill mountains disappearing," she recalled, noting, "At least the water has not yet been confiscated by man."

Harriet and Harold returned to Trenton by way of Erie, Pennsylvania, Buffalo and the Catskills in New York, stopping briefly in New York City before returning to Trenton. "When we returned, I wasted no time preparing for a prolonged absence that would take us farther than 25,000 miles from home."

CHAPTER FIVE

Heading into the Sun

On July 17, 1909, Harold, Maria, Albert, Honkie and Harriet departed for New York City, where the Locomobile was crated up and shipped overseas by the American Express Company.

"The big day had finally arrived!" Harriet said. "While a photograph was being taken of me sitting in the Locomobile outside my home, I happened to catch a glimpse of my maid Maria somewhat timidly peering from the front window. I couldn't possibly imagine what must have been going through her mind!"

Maria Borge had worked for Harriet at *Villa Carlotta*, Harriet's vacation home in Lake Como, Italy. Strong, big-boned and large in stature, Maria towered over most people. Although an imposing figure, Harriet described her maid as "typical of her country, always bright, cheerful, and sunny."

"I imagined Albert was inside the house somewhere tending to last-minute details in his efficient manner," Harriet said.

British born Albert E. Batcheler made up for his lack of physical size with an arsenal of practical skills. Albert, an experienced butler and valet, had worked aboard steamships that sailed out of London, England. Harriet described him as someone who could, "cook a good dinner or write a business letter."

Harriet explained that they had chosen to cross the Atlantic and begin their journey in Europe so that they would travel eastward with their faces always pointing toward the sun. "We sailed on the SS *New York* to Cherbourg, France, where we reclaimed the Locomobile in Paris."

No stranger to this city, Harriet recalled her excitement upon viewing her beloved city in a brand new way. "It was bliss indeed to glide along the beautiful streets, to be able to visit Fontainebleau and the many places of interest about Paris, in your own car, at your own time and pleasure, not feeling that you must hurry. And there was none of that quibbling over the *pourboire*, the French word for tip."

Motorcars were not uncommon in Paris, and up until the last ten years or so, more motorcars had been produced in France than in America. In Paris, however, the Locomobile drew attention, but for the wrong reason.

Harriet's enjoyment of her first Parisian motor tour came to an unpleasant halt. A French police officer, or *gendarme*, stopped the car, shaking his fist and babbling in French. With an angry expression on his face, he pointed at the smoke emitting from the Locomobile's exhaust pipe. It seemed that the car had spent too many days exposed to salt air during its transport. As Harold had put in extra quantities of oil in preparation, it was only now being burned off.

"We had an appointment with the Engineer of Mines for an inspection, and we had some distance to go. We could not understand what he was saying and he would not release us, nor would he allow us to run the car's motor. I feared this delay would make us late for our eleven o'clock motor inspection when we hoped to obtain our necessary travel permits."

This unusual scene quickly attracted a curious crowd that gathered around the Locomobile, distracting the police officer. Harold took advantage of this opportunity.

"'Hang on!'" he called to us." Harold stepped on the gas pedal and turned a sharp corner, leaving the irate officer lost in a cloud of the Locomobile's blue-colored exhaust. They arrived in plenty of time for their appointment and Harold let the car's motor continue to idle to burn off the surplus oil.

"A rather serious-faced inspector completed his examination of the car. Then he spoke to me in broken English, and I understood him to say, 'Madame, *si'l vous plait*, I would like to have a ride in your motorcar.' Well, after our first encounter with a French official, would *you* turn him down?" she laughed.

The inspector hopped aboard the Locomobile, and Harriet recalled how the motorcar wound so smoothly through the traffic of the busiest streets of Paris, crossing the River Seine and circling the Bon Marche. The car's performance met with the inspector's standards. Harriet was told her travel permit would be issued in three days

"Harold and I rejoiced in this news until we found ourselves face-to-face once again with the fist-pumping officer who had confronted us earlier. As I had no more patience for this man and his outbursts, I pointed to the American flag displayed on the car's dashboard, and shook my fist right back at him."

Her tactic worked. The officer, finally worn down, shrugged and walked off.

But another surprise was in store for them. Upon taking a drive around the Bois de Boulogne, a group of men rushed after them as they passed through the city's gates. "I then remembered that we were outside the city limits of Paris, and we had passed a station without getting our gasoline gauge measured."

Harriet explained that outside of Paris, one was able to obtain petrol for a few centimes less than in the city, so all petrol had to be measured when leaving and returning. It was required that one's tank have less petrol when one left the city, or face a tax, and a fine, and possible travel delays.

Harriet, Harold, Albert, Maria and Honk Honk had now been in Paris for five days. "I had learned more about that city, its streets, and its many interesting suburbs, than I had known in previous years after visits of weeks at a time," Harriet said.

She loved the freedom car travel presented and found it blissful to glide along the beautiful streets of the city at her own pace. "What a pleasure to visit such places of interest, in the Locomobile, without feeling hurried to remain on schedule, or be pushed and jostled in crowded trolley cars," she recalled.

It was now time for Harriet to turn her attention to her prolonged voyage and matters of supplies and camping equipment. Although she had made arrangements to stay with royalty and heads of states along the route, no one could predict the motorcar's progress, or the availability of necessary lodging in remote and unchartered regions.

"I needed a tent with lightness and strength," Harriet recalled. "And it had to be rain-proof." At the Vuitton Rue Scribe she acquired the perfect tent, designed with a unique telescoping framework that collapsed and could be rolled up into a small bag. She also purchased flannel-lined pneumatic sleeping bags, water canteens, and thermos bottles at an army supply house.

Just as she had demanded the best of the Locomobile, their new shelter had to meet her high standards. Special permission was granted by city officials and the tent was erected on the Place Vendome, a very busy and crowded boulevard. Once again, a curious mob formed around the car and its passengers.

"Our little experiment seems to be causing a lot of excitement," Harold had observed.

"He was right. We were creating quite a scene and I was nearly frightened out my desire to see that tent erected anywhere except in a wilderness."

Harriet, Harold, and the tent survived the crush of onlookers after which the tent was piled among two small steamer trunks. A hat box was fastened to the front extra tire with a tool box doubling as a seat for an extra passenger or guide. A canvas bag fitted with lock and key, laundry bag, water proof sack for their bedding, and an extension cot folded up and wound with a length of rope was stored around the front of the car's bumper. This served to help distribute the weight of the car.

Inside the Locomobile, room was made for rugs, toiletries, a pair of suitcases for Albert and Harold, a waterproof bag for sheets, and two small pillows that Harriet never travelled without.

"Why, we barely had any room for little Honk Honk," she recalled, laughing.

Their Parisian visit had come to an end and they prepared to move on. The entourage and their car were again swarmed by well-wishers and reporters while photographers aimed their lenses in their direction. "I announced to the reporters that before heading to Switzerland, I wished to take advantage of the health giving waters and the cure in the spa town of Contrexeville."

Harriet had visited Contrexeville before. But now, as the Locomobile rambled along the lovely tree-lined roads, and Harriet took in the French countryside from her car seat, she felt as if she was taking a continuous trip through a beautiful park.

On the road to this spa resort, Harriet was impressed by how nicely the roadways were kept. She observed old men, boys, and even some industrious women, as they broke stones into small pieces which were then mixed with sand and water to form a type of concrete used to fill holes in the road.

Harriet observed how at each corner, sign-posts had been erected to provide travelers with directions, and how milestones told of the distances that separated villages.

The Locomobile rambled through the crooked and narrow streets of quaint little villages and Harriet delighted in the sights found at each turn. Girls and old women sat making lace and knitting, and after four o'clock each day, as the end of the day drew near, sheep and cattle huddled together in front of their owner's door.

"Some even shared their master's living quarters!" she recalled, bemused.

Harriet inquired if this practice was unhealthful, to which a young girl smiled and pointed to her grandmother. "The girl told me this woman was over eighty years of age, and I'll tell you, a more bonny, sunny, healthful looking old face I had never seen!"

On the fifth of August, Harriet and her crew arrived in Contrexeville, and as she had before, found peace and relaxation in this restful place.

"I checked into the Grand Hotel d'Establissement for a three week stay, taking the cure there. From Contrexeville we enjoyed many side trips, including one to the birthplace of Jeanne d'Arc."

But even here, as she relaxed, it seemed that she could not resist a little competition. During the second week of her stay, Harriet was invited to participate in a competitive motorcar event called a Gymkana. The Locomobile was the only American car among forty registered for this affair where car and driver vied for a variety of awards and honors.

And like everywhere else Harriet ventured, she attracted her share of attention. "I was thrilled when I heard a man announce that my Locomobile, covered in beautiful roses, had won First Place Honors in the category of Floral Decoration!"

Next, she told me of how she had entered in another contest that required her to carry a full glass of water while her motorcar raced around a plowed field. "'Hold on to your glass Mrs. Fisher,' Harold had warned me. He promised 'I'll get you to the finish line with barely a splash.'"

And he did. Harriet victoriously returned to the course's starting point with the most water remaining in her glass.

"That's when I truly knew that Harold would be the most steady and reliable driver in any situation!"

On the twenty-sixth of August, after three weeks in Contrexeville, Harriet was rested and relaxed, and eager to resume her journey. "Upon our departure on a late August day, we were presented with armloads of beautiful roses grown by the local townspeople," she recalled, basking in her recollection.

But just outside of Contrexeville they found themselves victims of a roadblock. Harold slowed down as the path of the Locomobile was impeded by a line of local people. Harriet demanded to know what was happening to cause such a commotion. In response, broad smiles spread across the stern faces of the villagers. "They told me they had prepared a surprise farewell luncheon for Madame and her friends."

"During our stay in Contrexeville, we had enjoyed many a fine dejeuners," Harriet explained. "These fine people wished to have one more. They insisted that we come and dine under the shade of an apricot tree, where the townspeople wished us well and toasted to our journey with the good old wine of the country."

As they prepared to depart, the villagers cheerfully handed Harriet a large basket filled with a cooked chicken, bread and butter, a plum tart, and a cake.

"We were warned to beware of mischievous children along the roadside as we headed toward Switzerland, and they advised us to carry a long whip to keep them in order," Harriet said. "But we never encountered any of this trouble. Indeed, I would greet the people with a 'Gutentag' as we passed, peasants doffed their hats, and the children that were supposed to be so unruly threw little bunches of wild flowers into the Locomobile!"

The trip had been easy and pleasant thus far, but Harriet and her traveling companions soon learned that the rules and regulations, as well as the degree of comfort experienced in motor travel, would change with the geographical elements and cultural norms of the countries through which they toured.

They had more than mischievous little children to fear.

CHAPTER SIX

Car Meets Devil's Bridge

The safety and tranquility of Contrexeville was now just a pleasant memory. With every mile, Harriet was being drawn into a world of which she had no knowledge or previous experience. The thought of spending a little down time in the familiar Italian countryside brought her a degree of comfort.

As the Locomobile approached the entrance of Saint Gotthard's Pass in Switzerland, Harriet sensed Harold growing nervous. Car and driver were about to face their first real challenge with the crossing of this infamous pass and the trip over the perilous Devil's Bridge, high above the Devil's Gulch.

"I tried to make light of things and asked Harold to tell us the story of how the Devil's Bridge got its name, something he had enjoyed talking about."

"He obliged me and shared his knowledge with his fellow passengers. It seems that many years ago the mayor of the canton was quite troubled and disgusted, and resorted to some swearing and taking of the devil's name because every time they'd built a bridge there would come a storm to wash it out. Harold told how the devil heard of this and paid the mayor a formal visit to talk things over. In the living room of the mayor's home the devil asked him what the trouble was and the mayor told him that he would like to have a bridge built that would last a hundred years."

"'Fine, I'll build you one,' the devil said. But the mayor needed to know the cost of this bridge. The devil told him that money or gold meant nothing to him, but that he would take the soul of the first life who passed over the bridge."

"Upon its completion, the mayor crossed to inspect the bridge, at which time he came upon the devil who asked the mayor if he was so magnanimous and gracious as to sacrifice himself as the first life to go over the bridge. The mayor just laughed and released a big, black cat from a sack with a tin can tied to its tail. As it scurried away, the mayor told the devil, 'Go catch it if you can. That's your first life!'"

But the bridge, the gulch or the devil weren't the only hurdles Harold and his passengers now faced. First they had to deal with some steely Swiss efficiency.

"Upon our arrival at the gates of the Gotthard Pass, we were harassed by an arrogant Swiss guard. He told us that in order to keep the roads safe for pedestrians and horses, motorcars were only allowed to cross between five and seven in the evening, and chided us for being fifteen minutes early! He said we would be fined," Harriet recalled.

He further informed Harriet that the Locomobile had to complete its journey in three quarters of an hour or face yet another fine.

During the course of our interview, I would discover that depending on her mood, Harriet would resort to either cajoling or steamrolling her way to the desired result. In this case, she appeared triumphant, recalling how she cleverly handled this authority figure at the bridge's entrance.

"I cocked my head and smiled flirtatiously, and addressed the guard in German," she said laughing. "Well yes, I *know* we are early, but I heard there was a handsome-looking officer up here, and I thought I would prefer to sit and look at him for awhile rather than wait at the hotel."

Her strategy worked. The officer smiled, pulled down his uniform and braced back his shoulders! "We had a nice chat in German. He was quite taken with my car and confided in me that he had never been outside of his own country and the thought of a woman making a trip around the world was something beyond his comprehension! He told me that he had never even been in a motorcar before."

I smiled as I took notes, picturing this proud man of authority being charmed by Harriet's daring spirit, travel experience, and blatant sweet talk. Harriet was so thrilled by the results that she proceeded to invite the officer to join them on the ride up the mountain.

But not everyone was pleased.

"When Mr. Brooks heard of my invitation to this man, he was outraged. Why, his face darkened and he demanded to know just what I thought the car could do."

He reminded her that this uphill climb could be difficult and that the weight of another passenger would further strain the car that was already filled to capacity. While Harriet conceded Harold's concerns were real, she remained adamant about her invitation.

"I told Mr. Brooks that if the car could not do all I wanted of it, I would leave it."

Harriet continued, "For his part, the officer was so excited to go along, he forgot about the fine for having arrived at the gate too early. Hopping into the Locomobile, he informed everyone that he was indeed the chief of police, and set about proving it. As the car proceeded through the mountain pass, he gave Harold warnings about parts of the road that contained treacherous turns, and handled other parties who had the unfortunate timing to be on the road at the same time."

"He shouted at startled horses and pedestrians that dared to cross their path to get out of the way, for here was a Lady of Great Consequence, as that was my official title. We had our own crier, demanding, 'Make way there!'" Harriet said.

"But I feared for those who did not move quickly enough for his liking. He even took time to write down the name of a man who responded too slowly to his commands."

The car ascended to heights Harriet and her entourage had never experienced. Perched above Devil's Gulch, the ferocious roar of a waterfall made such a noise that conversation was almost impossible. At this elevation the landscape was barren, dotted with black rocks covered with gray moss.

Harold was relieved to see that the car's engine merely puffed a bit during this trial, handling the climb better than imagined. Harriet relaxed and admired the scenery. "I shall never forget our view of the setting sun over this mass of white-capped mountains."

The local peasants were surprised by their police officer's unscheduled visit to the mountain top. Apparently, he only ventured there every six months to log reports, and then only on foot. He proceeded to escort Harriet and her crew to an inn that was run by a German widow who was very welcoming.

"Harold, Albert, Maria, Honkie and I settled in as buxom Swiss maids tackled our trunks as though they were basket of cabbages," Harriet recalled, laughing. "I warmed myself by a crackling fire that greeted me in my room. We were later seated at a table for dinner with some of the other thirty-seven or so guests, enjoying a roast chicken with all the accompaniments, with a delicious omelet for dessert. All the other guests had walked up the mountain from Luzerne! They could not believe we had come by motorcar."

The road from Luzerne was narrow and Harriet reassured the other guests that she had taken the utmost care to respect those who had ventured on foot as most had never seen a motorcar. "I felt for those timid women as they clung to the sides of the rocks, or rushed madly into danger, not realizing that these snorting, monstrous-looking cars could be brought to a stop within a foot of them if need be!"

Harriet learned that at this altitude the cost of living could also be as high as the surrounding mountains. The Swiss officer had informed her that the prices at this inn were more reasonable than others, so she was startled when she received her dinner bill. "Why does one chicken cost four dollars?" she'd inquired.

She was told it was the altitude. It was impossible to raise livestock there and food supplies had to be hauled up the mountain from Paris.

Exhausted after her long day, Harriet paid her tab and then got a good night's sleep buried in the warmth of an enormous featherbed. Descending the mountain the next day would prove even more of a danger then the upward journey. Harold's driving skills were once again tested by the sharp hairpin turns of the mountain pass. Adding to their difficulties, a near-constant torrential downpour made the passage extremely slippery.

"Harold had warned me that one false move and the Locomobile and its passengers would surely slide off the mountainside."

"I dare say poor Harold's heart must have been pounding in his chest as he maneuvered the car safely down the pass through the Swiss mountains, down to Lake Maggiore in Italy," Harriet said. "I was equally relieved and happy to have passed through the Swiss mountains without incident and to learn that the Locomobile provided a warm and dry haven even during inclement weather."

As Harriet concluded her account, I noted that her hands were clenching the sides of her chair as if she was reliving her Devil's Path experience. She poured a little more of the amber liquid into her glass and took a small sip.

"We had no way of knowing how mild that little passage would compare to what lay ahead on other continents. We had no clue at all."

CHAPTER SEVEN

The Hospitality of the Italians

Harriet's face lit up as she recounted her first car trip to *Villa Carlotta*. "The sun was shining on the lake, welcoming us with a rippling smile," Harriet happily recalled. She was now enjoying the Lake Como region, another European locale so familiar to her, from a different perspective—the seat of the Locomobile.

"I thought to myself that this must be one of the most beautiful roads possible," She exclaimed. "I heard happy greetings of '*Ciao!*' and '*Benevenuti!*', offered by my staff of Italian servants."

Within a short time after their arrival, Harriet and her fellow travelers were being served breakfast in a small arbor of green magnolias, serenaded by the songs of birds.

A curious Honkie quickly started sniffing and digging about on the grounds of his mistress's sprawling vacation home. He tore about freely with no respect for the beautiful flower borders. I could imagine that this poor little dog wanted very much to run about on the velvety green grass of the region after being trapped in a motorcar and hotel for so long. But this was not appreciated by Gulio, Harriet's gardener, who was horrified by the dog's antics.

"'*Cane cattivo!*'" Gulio shouted at Honkie in Italian. "Yes, *cane cattivo*, a very bad dog, indeed, I had to agree. I reprimanded Honkie and told him that Gulio was so very proud of his begonias and we couldn't have him going about destroying them."

Harriet enjoyed several weeks at *Villa Carlotta*, calling upon old friends like the people she referred to as the "Marquese and Marquesa" Trotti, who welcomed her at their 17th century villa surrounded by lush gardens on Lago di Como, filled with what Harriet described as an air of "at homeness," despite its fifty rooms.

She seemed to grasp the unique history of each home, palace, and villa she visited, the meticulous planning that went into the design of the local landscapes, and the strong family bonds that were prevalent in the culture of these families.

Her love for this region was palpable. As she spoke of it, and its people, I felt as if I was there with her, basking in the Italian sun with vistas of rolling green hills filled with magnificent clumps of copper beeches, maples and firs, grouped in the most picturesque manner, with Lake Como sparkling in the distance.

"The Trottis loved to tell of how they had planted a tree on their wedding day, and how together they had laid out and planned the beautiful gardens," Harriet shared. "And it is so charming to see the Marquesa knit and crochet garments for the young members of the large peasant family whom she employs. She treats the peasants who work at her estate like family. I have never heard an unkind word on my visits there, and their admiration for America and its citizens is marked."

Over tea with another friend, the Countess Zucchini Solimney, Harriet admired the lake beyond. "Why, it looked just like a turquoise set in living green." Later, she chatted with the Duchess of Villa Melzi about the duchess's vineyards in Venice where she dressed like the workers and lovingly toiled in the fields alongside them.

Harriet spoke of her friendship with Count and Countess Taverna, whose palace in Rome was considered one of the country's finest. The always industrious Harriet was especially impressed that the countess had turned one of the family palaces into a school for teaching girls the art of lace-making. "As the girls learned a skill to help them make a living, a teacher was always on hand to read to them and to help them improve their minds while their fingers were busy!"

But Harriet's stay in Italy was not solely filled with visits to nearby villas of friends. While she was planning on making some automotive history, she also bore witness to some history of the aviation kind.

"One fine September day, we made up a party with plans to motor down to the city of Brescia and then to the vast plain of Montichiari, hopeful that we could view some air flights."

The prospect looked promising as the road was filled with all kinds of vehicles, trolleys, carts, carriages, wagon, bicycles and motorcars making their way to the field. Harold followed the traffic.

"Look, red flags are flying, there will be flights today," Mr. Brooks observed.

The Locomobile rumbled onto the field and waited patiently amid a jam of other vehicles. In the dusty field, Harriet and her party lifted their faces to the sky and squinted in the sunlight. From the seat of the Locomobile Harriet called, "Look! Over there!" Everyone watched in awe as a monoplane rose above them. "It looked just like a huge dragonfly!" Harriet remembered.

As fate would have it, they were witnessing the flight of the Blériot XI, flown by Louis Blériot. The pioneering French aviator had made an historic flight across the English Channel just months earlier. This achievement would not only win Blériot a lasting place in aviation history, but also assured the future of his aircraft manufacturing business. Of this accomplishment the British newspaper *The Daily Express* had declared, "Britain is no longer an island."

The excitement intensified when it was announced that the famous American aviator, Glenn Curtiss, a contemporary of the Wright Brothers, would now be attempting to break the record for the highest sustained flight ever with the hopes of claiming the Great Prize of Brescia, valued at 30,000 lire.

Thousands watched as Curtis completed six trips around the perimeter of the airfield at an altitude of one hundred feet. Forty-nine minutes and twenty-four seconds later, the plane landed as lightly as he had taken off. In the end, Bleriot took honors for reaching the highest altitude of the day.

"Then Mr. Curtiss's biplane rose lightly and swiftly to a height of about thirty meters, which was maintained throughout his entire flight," Harriet recounted. "You can imagine the suspense as thousands of us watched. Until then, nothing in the way of long flights at this altitude had been attempted. Word spread like wildfire as Mr. Curtiss began his fourth and fifth round! After his sixth round, and having flown for forty-nine minutes and twenty-four seconds, Mr. Curtiss's plane touched ground as lightly as it had ascended."

But Harriet and her party returned to Brescia too soon, and missed the flight of Henri Rougier, another French pilot who broke the record for ascending to a height of one hundred and sixteen meters, besting Curtiss.

On the following day, Harriet received the special honor of meeting Glenn Curtiss, noting that despite all the honors and attention he had received she found him to be quiet and unassuming.

"I remarked upon our meeting that his biplane reminded me of a giant seagull. He smiled and seemed pleased with my observation. He told me that was exactly what was intended when it was designed."

A fascinated Harold did not miss the opportunity to snap a photograph of Glenn Curtiss alongside his record-breaking flying machine, perhaps the most historic photo taken during the course of the entire motorcar trip.

"Later that afternoon our car was joined by over a thousand other fans in their motorcars as we watched as Henri Rougier tried to beat Curtiss's record for speed. But we missed all the excitement as we had already returned to *Villa Carlotta* by the time Mr. Curtiss bested Rougier during his second go round."

When not exploring the Italian countryside by car, Harriet took to sailing freely about Lake Como in her motorized yacht, the *Carlotta*. "Unlike the roads on which I rode, there on the lake I can zip about as fast as I wish without being warned by police officers: 'A little too fast, Madame.'"

On the twenty-second day of September Harriet's great competitive spirit emerged again when at a festival in Cadenabbia, on the west coast of Lake Como, Harriet took First Prize honors for Motor Boats. For this, she received a silver cup and a hand painted banner presented by her good friend, the Marquesa Trotti.

Three restful months had passed; it was time for Harriet to bid "*Ciao*" to the safety and comfort of these warm and familiar surroundings. She was invited to spend her final weekend in Italy with her friend Madame Brocca Rospinin, in Magenta, where many others gathered to wish her *bon voyage*.

I inquired what the members of this Italian nobility thought about their friend's plans for her daring journey.

"My Italian friends were fascinated with my car, and my intended trip. However, they all shook their heads and said that I did not know what was before me, which I freely acknowledged," Harriet simply replied.

"It was an exciting and happy time," she recalled. "We were returning to our voyage, gliding down the Riviera coast in my Locomobile, weaving through beds of pink and white carnations that lined the sparkling blue sea. I felt as if nothing could go wrong."

But upon their arrival in Marseille, France, Harriet was devastated to learn that one of her crew members would not be sailing with them to India, and no amount of cajoling, charm or fiery demands could alter this unforeseen situation.

CHAPTER EIGHT

"Honk Honk must not be forgotten!"

"We are sorry, Madame, but dogs are simply not allowed on board. No exceptions," Harriet dramatically repeated the news she had received when they arrived at port in Genoa, Italy. Despite all her pleading, protests and begging, Honkie would not be allowed to sail with his party on the ship that would take them the long stretch from Genoa to Egypt, and then on to Bombay. Arrangements would be made for him to sail on another ship.

"I declared, 'Honk Honk must not be forgotten!' and set out to make certain my dog's passage would be as safe and comfortable as possible."

Harriet provided the little terrier with a covered box for sleeping, a drinking cup, brush and comb, dog biscuits, and a pair of Harriet's slippers. "Then I wrote a note addressed to his future caretakers and placed it in a waterproof envelope attached to the dog's collar."

Across from me, Harriet pulled out a letter from her writing desk and began to read. It was obvious from her voice that this remained an emotionally charged incident.

TO WHOM IT MAY CONCERN.

My name is Honk-Honk, and I was given to my mistress as a mascot for her motor trip around the world; but as dogs are not permitted on the steamer that My Mistress sailed on, I, a Boston Bull Terrier, am obliged to be sent by another line. I don't bite, only love to play: and if there is nothing else, will some kind-hearted person give me My Mistress's slipper to play with? Then I won't cry.

I don't eat meat at all, only bread and soup, with plenty of fresh water, and occasionally a big bone, which will amuse me for hours; also if I may be permitted to play on deck, I'll be very good and not give any one any trouble. When I arrive safe those in charge of me will receive the gratitude of Mrs. Clark Fisher, at Bombay; also the gratitude of Honk-Honk.

Harold was dispatched to the custom house in Genoa where he had the car unpacked and recrated. Under his supervision it was hoped that the motorcar would be shipped properly by the American Express Company for a successful delivery to Bombay where, unscathed and satisfied, car and owner would be reunited. The next stretch of the trip would take place without motorcar or dog.

After a prolonged stay in Marseille, Harriet and her crew set sail on the *Mantua* on December 10, 1909, arriving in Port Said, Egypt, the morning of December fourteenth. Coming ashore on small boats called lighters, Harriet was overwhelmed by the sounds of the exotic languages that greeted them. "For a moment my heart failed me, for all my previous experiences in travelling seemed to have been of no avail. I felt absolutely helpless," she recalled. "For the first time in my life I was witnessing the different nationalities of the Eastern countries. Such excitement!"

Harold, Albert and Maria were left to watch the luggage while Harriet found an English-speaking man who agreed to help her purchase tickets for their train passage to Cairo.

This portion of their travel made Harriet anxious. "By the way," she said to me in a confidential tone, "this was the first time I had been on a railroad train for many months—yes, years!"

Since there were no other options, Harriet endured the trip and became even more grateful for the pleasure of riding in an automobile. The train followed the route of the Suez Canal, and Harriet was distracted by the many curious sights before her. She marveled at the structure of the famous canal called "The Highway to India," created as an artificial sea-level waterway connecting the Mediterranean and Red seas. "What a wonderful piece of engineering, but it cost so many lives and so much money while being constructed," she wryly noted.

From the train's window, bands of pilgrims were curiously observed as they traveled on the backs of camels, making their way along the canal's narrow bank toward Cairo. "I was told they were traveling to spend Christmas night with their dead."

As she had in the Swiss Alps, Harriet admired the unique qualities of another spectacular sunset. "Before my eyes, the desert stretched for miles, dotted with small mud huts and herds of sheep and little donkeys that gathered among clusters of palm trees. As the sun set, the desert was lit up in a golden glow; the sky was streaked with yellow, blue, and green, and every color known."

The train ride to the Cairo station had been hot and dusty. Arriving in that city, a fatigued Harriet and crew were beset by hordes of local guides. "Each seemed to have pockets filled with endless recommendations for tourists! We chose a guide and informed him we wished to stay at the 'Shepherd's Hotel,' upon which we were put on an overcrowded bus."

At the hotel, they were greeted by a dapper manager sporting a pink carnation in the buttonhole of his shirt. He bowed to and salaamed in the greeting typical of his nation while he directed his staff of brown, bare-legged Egyptian men. Harriet observed that these attendant's heads were wrapped up in yards of cheesecloth, and inquired of the meaning of this custom.

She was informed that upon their deaths, this material would be used for their funeral shrouds. "I couldn't help but think that always in life they carry that muslin with them."

But there were light moments to be had too.

"In Cairo, Mr. Brooks announced that he wished to ride a donkey," Harriet recalled. "He told us that he was thinking about buying a horse when he got back to America and wanted to practice in Egypt on a donkey."

This episode brought Harriet much amusement. "Mr. Brooks sat upon that donkey's back and the animal pitched and bucked, sending his unsuspecting rider into a double somersault over its head! Mr. Brooks landed hard on the ground and his angry eyes met the white-eyed gaze of the hostile animal!"

"Albert had a notion that he might have more success and decided to have a try."

But the proper butler fared no better. "Poor Albert was also thrown by the donkey, performing a perfect single somersault before crashing to the ground," Harriet said. "From that point on, Mr. Brooks no longer spoke of wanting a horse, and Albert chose to ride in something I called a sand-cart, if I recall, even though it was rough going!"

As she would throughout her entire journey, Harriet always seemed to take the time to keenly observe the customs and status of the local people. In Cairo, she noted that the children ran around half-naked and the few women she saw were those of the "better class" who covered their faces while being driven in carriages.

Outside of local shops, men sharpened knives while using their hands and feet at the same time; one foot turning a handle with knives in hand. Wood turners worked with the most primitive tools, and men sold water that was carried in dirty-looking calfskin pouches hung around their neck with a string.

"The mosques were interesting," Harriet said. "The students sat on the floor and kept up a constant rocking motion, all swaying in the same direction while studying. It made me feel seasick just to watch them."

Harriet was alarmed to find that many people in the city were blind or had "sore eyes," as she described them. "I was told that in many cases, when a son is born, the mother placed poison herbs mixed with goat's milk in their eyes to blind their sons. They believed this would prevent their sons from becoming soldiers and going into battle."

On Christmas Eve, Harriet and her party travelled in caravans to visit the tombs of the pharaohs. Despite the solemn nature of the season, they found themselves among children quarrelling like "little wildcats," and women trying to pull out one another's hair at the bazaars along the way. "Flies were everywhere. I was disgusted to see helpless and sick children with flies crawling all over their little faces."

Along with thousands of others, Harriet and her party joined the massive procession going up into the tombs. Here celebrants put on impromptu plays and dances to celebrate the season. "The spirit of Christmastide was in the air. At four o'clock Christmas morning, I found myself among worshipers who solemnly knelt and prayed to Allah as the sun rose. I found it hard to resist joining this diverse multitude in the thanking of one's own personal Allah for His many mercies and asking for His protection on the rest of one's journey."

Harriet recalled that Christmas night with the great pyramids with the Sphinx always on guard in the moonlight. On the evening of December twenty-seventh, Harriet, Harold, Maria, and Albert returned to Port Said on the backs of camels where they learned that the *China*, the steamer on which they were expecting to sail, had been damaged by a storm. They were delayed five days before departing on the *Persia*, en route for Bombay.

Their days in this exotic land were filled with the faith that they would all be blessed as they entered a new year, venturing unchartered roads and rivers into the great unknown.

CHAPTER NINE

"I shall be very pleased to send you a card from Calcutta"

Harriet and her travel companions celebrated New Year's Eve onboard the S.S. *Persia*.

"Oh, our young Mr. Brooks did not much enjoy the sea portions of our journey," Harriet mentioned. "On this portion of the trip, he complained that days at sea were 'long and red hot' and the other passengers uninteresting. Of the captain's 'Divine Services,' he stated that he did not care for 'ready-made sermons,' and on New Year's Day, Mr. Brooks matter-of-factly shared that he had made no resolutions, so he had none to break."

They arrived in Bombay on January 9, 1910. Harriet checked her party into the Taj Mahal Hotel. Then she wasted no time. She had a very important mission; it was time to reclaim her beloved dog.

"'Honkie!' I exclaimed with joy upon reuniting with him. I was so relieved to see that he had made a safe journey."

Harold headed to the shipyard, anxious to reclaim the Locomobile. Although the car had survived its voyage relatively intact, a board from the crate was missing and the salt spray from sea water had caused some corrosion of the car's brass work. Upon further inspection, he became irate when he discovered that the crate's boards had been nailed shut rather than secured with screws, causing him two hours of hard labor to unpack the crate in the intense heat of the day.

"Mr. Brooks complained that this had been quite a waste of his time and that those men in Genoa were useless!"

The next day, Harold took Albert with him to clean up the car in preparation for its police inspection. The car was issued a license and they were treated to a sailing tour with the police captain on the local harbor.

"They also enjoyed a dinner Mr. Brooks described as 'delicious and dignified' at the Gloucestershire Registered Officer's Mess," she recalled.

It was time to stock up with some essential supplies. Harriet knew that there would be no market or shops where they were headed. "I set out to acquire the perfect cooking utensils and food staples for our long trip through the wilds of India."

At an Army Navy Store she went on a shopping spree, purchasing a lantern, a hatchet, two guns, a coffeepot, teakettle, stewing dishes, frying pans, a soup pot with an "alcohol light" to provide heat for cooking, and two water buckets.

"The dining service for four fit perfectly in a large tea-basket." she said. "Many people were curious as to what kind of provisions I'd purchased for a trip of this magnitude." She pulled a list from a drawer of her writing desk and recited a litany of food items. "Seven pounds of flour, five pounds of coffee, three pounds of cut loaf and one pound of granulated sugar, a can of baking powder, three small jars of Liebig's extracts, three boxes of soda crackers, six jars of condensed milk, six cans of condensed cream, a jar of curry, three cans of Australian sausage, a jar of canned bacon, two jars of potted chicken, two pounds of boned partridge, and a quart of onions."

These were all packed in light wicker baskets and stored between the rear passenger seats, in company with the two Indian water buckets.

The party set out to make practice drives along the colorful Bombay Harbor. Harriet described the scene here as strikingly picturesque. Here there were crowds of people dressed in brilliant costumes, customary of the locals, a mix of what Harriet described as Hindus, Jews, Muslims, and Parsis.

The roads were crowded. "Harold was forced to play a dangerous game of hide and seek with bullock carts," Harriet recalled. She explained that a bullock cart was a wheeled cart pulled by oxen. These gaily-painted carts had two very high wheels, and were composed of only three or four flat boards, with no sides. Each held as many as eight to ten passengers and were steered only by long poles with ropes that ran through the nose of the bull that pulled it. "The drivers keep to the left in English fashion, but just when you are about opposite Mr. Bullock, he suddenly turns to one side, and you have to be mighty sharp at the wheel, like Mr. Brooks, to prevent being hit."

"I can still hear him shouting 'Hang On!' so often. Mr. Brooks would then swerve hard to avoid being rammed by the long poles used to manage those snorting bulls." Sometimes just the sight of the Locomobile so startled the drivers of these carts that in trying to pull out of the car's path too abruptly, their passengers and goods unceremoniously spilled to the ground.

"But these people just picked themselves off the dirty ground and happily bowed and smiled at us after we so inconvenienced them."

"We saw small groups of people paying rapt attention to snake charmers who had a dozen or so of those scaly creatures, some scorpions, and mongoose, hanging about. One could not go a block without being accosted by someone gesturing and smiling and wanting so show off his skills, or goods."

The mid-day heat was dangerous. "The first thing a tourist should do there is to get a *topee*, which looks like a safari hat, and a thin *pongee* silk suit or gown," Harriet said. "It is also advisable for one to carry a small bamboo stick to whip the bare legs of the natives who are a little too persistent when begging or selling their wares." Traveling the Queens Road toward Malabar Hill, Harriet's attention was drawn to flocks of buzzards that sat and chattered on surrounding city walls. Harriet shuddered as she recounted how local coolies carried human remains up onto the rocks where these birds would tear flesh from bones. "I was told that at night the jackals come and finish what is left of these human forms."

They took a day trip to the ancient Caves of Karli, so far from any railway that one needed a motorcar or horse to travel there. Harriet described these caves, with their intricate wall carvings and solid pillars, as the most beautiful in India. "They are so far up the mountains we had to be carried up in a *dandie*, a bed carried off the ground, by four strong men hired for twenty-five cents."

To see how well the Locomobile would handle the hills that would challenge them from Bombay to Calcutta, they took it on a trial run to Poona, a city about one hundred and thirteen miles from Bombay. As she would for many such outings, Harriet had packed a basket with tea and lunch and invited locals for a ride in her car. On this occasion, she had invited a Mr. and Mrs. Cassie to join them. She had met this couple during their sail to Bombay.

"Motoring is fairly underway in Bombay, and most roads are of excellent condition. Drivers went slowly and carefully and the police were helpful to oblige in any way."

Mr. Brooks navigated the Locomobile up a hill that no other car had been able to master without the radiator water boiling over. They were told that Harriet's vehicle had been the first large car to ever ascend the Bhor Ghat, explaining that the word *ghat* referred to a large set of steps that bathers used to reach the banks of a holy river.

"The Locomobile handled that *ghat* beautifully and this attracted a good deal of attention and excitement," Harriet said. "I was feeling anxious that we might run into some trouble, but Mr. Cassie spoke Hindustani and was of great assistance."

In Bombay, Harold changed the car's rear right tire, putting on a new "shoe" for the first time since leaving Paris. On January eighteenth, he spent the day preparing the Locomobile for its journey across India, and making arrangements for gasoline to be sent ahead.

But just before they were to depart from Bombay, Harriet was surprised to discover a young man sleeping on a quilted mat positioned outside her hotel room.

"I inquired what he was doing there. He told me his name was Antonio and that he was from Portugal. He explained that he wished to travel with me across India as my translator."

Harriet wisely knew that she was in need of this service and agreed. "His English was fairly good and we agreed to a fee of fifteen dollars a day. He would sleep outside the door of my tent whenever it was necessary. He traveled with a small tin kettle and a little box to carry his provisions."

Not surprisingly, many people doubted that Harriet could make it across a region that in some parts had not yet even been mapped by the Engineer Corps of the British Army.

As she paid the hotel bill, Antonio and two Hindus carried down all the pieces of her party's luggage, piling them into the Locomobile.

"The skeptical manager of the hotel looked on and asked me, 'Madame, do you expect to take *all* that stuff with you on your motorcar?' I answered, 'Yes, I certainly do.'"

"He replied 'But, madam, you will never get twenty miles out of Bombay with it.'"

"Oh! He was so irritating. But I calmly asked him why he thought so."

The manager told her that she would most certainly break down and would be robbed, too. Then he walked over to a group of men who had gathered at the other end of the piazza and engaged them in a lively conversation, before returning to her.

"'Mrs. Fisher,' he said to me, 'Those gentlemen over there are motorists, and they are making a wager that your undertaking to cross India is an impossibility.'"

Before a stunned Harriet could even reply he further informed her that there was not an English officer who would trust his wife fifty feet outside camp here in this country.

Harriet found her voice. "'No?' I replied to that manager, speaking loud enough to be heard. 'Well, I am going to trust myself, and I shall be very pleased to send *you* a card from Calcutta informing you *all* of our safe arrival there.'"

The manager obligingly gave Harriet his card and a postal on which to send her message.

"'Mrs. Fisher,' he said to me, 'May I present two of those wagering gentlemen?'"

Harriet agreed to this, as she wished to set them straight.

"One asked me, 'Madam, how do you expect to get petrol as you go along?'"

Harriet explained that the car carried about four hundred miles worth of petrol. The front tank held eighteen gallons, and the rear tank twenty-two. There were also four gallons of oil onboard.

"'I've also made arrangements to have petrol delivered at the different stations located on a map and I am pretty confident that I will reach these stations before our supply runs out,' I told them."

But Harriet was aware that they were only allowed to receive twelve gallons of petrol in three four-gallon drums sent to the care of one person. She cleverly figured out she could have supplies sent in the name of the others in her party, ensuring they would have a steady supply of petrol and oil.

"The other man asked me, 'But where will you spend your nights?'"

Harriet told them when not sleeping in her custom-made tent, they would seek shelter in government run bungalows called *daks*, and rest houses, until they reached Calcutta.

But as she was speaking to these men, a concerned Harold had been listened in and knew there might be some truth in what the manager said.

"Mr. Brooks confided to me that the rear spring was 'below flat.' I asked him if I should be concerned about the car. I liked his answer very much, for Mr. Brooks assured me that he wouldn't allow that manager's doubts, or those of others, to discourage him. He told me that the Locomobile was the most reliable car made anywhere in the world, and it would keep us safe in any situation."

Although government officials warned her not to proceed with her 2,300 mile voyage from Bombay to Calcutta, Harriet would not be dissuaded. She was anxious to head out on her journey.

At eleven o'clock on the morning of January seventeenth, the Locomobile rolled onto the Queens Road and departed Bombay. Just a few miles into their Indian journey, the view did not look promising. "There were so many half-naked, dirty and ragged-looking people everywhere," Harriet recalled with dismay. Noting the number of corpses that lined the roads, she grew worried. "There had been much talk of the plague and smallpox."

But Harriet explained that she believed the Hindus to be very "cleanly" for they were always washing. Unfortunately, this washing took place where the waters from different wells ran back into the wells from which they drank. "But this water was always well-cooked before taking."

Conditions improved as they moved away from the city and into rural regions. Due to the steep *ghats* that had to be maneuvered from Shapura to Tagpturi, the going was slow. They arrived at Khardi, in the Thane District, at five o'clock that evening after only advancing ninety miles in six hours.

"It was hot and we were all thirsty. Albert was obliged to keep the kettle boiling for three hours to supply us with drinking water. We had no ice and had to cool the boiled water by putting it in a *chattie* and tying the bottle on a tree limb," Harriet recalled. "Sometimes I was put to work swinging the bottle to cool the water!"

"At one thousand feet above sea level, Khardi is an area of great natural beauty. It is impossible for one to picture adequately the views that presented themselves to us," Harriet said. "From points north, south, east, and west lay barren mountains, with an occasional clump of trees with little mud huts that looked like straw-covered mounds."

There were no *dak* bungalows or rest houses in this area. It was time for the tent to be put to its first trial in the wild and a good night's sleep would be had by none, especially Honk Honk.

CHAPTER TEN

Wild Nights in the Jungle

"My dear girl," Harriet said to me. "I've been chattering away like a parrot in the wilds of India. I haven't even allowed you to ask any questions! Please, let's walk and take lunch underneath the lovely apple tree out back. Maria has been cooking some kind of sauce with our tomatoes. It takes me back to Italy and has made me hungry. I've arranged for her to bring us a delicious dish she makes with the eggs laid by my own hens. It is like a pie made of spaghetti and egg and cheese," Harriet explained. "It is delicious!"

I took this opportunity to sharpen my pencil and rest my weary hand. We left our hats in the house and rolled up our sleeves. Harriet's mind might have been back in Italy, but out in the hot sun, taking in a vista of fields and rolling hills, I felt like anything was possible. I imagined myself in Khardi, ready to tackle the dense jungles and steep *ghats* of the Indian continent.

Harriet summoned two young men to set up a small table and chairs for us. Albert followed with a tray that now held a carafe of pale red wine. We sat and Harriet poured for the both of us.

"Here's to a beautiful Sunday," she said, raising her glass and tapping it to mine. I took only a small sip. Giddy from her stories, and wary of the heat, I wanted to stay as sharp as my pencil.

Before we resumed our conversation, Billikins and the two dogs reappeared. Honk Honk and Jappy settled down under the shade of the table, but the monkey had other plans. He quickly scaled the apple tree, climbing up high out of sight.

"Billikins!" Harriet called up to him. "Leave those apples alone. They are not ready for picking!"

Now Albert had come out of the house, joined by Maria. Dressed in a white blouse with a plain black skirt, Harriet's maid carried a large tray with the promised meal that did indeed resemble a pie, along with some other delicious-looking items. They all stood while Harriet peered up the tree.

"Watch your head, Miss," Maria said to me, with a soft Italian accent. Her dark hair was piled on top of her head, and her sharp features seemed to soften when she smiled.

With that warning, a small half-ripened apple landed at the base of Harriet's skirt. "Billikins, come down here, now!"

"Why if this doesn't bring back memories of our time in Nebraska," Albert said. "We had stopped to let the animals out of the car for some exercise, and Billikins climbed up a tree. He thought it was great fun to shower us with fruit and would not come down."

"Was that Colorado or Nebraska, Albert?" Harriet asked. "But, no matter, he did it!" she went on without waiting for an answer. "It was only when I cleverly had the car started, and we pretended to leave without him, did I see a monkey move so fast, fearing he would be abandoned."

Harriet, Maria, Albert, and I had a good laugh at the story. Billikins, perhaps smelling the food and hoping for some more lunch, scrambled back down the tree.

Maria and Albert served us and left us to our talk. As they departed, they spoke to each other with an easy banter, marked with bouts of laughter as they headed toward a small bungalow on the property. I was struck by how Maria towered over the man who had become her husband not long after arriving home from their long journey.

Harriet noticed my curiosity. "Funny how fate can take one so far from their place of birth," she said. "Do you think that Maria Borge, growing up in a small town in northern Italy, thought she would marry an English butler, travel the world with her boss in a motorcar, and then settle in a place called New Jersey?"

That scenario did seem quite unlikely, but the thought of it made me smile. "They were bonded by your desire to see the world," I said. "It's a testament to you that they made such a grand commitment to each other, and to you, after such strenuous endeavor."

Harriet stared at them as they moved out of sight, as if in deep thought. "Yes, some of us have been so fortunate," she said. "Now, getting back to our interview. Do you have any additional questions about my motor trip?"

"I do," I said, glad to refocus our talk on the trip. "What was it like spending evenings in such strange places? I imagine it being quite scary."

Harriet recounted that first evening in Khardi, when they were reminded of just how far from civilization they found themselves. "Sleeping under the stars for the first time proved to be surprising noisy," she began. "In the distance the constant beat of drums echoed from a local village. They never seemed to stop, and Honkie, tied to the Locomobile, would not stop barking at so many strange noises."

"When I complained, Mr. Brooks pointed out that Honk Honk made a great watch dog."

At this point in her trip, Harriet appeared to have absorbed the magnitude of the voyage on which she had embarked. "The sensations that come when one realizes that one is really in a foreign land surrounded by natives are decidedly peculiar," she tried to explain. "Many natives delighted their souls by gazing at us. They were extremely polite, but never came within fifty feet of our camp unless invited to do so. They were willing to serve us by bringing water, or wood, or by doing anything that was requested by me, the 'White Lady.'"

At this time, a great religious festival was taking place in India, one that occurred every twelve years. Thousands of pilgrims shared the route of the Locomobile as it began its second day of motoring into the interior of this vast continent. Harold was instructed to choose a course that had him navigating one hundred miles of level road from Igatpuri to Nahsik. This municipality of the western Indian state of Maharshtra was located near the banks of the Godavari River, and was densely lined with ancient temples.

These pilgrims journeyed to Trimbak, the location of the sacred Trimbakeshwar Shiva Temple, to bathe in the holy waters of the Godavari at its source.

Harriet described the scene in colorful detail. "Here one sees orange, red, and white turbans. Mothers carry their infants on their hip. We were greeted with a *salaam* given by the touching of the right hand to the head, which was then passed gracefully to the heart!"

They made their way to Munar, on to Malegaon, and then to Dhulia where they received their first supply of petrol.

"The chief of police there was very interested in my trip. He gave orders for sixteen bullocks to meet us at the banks of the Tapti River to assist our passage through the sand."

But even with their assistance, the crossing of the Tapti River presented a challenge, as several hundred yards of deep sand lined both of the river's banks, requiring the car to be pulled by bullocks. "The sand was so deep and soft in places that the rope that pulled the car broke. I was glad to be able to offer my own fine manila rope which I had brought for this very purpose."

When they were not required to spend the night in the tent Harriet found that the quality of the government facilities made available to them varied greatly. "We always supplied our own linens and mattresses. In some instances we found it necessary to explore dark corners for snakes and scorpions."

In Mhow, a railway district headquarters, they obtained their second supply of petrol, which was purchased for about eight rupees. They were tired and only found a very dirty bungalow in which to sleep.

"In this city, we met an English woman who was in tears. It seemed her husband had just been transferred to the station here and her two little girls had just about been eaten up with what she called 'crimson ramblers' or what we in America call bedbugs!"

It was quickly decided that the crew would move onto Indore, where they were able to locate a clean bungalow. Harriet called the manager of the place an "old robber" when she learned of the price they would be forced to pay for their lodging.

"We refused to take a meal there," she recounted. "But Albert managed to give us a good dinner of baked beans, tomato salad, boiled potatoes, and fried eggs. I recall a man named Mr. Ross dined with us, and despite our simple fare he told us it was the best dinner he had enjoyed since having come to India!"

But later that evening, Honkie, attached to the Locomobile, howled in fright. Harriet rushed to see what the commotion was all about. "'Get away!' I shouted at a pack of jackals that had circled him." As they prepared to attack, Harriet untied Honkie and rescued him from being their prey, just in the nick of time.

"From that point on Honkie chose to sleep with his mistress," Harriet said. "Harold was not too happy at this point, either, for it was in Indore that we had our first tire trouble with two punctures and a blowout."

Harriet and her party left Indore around eleven o'clock the following morning, arriving in Sarangpur at six o'clock that evening, a trek of about 125 miles.

"For the most part it was a charming spot," she recalled. "Two policemen had been sent there to take extra care of the *dak* bungalow during our stay. The native women brought us cakes, but we had to draw our water from a pond where dead animals were lying about."

While there Maria took the opportunity to wash the party's clothing in a tin bathtub with water carried in the hot sun from a pond located almost a mile away. The clothing was hung in the bushes to dry.

"It was sixty-five degrees in the shade," Harriet noted of the harsh weather conditions.

And other matters of great importance loomed large. "For the first time our food supply had run low. We had consumed all of our canned goods and depended entirely on biscuits. Mr. Brooks went out gunning for game because we had run out of chickens and we had only two eggs in our stores."

As Harriet and I leisurely lunched on the grounds of Bella Vista, I tried to imagine how someone would find an egg, or anything edible, in the wilderness.

The pressure was on Harold, Albert, and Antonio to forage for food. Harold set out to hunt fowl. He successfully brought in some fine pigeons, but he was distressed about a hunting misfortune, apologizing for having shot a beautiful parrot by accident.

"Poor Harold. He knew how much I loved birds, and what beautiful birds they were, throughout India. Mynahs, green parrots, swarms of peacocks that made noises like humans."

Harold had other reasons to be concerned as the shooting of a bird was not to be taken lightly. Many Hindus believed that the spirits of their ancestors assumed the shapes of birds. Harriet had been warned by locals that they were never to shoot these creatures as they were considered sacred by the natives. "Why we were told that if we were even to be found with feathers our immediate slaughter would be demanded!"

Fortunately for Harold, his digression went unreported, as did Antonio's as he returned to camp with two chickens in hand. Albert proceeded to prepare a special treat, cooking them with curry and rice.

"Rice was always plentiful. We would often find peasants sitting along the roadside, miles from nowhere, with flat baskets or cloths heaped with rice for sale. I would often spot a frail peasant woman carrying a child on one hip, staff in hand, with a bundle of bedding wrapped around her neck, all the while balancing a round brass basin on her head that was filled with water."

Back on the road, the Locomobile continued its battle with the bullocks. "At one point, the roadway and the fields appeared to be alive with them." Harriet described these animals as clever, small footed and bright eyed, possessing perfectly shaped horns and a hump just between the shoulder.

"As we drove along, about five bullocks suddenly stood still. They lowered their heads and bellowed loudly, switching their tales. They looked like they meant business. Two of them attacked the side of the Locomobile, while the others charged the car's front."

"'Give me stick, quick!' cried Antonio, who was able to ward off one ferocious bull. Then Mr. Brooks leapt over the car's roof and, using a piece of rubber hose, belabored the bullocks up in front of the car that were ramming their heads in fury against it."

Finally, some local coolies came to their rescue. They shouted and made a great noise and beat the bullocks with sticks. Back in the driver's seat, Harold drove off just fast enough to fill the eyes of the bulls with dust.

At this time, much to Harriet's delight, the travelers were excited to be heading toward their first visit with Indian royalty. "Interestingly, on the occasions we met Indian royalty, all of the Indian princes asked me how we managed to share the roads with the bullock carts!"

Arriving at Goona, part of a region known as the Gwalior State, at eleven o'clock in the evening, the party was exhausted.

"There was a rest house there and we paid seven rupees apiece for two rooms and a little kitchen for our one night stay. This included all of our water and two bedsteads, but no mattresses, just the straps to support them. We made do with some linens. No extra charge was made for the dirt which was plentiful."

Harriet enjoyed their stay at Goona, describing it the most magnificent night anyone could ever imagine. "The balmy air was perfect, and the odors from the flowers mixed with the dew of the night air with their spicy breath."

Harriet explained that the keeper of the rest house was Eurasian. He was well-informed and believed in the use of different herbs and recipes that the Indians used for medicine or cures for all kinds of ailments and diseases.

"The lonely caretaker of this property had lost his wife only three days earlier and longed for company," Harriet said. "But Mr. Brooks found him tiresome and complained that he would talk us to death."

The caretaker had a mysterious air about him, and directed his audience's attention to the sky.

"'That star will protect you on your journey and prevent you and your party from coming to any harm,' he told me. We all looked up, and on that night of the twenty-seventh of January, we had our very first view of Halley's Comet!" In Goona, Harold was ready to receive his next supply of petrol. But the station master, upon discovering that they were two cans over their limit, had these extra supplies forwarded to the future destination of Agra.

Harriet learned that she and her party had been invited to be the honored guests at a banquet given by the Maharaja of Gwalior. "I happily accepted, for I looked forward to more luxurious accommodations and to meeting the Maharaja Madhave Roa the Second."

The Maharaja had been chiefly responsible for the advancement of the railway system of India. Harriet had been told that he had built the Gwalior Light Rail in 1904, using his personal funds to purchase engines and other materials, and using his own subjects for laborers.

"Despite my dislike of rail cars, I *was* anxious to meet this distinguished industrialist and royal figure who was the proud owner of thirty-two motorcars!" an impressed Harriet recalled.

CHAPTER ELEVEN

A Royal Reception at the Gwalior State

"Her Highness of Gwalior only receives ladies in her private room," Harriet was informed upon her arrival at the royal palace.

"'Are you fond of bridge?' Her Highness inquired of me upon our meeting."

The royal couple had no children and Her Highness appeared to lead a lonely life. She told Harriet how fond she was of the card game and confessed to Harriet that she did not know what she would do with her many long hours if she could not play. She went so far as to say she would like to, "give a vote of thanks to the person who invented it."

"Her Highness was not a worldly woman and thought that anyone who spoke English must be from England," Harriet said.

"But I was made to understand that His Highness was advanced in all his ideas and was considered a loyal subject of England, with many English diplomats in his employ."

The Maharaja owned many palaces and traveled back and forth between them as the seasons dictated. The manner in which he entertained visitors was legendary. Harriet was told that some guests were sent on long rides on elephants to explore "his jungles." In true form, he saw to it that his American guests had an unforgettable visit.

Harriet and her companions were lavishly entertained in a grand room decorated in yellow and white and lined with lush potted plants. The table at which they dined was shaped like a long horseshoe with miniature silver cars that ran up and down a track. The cars traveled along the table, stopping to deliver sweets and small cakes, cigars, cigarettes and liquors to each diner.

Up on a balcony, musicians serenaded them with what Harriet described as "Oriental" music. The songs were nonstop, with new musical groups replacing those that were fatigued.

The next day they prepared for a grand tour arranged by their host. There had been no rain in this region for several weeks and the dust hung heavy in the hot and arid locale. As they departed the Gwalior State, they were engulfed by great clouds of it in a dark copper color that rose up from the parched roads.

"Our boy, Antonio, had been painted white. But now he looked like a tremendously serious clown. In the dust, he had taken on a dark copper color and his eyelids and hair were simply pasted with red dust," Harriet recalled with amusement. "As for us, the dust turned our party into veritable Indians in color!"

They made a seventy-three mile trek to the city of Agra on a well-maintained road. But the ferry crossing over the Chambal River, a tributary of the Yamuna River in the Madhya Pradesh state, proved challenging. "I feared the Locomobile and its contents would be pitched to the bottom of the river!" Harriet recollected.

They stopped to rest at an Inspection Bungalow just outside of Agra and enjoyed a meal prepared by Albert. "We had managed to purchase some carrots and some delicious green peas. We also had a little flour in our supplies and Mr. Brooks had succeeded in killing four pigeons."

At sunset, Harold surprised his colleagues when he came back from hunting with two partridges. "Everybody unfeignedly rejoiced in this welcome change from pigeon and an animated conference was held as to how the partridges should be prepared."

Antonio had advised Harriet to pack as many limes as possible, and these were hanging in a small net sack on the side of the car. A combination of sugar and limes was added to boiled water to make refreshing limeade.

In Agra, they registered at the Lauries' Great Northern Hotel which Harriet described as "fairly good." As there were not many choices for hotels in the region, the landlord often took advantage of those they found foolish enough to travel so far from home.

As was typical of most of the local hotels, this one was a one-story structure built in the shape of a hollow square with a courtyard located in its center. In this arid climate, a fountain that contained no water stood surrounded by plants Harriet described as "indifferent" for great lack of moisture. "Here, even the most ordinary tree or weed was allowed to grow," she recalled. "Anything that was green."

As was the case in most rest houses and hotels, Harriet provided the bedding, pillows, linen, and towels for her party. The bedrooms were typically furnished with only a dusty piece of matting that covered a stone floor. There were no modern toilet conveniences, but off the bedroom area a small room contained a tin tub and a commode.

"Twice each day, an attendant, called a sweeper, would bring us fresh water," she explained. "Travelers to this region should never use unboiled water, even for brushing one's teeth, as many took ill from drinking this water." Harriet also insisted on acquiring a mosquito net to protect against their poisonous bites.

Across India, there was always great interest paid to the Locomobile upon its arrival at area hotels. "The proprietor and his entire staff would come out to inspect the car and to greet me, the *mem sahib*, which was used as a form of respectful address for a European woman," Harriet explained. "Among them there would always be the old *Baba*, the one responsible for all the books and accounts. You could usually spot him with his long white beard, and smiling face that was patience personified."

Harriet noted how she was never required to record her name in the hotel's book as train passengers were required to, and how her accommodations were always ready for her arrival. "I suspect that my Indian boy, Antonio, would telegraph the hotel to let them know that 'a personage' was on the way."

In the city of Agra, there were only two automobiles and a ride in one was a great novelty. Harriet invited a couple from Ireland by the name of Mr. and Mrs. Seagraves to spend a day touring with her in her car. They visited shops where men embroidered beautiful robes, and markets that sold bronze, emeralds, and pearls.

"Did you get to visit the Taj Mahal?" I asked, knowing that it was located in the city of Agra. With its elements of Islamic, Persian, Ottoman, and Turkish architecture, and its dramatic history, the Taj Mahal, or Crown of Palaces, was a place that held great fascination for me. I had seen pictures of the fantastic white marble structure that had been built in 1631 by the grief-stricken Mughal emperor, Sha Jahan, in memory of this third wife, Mumtaz Mahal. She had died during the delivery of the couple's fourteenth child.

"Yes, we reserved one entire day to explore the Taj Mahal and its grounds," Harriet replied. "We wandered freely about the white marble mausoleum with its sides that looked like beautiful pieces of lace, some of them inlaid with mother of pearl and colored stones. We had arrived with our tea-basket and were permitted to have our supper on a beautiful marble corner. We dined as we waited for the moon to rise. It was an experience I will never forget."

"Mr. Brooks simply declared, 'This is the most gorgeous and beautiful thing!'"

She spoke of a magnificent silver lamp inside the tomb and explained that it had been presented by a man named Lord Curzon, whom she described as the person credited for preserving the magnificent wonder. "Without his thoughtfulness, this place would have crumbled away or would have been carried piecemeal away by the souvenir-hunting tourist," she explained.

Harriet seemed to be totally absorbed in her recollection of this magnificent monument filled with romance and melancholy, asking, "I often wonder if in these modern days anything as beautiful and lasting will ever be accomplished. Will any man in this present age remember his wife with so beautiful a memorial?"

CHAPTER TWELVE

On to Delhi

On the morning of February fourth, the tanks of the Locomobile were topped with petrol and oil as Harriet prepared for passage to Delhi, a city that stood about one hundred and thirty-three miles from Agra.

"Before heading off we received our mail. I had to reprimand Mr. Brooks when he objected to me snatching his mail right out of his hands before he could read it," Harriet said, laughing. "I heard him remark to someone that Mrs. F could be so difficult!"

But fifty-five miles later, things were a little more restful as the party stopped in the ancient town of Aligarh. "We lunched under the shade of a beautiful spreading tree. The odor of the straw in the rice fields reminded us of harvest time in America."

Just outside the city of Delhi, the Locomobile waited for its turn to pass over a newly constructed one-way bridge. As they idled, they were approached by a uniformed officer on horseback.

"I said to Mr. Brooks, 'Look at that odd man.' He was trying to *salaam*, but his horse was being spooked by our car. The Locomobile must have looked like a two-eyed monster to that poor horse!"

The agitated man jerked around in the saddle, struggling to bow while remaining on his mount. He finally calmed the agitated animal, and halted traffic so as to allow the motorcar to pass before all others.

"I marveled at a parade of men who walked alongside us carting huge mounds of long grass and sugar cane on their backs. Under the weight of their cargo, I could only see their brown legs. It would be a load for any ordinary *horse* to carry."

At the Great Mosque in Delhi, Harriet observed thousands of people praying on the bare stone floor. "They looked toward the sun and praised Allah with a chant that stayed in my memory for years. Then, they all disappeared and were almost immediately replaced with people selling all kinds of wares."

At this point Maria returned to us at our spot under the tree, bearing a welcome pitcher of lemonade and two cups on a tray.

"Thank you Maria!" Harriet said. "Maria, do you remember how I bought those perfectly tamed little birds at the bazaar at Delhi?"

Maria smiled and nodded. "Yes, I do. You and your pets." She headed back toward the house with a funny little nod and a dismissive swish of her hand as if to indicate that there was a humorous inside story about these birds.

"After I purchased those birds, a small boy showed me how to attach a string to each of their tails so I could get them to the hotel until we could find a proper cage," Harriet explained.

But Harriet wasn't the only one intrigued with the local wildlife. Wherever they drove, packs of curious red and black squirrels and chipmunks crowded the Indian roadways by the thousands. They entertained the humans, but for "vicious hunter" Honk Honk, they proved to be easy prey.

And then there were the monkeys.

"Throughout our travels in India, monkeys were always on both sides of the road, chattering away in their monkey jargon, and giving forth weird screeches. Antonio informed us that the natives of India cherish monkeys. Antonio captured the nation's deep affection for these animals by sharing a story that had been told to him by soldiers who had been camping along a river filled with hungry alligators. The soldiers relayed how a baby monkey, while playing happily among the trees, had fallen from a bough into the river below him. As the alligators swarmed around the unfortunate baby, hoping for a fresh meal, a squad of monkeys had responded to the distress call of its mother."

"'Monkeys rushed from all directions to help,' Antonio went on. 'They joined paws and formed a monkey chain that let the mother monkey reach her baby. She snatched him from being taken by the jaws of the alligators.'"

For good measure, the monkeys tossed coconuts at the big scaly creatures until the baby was sprung back into the tree and was once again safe in its mother's arms. As she held her baby she let out a howl of joy.

"What an interesting story it was!" exclaimed the animal-loving Harriet.

Before setting out for a day of touring the area around Delhi, Harold endured much aggravation in the hot sun while putting a new Dunlop tire on the car. "Poor Mr. Brooks," Harriet said. "It didn't help much that I became angry with him after he had spilled some perfectly good coffee in the car that morning."

Harold's mood did not improve on the next stretch of the trip. Touring near Delhi, the Locomobile was forced to climb countless *ghats*. These deep sand-covered steps had continued to be a constant challenge for car and driver.

"At times, it seemed as if the car was fairly holding her breath before her throttle opened up with a renewed conviction to continue on, and with an almost human-like sigh, she struggled to the top of each hill."

Harriet gave a sigh, too, but one of happiness. She was filled with excitement about her visit to the city of Allahabad where she would be reunited with a man she referred to as Judge Nehru, someone she had become acquainted with on a steamer excursion.

Her anticipation would be justly rewarded.

CHAPTER THIRTEEN

The Gracious Hospitality of Judge Motilal Nehru

They approached the city of Allahabad. Its original name was Prayagan, which meant "place of offering," because it was located where the sacred Ganges, Yamuna and Saraswati rivers met. Filled with ancient temples and palaces, this city played an integral role in Hindu scripture.

Harriet recalled that not everyone was enjoying the ride. "The roads were very bad at this point and because it was so arid, large clouds of dust made it nearly impossible for Mr. Brooks to navigate or to even see where he was going."

The local people, not used to seeing motorcars, often fumbled into the path of the Locomobile and Harold grew increasingly aggravated. "He would complain impatiently 'Now look, I have knocked a man down and because of his carelessness the glass of a car light is broken!'"

But nothing could ruin Harriet's good mood, for she was particularly excited to be entering this sacred city. "I had high hopes of seeing my new friend, Judge Nehru."

As I mentioned earlier, although I had read Harriet's account of her journey, I had observed that she often casually referred to royalty without making it clear the significance of these individuals.

In this case, Judge Nehru was Motilal Nehru, an important and powerful Indian political figure, leader of the Indian independence movement, co-founder of India's Swaraj Party, and father of its first prime minister, Jawaharlal Nehru.

The thought of visiting the judge's grand home, and the promise of adventurous rides on the backs of elephants, filled Harriet with great anticipation. But her happy expectations were short-lived.

"Upon our arrival to Allahabad at nine o'clock in the evening, we received no official invitation from *any* dignitary." she recalled with disappointment.

"In fact, we had to settle in for the night at the Great Northern Hotel, which was truly a miserable excuse for one."

Early the next morning, Harriet was awakened by a great commotion. Outside her window Antonio was speaking with two servants who profusely gesticulated and bowed toward him.

"I called Antonio over to me and inquired as to what seemed to be the problem," she said. "He informed me that the servants told him there were people waiting to see me in the hotel's drawing room."

Harriet went to meet her visitors and found a woman named Miss Hooper, Judge Nehru's personal attendant, and the judge's young daughter. They were very relieved to see her. Due to some misunderstanding, the judge had expected Harriet's arrival the previous day and he was gravely concerned that she and her party might be in some sort of danger.

"I was informed by Miss Hooper in a clipped British accent that Judge Nehru has requested my presence at the palace immediately."

"I had protested that I could not possibly come at once. It would have been quite an imposition for the judge and I had not even met Mrs. Nehru."

But the woman insisted. "I was told that was of no consequence and that I had been personally invited by the head of the house."

Maria encouraged Harriet to accept this special invitation, informing Harriet that their filthy hotel rooms were inhabited by a number of crimson ramblers (bed bugs).

Outside the Great Northern Hotel, Harriet found a fine Fiat automobile with a tonneau lined with red satin waiting for her. Her party followed in the Locomobile as they rolled through a beautiful park-like setting lined with miniature lakes, a property owned by the judge.

"We soon arrived at the magnificent white marble palace. It was nestled in a lush landscape filled with rose bushes, date palms and coconut trees," Harriet recalled the stunning residence known as Swaraj Bhavan, or "Adobe of Bliss."

"We neared the grand entrance of the palace and my heartbeat quickened by the spectacle of at least seventy-five servants and two enormous elephants that knelt in welcome! They were the largest elephants I had ever seen, bigger than Jumbo of Barnum's Circus. They were dressed in magnificent gold and silver band-embroidered *howdahs*, the carriages placed on top of their backs. I was later told those seats cost over twenty-thousand dollars. Imagine that!"

At the palace entrance, Harriet was greeted by two of the judge's nieces. They were elegantly dressed in white saris adorned with stunning gemstones.

Harriet sensed these shy girls were as nervous as she. "But our uncertainty soon wore off under cordial greetings," Harriet happily recalled.

"Although India is a British Colony, it was far more an exotic place than can be imagined. I ask you to imagine what it meant to one who was thousands of miles from home, in a strange land, where a strange language was spoken, to suddenly find oneself transported into such a magnificent home, with all one's dreams and fancies of oriental grandeur realized!"

Given my limited travel experience, I told her I honestly could not.

In this lavish setting, Harriet recounted that she was spared no luxury and attended by a pair of servants at all times. "Madame, you are the first white lady that we have had the honor to entertain in our home," they informed me.

But Maria was not so impressed by all the fuss. When she attempted to take possession of their apartment, she experienced some unexpected interference from the two female servants assigned to her mistress.

At the time, Maria had confided to Harriet that she did not trust these women.

But Harriet reminded her maid they were honored guests of the judge and had to go along with his rules. Maria reluctantly handed over a bag of jewelry and personal papers to the care of her new co-servants, despite her fear those items would be stolen.

Harriet sensed that since his arrival at the palace, Antonio had appeared to be more formal in his actions, perhaps awed at suddenly finding himself in this special place of honor, one he never dreamed of seeing. She suddenly noticed that Antonio and all the male members of her party had disappeared.

"I asked the servants about the whereabouts of the men."

She was told that Harold, Antonio and Albert had been sent away. "No white man can stay under the same roof as the Indian servants," I was informed.

The men, Honkie, and Harriet's pet birds were put up in a tent one hundred and fifty feet from the palace.

"Mr. Brooks told me not to worry about them. Their sleeping accommodations were quite comfortable, though just a little cold in the morning."

At breakfast the next morning, Judge Nehru greeted her like an old friend, despite having made her acquaintance only once on an ocean liner. As was their custom, the gentlemen and the ladies sat on opposite sides of the table.

"In this perfectly arranged English dining room he relayed to me that his wife was not feeling well and he regretted she could not be there to welcome me. He told me that he was so relieved our trip from Bombay was a safe one, and he said that he too had owned a motorcar for two years, but did not even dare drive to Delhi, fearing the roads would prove too difficult."

Judge Nehru regarded his nephews as sons and as they married, the newly formed families were invited to come to live at the judge's home. As the families grew larger, an additional home was built with its own center court.

Harriet was intrigued by these courts with their white marble rooms and flowing fountains. "How restful, peaceful, and beautiful they were."

After breakfast, she got better acquainted with the ladies of the house.

"They addressed me as 'Mrs. Fisher.' Although they kept up an English manner of living, many of them preferred the native way. They asked me which form I preferred."

Harriet informed them that as a guest, she wanted to experience the Hindu manner of living. She was promptly escorted into a boudoir of one of the nieces lined with velvet cushions on which Harriet proceeded to recline in Hindu fashion.

The young women were anxious to have exchanges about cultural and societal norms with their well-travelled visitor from the West. "They confided to me that Hindu ladies never went about or visited except with their husbands."

"They had formed a woman's club as an excuse to venture out. But they confessed that their group only consisted of five members. I guessed correctly that they were the five."

"In this culture," Harriet explained, "The raising of boys was highly valued, as a boy was considered a future soldier. I was made to understand that where two girls have been born in a family that had as many boys, the birth of a third girl would mean that her life would end with her birth. The poor mother would not even see the little one, and this was perfectly legitimate!"

The nieces explained to Harriet how different marks on the foreheads of their people indicated to which caste, or social group, they belonged. They spoke of their efforts to prevent the custom where girls as early as age seven were married to boys no older than nine. These young bride-elects were customarily sent to live with their mothers-in-law and trained in all the ways to serve their new husbands best.

They told Harriet that they were under the assumption that education lessened the desire for a man to possess more than one wife at a time.

"I had asked them 'What about love? Did that not come into play?' They all laughed at the idea of love such as we know it in America," Harriet remembered. "They were amused at the idea of any sentiment between two people as man and wife, outside of their own children."

"They informed me that in their country, there were no options for women, and that divorce is rare, and that those females who cannot acquire a husband are considered to be under a curse, useless to society."

The talk soon turned to Harriet's own personal affairs.

"They asked me if I loved my husband. Yes, I told them. Another asked if I was a widow. I affirmed that I was. They wanted to know if life was the same for me after my husband's death. I told them no, and that it never would be, but we in America consider that widows have work to accomplish in the world after the husband's death, just the same as during his lifetime."

Harriet noted that her new friends appeared to be fully informed of the value placed on widows in America and in England. They knew that widows stood a greater chance of marrying than spinsters.

They shared with Harriet that in their nation, men were treated like gods. "They told me that there a woman, upon losing her husband, had lost her value and in many cases her own life and that in certain regions of India, a widow was destined to be burned on a funeral bier alongside her husband's body."

"These modern-thinking women expressed gratitude that the British government had now forbidden this practice and for the efforts that had been made on behalf of all women of India," Harriet said.

Of particular interest to Harriet, the judge's nieces had also shared with her how travel was discouraged by their religion. "They relayed to me that it was considered a sin for a Hindu to travel very far away from home unless it was to make a pilgrimage to the sacred river."

They further informed her that if a Hindu was planning to leave home, he must fast for a number of days before, and had to feast with his friends before his travels and after his return home. This bold traveler was also made to pray continually and to pay a penalty in pearls or gold to a priest who prayed for his safe return during his absence. If he did not do this he would lose caste.

"I inquired about the absence of children on the grounds of the house," Harriet said. "I was told that the wealthy class never had their children in evidence. They are kept in the nursery with their proper nurses, and their mothers visit and spend hours with them. I must say they were the most polite and good-tempered children I have ever met!"

"We were all kept busy at the Nehru palace. Even the judge found good use for Mr. Brooks's experience as a boat mechanic."

Judge Nehru asked Harold to check on some problems he was having with the engine on his motorboat. Upon inspection, Harold discovered water in the gas tank and that the needle valve had rusted. He reset the ignition, removed oil and petrol from the crank pit and changed the boat's battery. After Harold had it up and running smoothly, Judge Nehru and his young visitor took the boat for a ride on the sacred waters of the Ganges River.

Indian worshipers making their twelve-year religious pilgrimage to the sacred Ganges crowded the banks and water of the river. Young Harold watched in horror and amazement. He found nothing sacred in what he observed and reported with disgust to Harriet. "He told me that hundreds of people were bathing to purge their souls in the filthiest water imaginable. And they were drinking it, too, carrying jars of it away with them despite the fact that many dead bodies were sunk in it."

Harriet, and her entire party, would experience their own journey to the banks of that sacred river, as the judge had arranged for an elephant to be at their service the next day.

"We ventured out early, so as not to suffer from the heat of the afternoon," Harriet said. She later learned that Judge Nehru had been required to obtained special permission from the government to permit the elephants on the street at that hour as the elephants spooked the horses of the English officers. "What a gorgeous sight met our eyes as we gazed at these enormous creatures all dressed in holiday garb. The *howdahs* on their back resembled golden chariots!"

Harriet was assigned the seat of honor, accompanied by two of the judge's nieces and Maria. Harriet laughed and recalled, "I looked over at Harold and he looked as though an automobile would better suit his taste. But he climbed the ladder to the top of his elephant and took his seat."

Harriet was told that the elephant upon which she rode was fifty years old. But Harold rode on a twenty-year-old female who was so mischievous that she required several men to keep her in order.

The elephants were made to kneel in order to allow the passengers to settle in, which was easy enough. However, once they stood, their passengers were thrown backward, then forward, and then side to side.

They rambled on down to the banks of the Ganges moving in a combination swinging-seesaw motion. "I must say that on the whole, almost any river in America, even the muddy Delaware, is more picturesque than the Ganges. The only difference is that on the banks of this sacred river, men have built beautiful temples and shrines as testament to their belief in the holiness and purity of its waters."

Harriet was thrilled to be among the millions of people that had gathered along its banks. "We had a perfect view from the elephant's back. Judge Nehru had said there was no better way to see this grand throng and he was correct."

And what throngs they were, Harriet recalled. "We passed groups of naked men just sitting on hot ashes. I knew how hot they were, for when I got down from my perch and put my fingers in the ashes, they blistered my finger, and also proved that I did not belong to a sacred tribe!"

Every few minutes an elegant *dandie,* a bed carried on the shoulders of servants, could be seen transporting Hindu ladies of great social position. They were carried in secrecy to the river's edge for their sacred baths, which were said to wash away sins. "No one was permitted to look upon the faces of these ladies," Harriet confided in disbelief. "But on this occasion, the judge's nieces showed their faces in public for the first time as a show of independence!"

Some people were having a merry time and children ran about playing all sorts of games. But here and there, Harriet shared bread with the beggars she met along the river bank. "Throughout India, poverty was, and remains, a real thing."

As she spoke on the sensitive topic of abject poverty so prevalent on this continent, I remembered that Harriet had received an eloquently written plea for assistance during her brief stay in this city. "Mrs. Fisher...I mean Harriet," I said. "I recall reading about a very sad letter you had received from a local orphanage in Allahabad."

Harriet nodded. "Yes. That letter stays with me," she answered. "It was so poignant. Its writer described the distressed conditions throughout India, its extreme poverty, sunken faces and worn out naked bodies of the natives. It compared the few palatial towns to a few twinkling stars peeking out between a cover of dense clouds. It spoke of the tourists who believed that 'anything that glitters is gold,' and left the continent in the false belief that India is happy."

I knew that Harriet had unflinchingly printed the entire letter in her book. She had learned firsthand that in many regions of India, when a person asked you for food they really meant it. "Money is useless when there is no food to buy."

Later that day, the judge had another surprise for Harriet. After luncheon, she strolled with the judge and his young daughter through a fragrant rose garden on the grounds of the home. "It was so beautiful that I found it hard to believe that I was walking in what one missionary had described as a heathen land."

As they walked the young girl gathered a bouquet of blue and white violets for her special guest. "When it had been learned that one of my favorite flowers are violets, I found them placed on my coffee tray each morning."

They entered a small temple where Harriet was invited to take a seat on a luxurious floor cushion. "I was shortly surprised by the sound of rain on the roof. I could not understand how water seemed to be falling on this building when the sun was shining so brightly in such an arid place."

In a region where rain did not fall for as long as eight months at a time, the clever judge had designed a system of pipes that made it possible for water to flow on demand from the most sacred of sources.

But Judge Nehru did not offer an explanation. Instead, he led his astonished guest back out to the garden, stopping before a ferocious-looking sculpted image at the entrance of a cave called "The God of the Ganges." Judge Nehru proclaimed, "And Great Allah said, 'Let there be water,' and there was water from the Ganges." Upon the judge's words water miraculously gushed from the mouth and nose of the intricate carving.

"I looked about for some hidden button that might have been used to bring about this seemingly miraculous presentation," Harriet said, hoping for some mystical explanation.

Finding none, she finally inquired, "What wonderful mystery *is* this?"

Harriet appeared to be a bit disappointed when a man suddenly appeared and asked, "What do you think of that, Mrs. Fisher?" She was informed that the source of this spectacle was merely a colleague of the judge who had turned on the water from the rear of the cave. "It was all so mysterious and beautiful that I was sorry to have my mind disillusioned," she recalled with a sigh.

But Harriet's spirits were quickly revived in the tea room of the judge's house. "For the first time in my life I had a cup of real tea! I lost track of my numerous requests for refills."

During this occasion of tea drinking, Harriet recalled that a man had suddenly appeared in the room. His costume consisted of a piece of soft white muslin that was tied around his waist. He wore an English shirt over this, fastened at the collar with a pearl stud with more pearl buttons down the front. Not being tucked in, his shirt flowed loosely, and gave the impression that he had been suddenly called out before his toilette was completed, with his brown bare legs appearing below his shirt.

Judge Nehru took charge of the situation. He uttered something to this gentleman in Hindi. Harriet remembered that whatever had been said produced a blush of crimson on the man's face, a countenance that now displayed an expression of pained confusion. He quickly fled the room.

Harriet nodded her head and grinned as she enjoyed her recollection of this amusing scene. "Nehru apologized, 'Mrs. Fisher, I hope you were not shocked. I did not intend for you to see my friend in his costume. He really knew no better. I told him he might shock you by appearing in the drawing room with nothing on but his chemise!'"

Harriet was quick to make the best of the situation. "I told them that this scene suggested to me the well-known story of the Irishwoman's retort to the Chinaman who complained of feeling cold."

Harriet let out a loud chortle. As I had not ever heard of this "well-known" story, and wasn't sure if I wanted to, I did not inquire of the story's ending.

To Harriet's surprise and delight, her attempt at humor brought great amusement to those in the room. Harriet had been under the impression that Hindus were a very serious people and she took the opportunity to have some more fun with her hosts. "Well, I unloaded every old joke and story I had ever heard. I could hardly believe my own eyes and ears, for a more cheerful and merry family party I had never seen in any country."

And Harriet was to receive yet another surprise.

"Mrs. Nehru wishes to meet you," Miss Hooper announced to me after tea.

Harriet was promptly escorted through the court to another part of the sprawling house where two servants stood at an entrance with a door.

"The door was thrown open, and I stood for a moment, almost wanting to rub my eyes. Before me I saw nothing but a beautiful mass of color," Harriet remembered. "On one side of a raised platform covered with magnificent Turkish rugs sat Mrs. Nehru. She was a tiny little woman with great brown eyes and a face of great loveliness."

Mrs. Nehru beckoned Harriet to approach and as she did, reached out toward Harriet, grasping both of her visitor's hands in her own.

"She offered me her cheek for a kiss. I was later told by Miss Hooper that this was the most sincere welcome that could be offered a visitor in a Hindu home."

The judge's wife implored of her guest if she had been made comfortable during her stay. Harriet spoke to Mrs. Nehru as Miss Hooper translated. "Your husband has shown me the most gracious hospitality. He has offered us all a truly at-home experience. Nothing more could have been done during our visit to make us feel more at home," I assured her.

Harriet knew the woman was frail and feared she was trespassing too long on her strength. "I made my farewell *salaam* by putting both palms together and giving the Hindu salute that I had learned by observing the Hindu ladies."

Harriet was left alone to write letters, read, and rest until her farewell dinner.

On this, the eleventh of February, Harriet was given a lavish meal in her honor. She made her entrance in a beautifully-embroidered silk sari provided by the judge's nieces.

"They told me that this was an outfit appropriate for a widow," Harriet said. "It was made from ten yards of straight goods cut the length of the skirt, pleated in front and back, and tied in the indescribable knot that only a Hindu knows how to tie."

Two yards of extra material was looped over Harriet's head and then draped over her shoulder. A rope of pearls with tassels was tied around her head that came to rest hanging over her left ear.

"I gazed at my image in the mirror," Harriet recalled. "I had never felt lovelier. I barely recognized myself."

During this special dinner served in western style in an English dining room, Harriet, Harold, and Judge Nehru were the only diners to partake of meat. Harriet was told that the Hindu servants would not even cook meat and a Mohammedan chef had been hired for that express purpose.

Harold enjoyed many of the Indian delicacies, such as a Farina-like pudding. He was impressed that the men's puddings were topped with a sheet of gold leaf with silver toppings for women. Honkie, on the other hand, enjoyed so many sweets and goodies that Harriet worried about her little dog's health.

"From the next room I heard music that was at the same time weird, thrilling, and charming. At dinner's end we retired to the drawing room and lounged on cushions arranged in a semicircle."

Here Harriet found the source of the music—five musicians dressed in costumes with embroideries worth their weight in gold. Upon their heads rested turbans woven from beautiful cloths in colors that she found fascinating.

"Do you women like to dance?" Harriet asked the judge's nieces.

"They laughingly told me no! They said 'Dancing makes people look like monkeys! Dancing is only for those who have to do it to make a living.'"

Harriet became aware at this point that people in the room were saluting her. "'What are they saying?' I inquired of my host. Judge Nehru interpreted for me. 'They are calling you the Princess from the Land of Promise,' he said."

One of the most enduring gifts of Harriet's stay at Judge Nehru's home would be her introduction to his nieces. But during her farewell dinner, she was also introduced to other honored guests, including His Highness the Maharaja of Baroda and his wife, Her Highness the Maharani.

Harriet was impressed to learn that although Her Highness practiced the strict traditions of her rank and caste while in India, when she traveled abroad with her husband, she was open to the ways of Western culture.

His Highness of Baroda was so impressed with Harriet's historic trip, and her Locomobile, that he made arrangements for his family to accompany her during her tour of Japan, traveling in their own thirty-horse-power Fiat.

This idea thrilled Harriet, who seemed to have found a kindred spirit in Mrs. Baroda. "I could sense the Maharani was a woman of great charm," Harriet recalled. "And I very much looked forward to our next meeting."

Harriet regretted having to leave this lovely place. But her pet birds would remain.

Just before leaving, Maria came to her in a state of dismay. "Senora, Fisher! *Il gabbia per uccelli!*" Maria explained to Harriet that when she was changing the water in the bird cage, she had left the door open. The little birds had quickly fluttered out the window and disappeared among the treetops.

"'Don't worry, Maria,' I consoled her. I am glad to know that they are free again in their beautiful native land."

From the way Harriet uttered these words, I sensed that there were times when she longed to be among them, flying freely about that beautiful place that held a special place in her heart.

The following day Judge Nehru and his family bid farewell to their special guests. Her stay may have only lasted just a few days, but those days would remain in her memory for the rest of her life.

Harriet relived the tearful parting of friends. "They said that they hoped to meet the Princess from the Land of Promise again someday."

CHAPTER FOURTEEN

His Highness of Benares and the Burning Ghats

It was now one o'clock in the afternoon. The sun sparkled high up in a clear blue sky, bathing the quiet landscape of Bella Vista in a golden hue. Harriet and I had spoken for several hours straight, and here we were, not even out of India.

I had always been fascinated by this exotic country, and although I found her stories thoroughly intoxicating, at this rate I feared there would not be time enough in the day to cover her entire worldwide journey. But I couldn't help stating an observation.

"Harriet," I ventured. "Your tales of India recall for me the many hours of my youth spent reading Rudyard Kipling's *The Jungle Book*."

I spoke of the themes of loyalty, courage, and persistence that ran throughout his stories; ones that were linked to the cultural traditions and encounters Harriet had experienced in India.

"It sounds to me like you had lived your own Kipling stories, at times."

"Yes, the journey through the palaces and wilds of India were filled with contrasts, captured so succinctly in that letter from the orphanage," she reflected.

Harriet explained that she genuinely wished she could have visited the orphanage, but her travel itinerary had not allowed for it. "You know, I am not indifferent to the plight of children."

I recalled Harriet's volunteer work on behalf of a children's hospital in Flushing, New York.

"One moment my little crew and I seemed to be scrounging up food, sleeping in a tent in the wild, just like peasants, and the next, transported to the most luxurious accommodations that I could not have imagined existed in my wildest dreams," she said.

"Throughout my travels in India, I had been told not to give any of these impoverished poor people a gold piece, as they would rather starve than use it in any way, except to make a necklace of ornament," Harriet said. "If I offered money, they would place their hands behind them and refuse to take it, instead, pointing to their mouths and placing a hand on their stomachs. We often shared our last loaf of bread with them."

With this, Harriet got up and stretched. "Let's walk back up to the house and continue our talk in the parlor. I have some newspaper articles I can share with you there. We can finish our tales of India and move on."

As we walked, I indicated that so far, her Indian voyage had seemed to have gone relatively smoothly.

"Yes, it had," Harriet confirmed, admitting she had been somewhat surprised. "Despite having been issued so many dire warnings, and being assaulted by the doubters and naysayers who seemed to come out of every corner as we drove out of the woods, pulling up to each of our accommodations while in India. Many could not accept our story that we had driven *through* the jungle!"

The extraordinary hospitality of the Gwalior State and the accommodations so graciously offered by Judge Nehru and his family were high points of her Indian journey. Up until then, she and her companions had experienced only mildly unpleasant encounters at some filthy or poorly managed government lodgings, and manageable threats from bullock carts, a few locals, and wild animals.

But on February twelfth, things would change, as the Locomobile ambled from the comfort and safety of Allahabad to begin its seventy-six mile journey to the sacred city of Benares. Harriet and her party were about to meet some unusual people, and have an encounter that would remind her of the inherent danger of her presumably well-laid-out plans.

Benares is an ancient city situated on the banks of the Ganges, regarded as the holiest of the seven sacred cities. This locale played an integral role in the development of Buddhism, although many of its temples had been plundered and destroyed during the 12th century.

"Despite all that destruction, there were over 5,000 temples and shrines to explore in that city; most dating back to the 18th century," Harriet noted. "Harold was most impressed by the multitude of primates that greeted him at the Monkey Temple!"

Arriving in this sacred city at approximately eleven o'clock in the morning, they checked into the first hotel they came upon. "But as we prepared to unload our luggage from the Locomobile, my attention was attracted to a fine-looking man dressed in Indian costume."

The man presented his card to the hotel manager, which caused quite a stir. The manager quickly exited the room and soon returned with another man. With great excitement, they bowed profusely as they presented Harriet with a card that introduced the elegant stranger as Sen. Roy, The Private Secretary to His Highness, the Maharaja of Benares.

"I saluted this royal messenger and awaited his command," Harriet recalled. "I did not know the meaning of his "Sen" title, but he spoke good English and proceeded to offer our party the hospitality of the rest house belonging to His Highness of Benares. It was a place where His Highness liked to entertain visitors of note, among them, the Prince of Wales. His Highness would be greatly grieved if Madam did not accept his hospitality in the same spirit it was offered."

The secretary told Harriet that he was to be at her service from nine in the morning to any time or hour of the night. It was further expressed that it was hoped that their stay in Benares would be a lengthy one.

"I hesitated. I had already pledged my business to the hotel manager. I glanced at him, and although he appeared to be a little wistful at losing this opportunity to host such a special visitor, he assured me saying, 'Madam, there is no alternative. I am at your command always.'"

"A cautious Harold questioned this choice. Mr. Brooks suggested all sorts of bad things that might happen if we stayed in a strange house where no one else was living. He feared all kinds of things, from us being robbed or led astray."

Harriet stood by her choice, and once again, they took their seats in the Locomobile. They followed Sen. Roy, who rode in an open carriage with two footmen and a driver. After they settled in at the rest house, they enjoyed a luncheon and some sightseeing with their guide.

"We visited mosques and mausoleums and were quite ready to rest when we returned home by two o'clock."

But their rest was brief. "We were exhausted, but one hour later, our royal guide arrived and whisked us away again for more touring, in the private carriage of His Highness, complete with footmen, coachmen, and two out runners."

Then an exciting announcement was made. On the thirteenth of February Harriet and her party were invited to pay a personal visit to the Maharaja of Benares at the prestigious Palace Ramnagar. At eleven o'clock that morning, Sen. Roy arrived with his carriage that delivered them to the banks of the Ganges where a veritable floating palace awaited them. "This boat was arranged with gorgeous red and yellow cushions upon which I reclined while ten strong men rowed us all across the Ganges to the palace," Harriet recalled.

Crossing the river, they landed on the palace grounds, where four barelegged men, dressed in red and yellow costumes, placed Harriet on a *dandie*. She was carried high off the ground, with Harold, Sen. Roy, and Albert following on foot. They all ascended a stairway covered in red velvet in honor of her visit, as was explained by Sen. Roy.

"I was delivered to a small antechamber where I was received by an elderly gentleman with a long beard who was wearing a gorgeous turban."

Outside the grand reception room, two more servants stood on either side of a curtain tied with a silver cord. "They untied the cord and suddenly, His Highness appeared! He was dressed so magnificently in a costume covered with pearls, rubies, diamonds, and sapphires. I was stunned, and for a moment I felt I could not speak to this royal and gorgeous-looking personage."

His Royal Highness, sensing Harriet's reluctance to approach him, came forward to give her a warm welcome. He graciously inquired of his honored guest, "How is it you have the courage to enter into the great land of India by car?"

Harriet said, "I quickly found my voice and replied confidently, 'Do I look frightened?' He said, 'Mrs. Fisher, I do hope you have received every attention and courtesy while traveling in India.' I assured him that I had."

"His Highness was intrigued with the Locomobile. He was eager to learn how I found the conditions of his city's roads, if I had met with any difficulties while traveling throughout India, and if the natives I encountered had been courteous and had not given me any annoyance. This last matter seemed to concern him greatly."

Harriet had been instructed not to ask for Her Highness, as His Highness actually had two wives, and neither was permitted to view any foreigners.

"But, I did get a glimpse of them later in the visit," she revealed.

"He asked me if I wished to see some native dancing, but I told him I preferred to visit some native workshops, and to see the Burning Ghats. His Highness offered me the full use of his yacht for this purpose."

"Our talk turned to business. 'You are the first lady I have ever met who knew anything about iron,' His Highness confided in me. He then proceeded to quiz me about my industry."

Harriet recalled how he blushed like a boy as he proudly told her about a pig-sticker he had devised that was made of iron. "He asked me if I would like to see it and to visit his museum," Harriet recalled with bemusement. "I told him that would be alright."

As Harriet prepared to leave, a servant presented the guests with velvet cushions upon which rested two chains, one silver and one made of spun gold. "These were to show the world that we were the honored guests of royalty. The gold chain was placed around my neck, which signified that I had been married," Harriet said. "Harold received the silver chain which indicated that he was in the state of single blessedness!"

"Before I left that day, I invited my royal host to go for a ride in the Locomobile. 'Ah, I think that is a little too rapid for this old world, according to my idea,' he said, declining my offer."

"As I got ready to depart, His Highness presented me with a photo of himself and asked if I would like it to have his autograph!" Harriet recalled. "And when we returned to the rest house we found a fleet-footed messenger waiting for our arrival. He was still out of breath and presented me with a gift from His Highness. 'What is that?' Mr. Brooks asked, examining the offering. 'Why this must be that odd pig sticker the Maharaja of Benares spoke of,' I answered, amused."

"Mr. Brooks smiled and noted that as it was indeed made of iron. Perhaps His Highness thought that the Lady Ironmaster would be impressed by his handiwork."

Although His Highness had declined an invitation for a ride in Harriet's car, Sen. Roy did not. As a passenger, he guided Harriet and her party to old ruins and obscure parts of Benares that were seldom seen by tourists, including a tour through the private royal park owned by His Highness.

The following morning, the fourteenth of February, Harriet received a call at five o'clock. "We were once again transported in the royal carriage to the banks of the Ganges. On this occasion, we found batches of marigolds onboard and we were told that as it was the first of the spring season, these yellow flowers were to be used to decorate all the idols, bulls, and their calves."

From the royal boat, Harriet and her party witnessed the Burning Ghats. Harriet had learned that it was the wish of every Hindu to be cleansed with the holy waters, cremated at the Burning Ghats with the sacred eternal fire, and then have their ashes tossed into the sacred waters of the Ganges. This allows the soul to proceed directly to heaven, without having to deal with karma and reincarnations.

Harriet's party watched in astonishment as a corpse was taken down to the river for its farewell bath. After the body was allowed to dry in the hot sun, it was then placed on a pile of wood and burned. Afterward, some of the ashes were swept up in the right hands of mourners and then tossed into the wind while a prayer was recited. The remaining ashes were swept back into the river.

Harriet recalled a man with a little child of about three or four walking down to the water where a calf was being bathed. "I was told that the child's father had paid the priest to have his child touched by the sacred calf." Harriet said. "The calf's tail was placed in the child's hand, but unfortunately, the cow did not appear to be lively enough for the father. Apparently, liveliness on the part of the calf indicates that the child will be blessed with good fortune, otherwise, the child was doomed to a life of misfortune."

She recalled how she had gazed upon the sun worshippers and fanatics that crowded the river bank. She was told that these people would sit there for hours, eyes wide open, gazing into the sun. They held teapots filled with water from the holy river that dripped slowly back into the river, each drop accompanied by a prayer.

"The faith, the absolute belief, of these people in the sacredness of the river is astonishing. The Westerner cannot conceive of it." Harriet declared.

The remainder of her stay in Benares found Harriet visiting local shops where she admired brass works, the skills of silversmiths hammering away at silver and gold, and men embroidering beautiful saris.

"I managed to resist the temptation to buy at this time," Harriet confided. "I lulled my desire by convincing myself that I might come again to this interesting land."

CHAPTER FIFTEEN

A Rough River Crossing and a Brush with Brigands

Bidding farewell to Benares, Harriet set her sights on her party's final Indian destination—Calcutta. They traveled eighty miles in order to cross the river at Dehri-on-Sone, which would prove to be a major challenge.

We made our river crossing arrangements with the English chief engineer who was stationed there to supervise the building of a solid stone bridge.

The evening before the river crossing, Harriet was obliged to spend the evening at a dirty old *dak* bungalow. "The attendant was an old man with a moth-eaten looking dog," she said with disgust. "But the devotion of the dirty old man to that dirty old dog was pathetic." Honk Honk was curious to meet this fellow canine, but Harriet kept her dog on a tight leash, not trusting the foreign one.

Early the next morning, they enjoyed their coffee and filled their thermoses with boiled water before heading to the river. They arrived at its bank as the sun rose, infusing the landscape with a rosy glow, but the outlook was not so sanguine. Here they found two long planks, each measuring about twelve inches wide, that were arranged to create a make-shift "bridge" that spanned from the top of a very steep bank down to where a lighter was waiting to transport them and the car across the water.

Harriet crossed over the planks on foot with Maria and Albert. Harold carefully maneuvered the Locomobile down the banks and onto the float. Harriet was informed that people had traveled miles just to see the lady with the motorcar. "I think I can safely say that this feat was witnessed by a thousand people!"

To prevent the Locomobile from slipping from the planks, ropes were fastened to it, both front and back. "We paid fifty rupees for the crossing and it took twenty-four coolies using long sticks of bamboo to propel the raft to reach the other side of the river," Harriet said. "The raft was made of iron and attracted the piercing rays of the sun. It was the hottest trip I have ever experienced."

Harold and Albert made good use of this time. Always on the lookout for food supplies, they loaded their guns and prepared for action. "Mr. Brooks met with some success, but Albert brought down a wild duck that must have been three hundred feet away."

These ducks did not appear to be as revered as other birds. One of the rowing coolies was so excited about Albert's feat that he jumped into the river and swam to retrieve it. These beautiful birds were called Golden Head Ducks and were very difficult to shoot. "It seemed almost wicked to kill anything so beautiful to satisfy human appetites," Harriet said with a sigh.

But the coolies admired the hunting skills of their foreign passengers. They fondled Harold and Albert's guns and fought for the blank cartridges to keep as souvenirs.

"For three hours I watched the well-developed muscles of our rowing crew and scanned the landscape," Harriet recalled. "Finally we reached the other side."

But now they faced a steep ascent up the opposite river bank. "'How shall we ever get our car up there?' I asked of Mr. Brooks."

They navigated to shore until the raft was nearly grounded, and began arranging the planks into a bridge-like structure. The prospect of transporting the car to land made Harriet overly anxious. "What if our car should slip and fall into the mud? How would we retrieve it, and in what condition would it be?"

They had no other options. "With brave hearts and trembling hands we waited for the raft to reach terra firma," she recalled. "Thank God for those brave little coolies! They carried rocks from the river bank with their bare hands to place on top of long poles of bamboo building a temporary buttress on which to rest our planks!"

Along the river, Harriet had noticed that bamboo poles were always used by the locals to propel their rafts. "I asked why they did not use oars, and was told there was no wood to be had. As the result of selfish acts of men, India is now suffering for the want of timber," Harriet explained. "If it were not for bamboo, and the discovery of coal in some Indian locales, these poor people would be in a bad way. This situation reminded me of the time I took the Locomobile for her trial run in America and saw how men were robbing our own prosperous land of its trees, and not even planting one tree for every four they cut down."

Harriet's party made land, which was once again witnessed by hundreds of curious onlookers who had gathered on the river bank to watch. Many assisted the coolies as the pulled and pushed several heavy boats abandoned on the shoreline to clear a path for the car. Thankfully, the planks used to get the car onboard for the launch had been brought along and were now used to rise up the Locomobile as it navigated through a myriad of tree stumps.

After a long, hot, and challenging day, it was time for a bit of rest. They traveled an additional twenty miles and were pleasantly surprised to come upon a bungalow. "It was lovely," Harriet recalled, "situated up on a high and dry knoll, surrounded with roses and azaleas in full bloom."

Harriet settled in, looking forward to a couple of uneventful and restful days. Maria washed and ironed their clothing. "Did I tell you that we carried a little alcohol iron? Maria used it to iron my blouses and the men's shirts to make us fairly presentable when we made our visits straight from camp."

The caretaker of this bungalow was so impressed by Harriet that he immediately placed a new carpet on the floor of her room.

Harold busied himself with some quail hunting. "Albert made a delicious dinner with his duck and Harold's bird. Curried duck and quail with rice, boiled potatoes, and some Indian mangoes procured by Antonio at a local bazaar en route."

They had no bread, but Harriet found a clever way to improvise. "As a child, I had learned to make a fire while spending time at a sugar camp in Ohio. I showed Albert how to build a good one right in the middle of the wilds. We made some delicious muffins out of our flour and baking powder and cooked them on a flat pan over the open fire. Listening to Harriet's recounting of this day, it struck me that she treasured these quiet, unplanned moments as much as she did her opulent stays at lush royal palaces where she was waited on every moment.

I also had a better understanding of how well her "employees" worked together as a team despite the differences in their ages and countries of origin. Each had a special value to Harriet, and an important role in this journey of a lifetime.

This quiet stay was about to end, however. "We were just about to settle in for the evening," she recounted, "When we were surprised to hear the sound of a motorcar approaching. We rushed to the piazza to see if we were all awake or dreaming."

Two men got out of a small car and approached the *dak* bungalow. "I must say I was pleased to think we would have neighbors for the evening.

One of the men addressed me. 'This is Mrs. Fisher, I believe, who is making a tour of the world in a motor-car?' I affirmed that I was indeed she. The men explained that they had been informed by locals that I was in the area and they had a special invitation for me. "'His Highness, the Raja, who owns this bungalow and all of this land, wishes to offer you the hospitality of his rest house as he is now away on a tiger hunt,' they announced."

"Harold whispered to me, 'Something is not right about this.'"

"Although the splendid hospitality I had enjoyed at the other palaces made me eager for my next royal visit, I heeded my driver's concern and graciously declined. I said, 'Thank you for your generous offer. But it *is* very late, and we have settled in for the night.' Harold agreed, telling the men that the next day would be better, but he also sensed an opportunity. He told them we were tired and that he had work to do on the car the next day. He wondered if His Highness could spare us some oil. He said we had not seen a place for six hundred miles and were getting low on supplies."

"The men were more than happy to oblige. 'Oh, yes, we can give you anything you want for your car! We have petrol by the barrel, oils, and everything.'"

Hearing this, Harriet informed the men that they should expect their arrival at noon the next day. A beautiful full moon had risen and bathed the surroundings of the bungalow in a soft glow. Wistfully acknowledging that this would be their last night in this enchanting place, it was agreed they should explore the sights of this peaceful landscape in the moonlight. Harold took his gun, Albert carried a thick stick, and Honk Honk accompanied them.

Their fun jaunt was cut short with a rustling in the brush and a sound that Harriet could not place. But Antonio could. "Cobras!" he shouted, and they all headed back to the safety of the bungalow in short order.

After a restful night's sleep, Harriet and her party woke and readied themselves for travel in the harsh morning sunlight. It promised to be a hot day. They dressed in their lightest clothing, donning the fewest items permissible for a luncheon with a Raja. "On this occasion, I envied the native his freedom from our Western dress," Harriet recalled. "It had been days since we had seen or spoken to anyone, beside our callers, and I was longing for companionship."

At nine o'clock, she gave the *dak* bungalow a lingering farewell look, and reluctantly took leave of the comfort of this charming place as she rolled away in her car. They followed the directions given to them by the man who had referred to himself as the "Royal Chauffeur" the previous evening.

The path was rough. At some points it was necessary for the Locomobile to leave the main road, which required them to cut away at tree limbs that blocked their progress.

On this unbeaten path, Antonio made inquiries in Hindi to any local he met. Harriet feared they might be lost. But as the Raja's men had explained that His Highness was presently on a tiger hunting expedition, and there was evidence of some tracking in the brush, Antonio believed they were on the right path.

It was now two o'clock and everyone was tired, hungry, hot, and inclined to be disagreeable. "Look!" said Harold, pointing to a little tent up ahead on the road. Its side curtain was turned up to reveal the little car that belonged to the Raja's men. An excited Harold sped up and honked the horn of the Locomobile to announce their arrival. But Harold's initial fears from the previous evening were about to be confirmed.

Harriet continued her story. "But our Antonio grew cautious. He held up his hand and commanded Harold to slow down. 'Me no like look of town,' he said. 'No Raja here. Me go ahead and find out. Mem Sahib stop here.' To our dismay, about a half dozen naked men appeared before us, and they were not giving us the welcome we had anticipated," Harriet recalled. "Their faces were painted with bright red and blue streaks, their long hair twisted like wool, tied with pieces of red cloth. They stared at us with vicious smiles, as a cat looks at a mouse when it knows the poor creature cannot escape!"

"Antonio stayed in the Locomobile and shouted out for the head man to come forward. The two men who had visited us the night before appeared. I smiled at them in friendly recognition, but I was alarmed. The faces of these men no longer bore the affable expressions of the prior evening. I felt a great leap of the heart as I suddenly realized how helpless we all were should these men prove to be unfriendly."

"I anxiously searched the surrounding area looking for the elegant rest house that had been promised by the visitors. All that met my eyes were a cluster of some old stone ruins. I now felt that we had been too hasty in accepting the invitation of strangers."

Harriet commanded Harold to keep the car's motor running. "I spoke in Italian so as not to be understood. Antonio took charge. 'Quick turn around,' he urged Harold but Harold had his own plan. Mr. Brooks, not wishing to show any suspicion, kept on, and we found ourselves even farther inside this circle of wild-looking heads, as more men appeared from tents. There were so many I could not count them all!"

"I called out to these savage-looking men. 'Good morning. I am sorry we are so late, but we lost our way. Where shall we find the rest house?' I said, keeping my voice pleasant and unconcerned."

"One of the English-speaking men pointed to some ruins of a building up on a hill and said 'You will be staying there' to me and Maria, 'and we will take care of the men.'"

Harold drove up the hill where they found men hastily removing a herd of cows from these stone ruins; others scraped the floors where these animals had been standing.

"This apparently was the beautiful rest house we were to occupy. It was quite odorous as you can imagine."

"I managed to remain calm. 'Where can we find the Raja?' I inquired of the men. 'He set off on an elephant earlier today,' one answered. 'He received news that tigers had been seen. He is sorry he could not be here to welcome you, but will return this evening and wishes you to make yourself comfortable in these quarters.' My inquiries as to whether there were any women in the tents were met with sardonic smiles."

"The men told me to please step out of the car to come and look at the rooms of the rest house, but we all remained in the car. Upon closer examination, I could see that these old ruins were a veritable prison. The windows were fastened with stones, leaving only small peep-holes for light and air," Harriet recalled. "There was a big door, with straps riveted on with iron, with hinges that would require the strength of a giant to open."

A group of these savages began to unstrap the luggage from the Locomobile.

"Harold called out to the men. 'Do not touch this car, we are not stopping.' Harold turned to the man who had promised him supplies and asked, 'Where can we get some of that oil you promised?' He received no reply."

"Mr. Brooks remained calm," Harriet recollected. "He carefully turned the car around slowly and pointed it in the direction from which we had entered the jungle."

Her hosts persisted. "They said to me 'Please come out of the car, Mrs. Fisher. These men will have your lodging ready for you soon and you must now come and see your rooms.' I told them that I preferred the fresh air. 'I would love to, but I regret we cannot stay as our arrival is expected at a big reception being thrown for us by some royal friends in the town of Gya.'"

"'You have friends at Gya?' they queried."

"'Yes,' I answered. 'And I am sure that as we are already two days late, an escort is likely to be out searching for us right now.'"

"I directed Antonio to speak to them in their own language. He confirmed my message. 'Yes, we received a telegram while at Dehri-on-Sone,' he informed them. 'I am sure our hosts are anxiously awaiting our arrival.'"

The savage-looking men crowded around the Locomobile chattering like a flock of parrots. Perhaps worried they might suffer the punishment of local authorities if any harm came to Harriet or her party, they finally broke away and allowed the motorcar to pass.

"I smiled and waved a charming goodbye. I yelled out to them, 'Please thank your Raja for his most generous offer!' You can just imagine the expressions on their faces!"

Harold drove back into the jungle, never losing his composure. "We reached the main road and I wished that our car could go at the rate of ninety miles an hour instead of fifty," Harriet recalled with a shudder.

Of this incident, Harriet's only regret was that she had not had time to take photographs of these savages. "I would rather have their pictures than their comradeship! They were an evil-looking lot of cutthroats. I had never seen anything like them and hope to never again."

Her only fear now was that the car's oil supply would not hold up. If the car could not go on they would be stuck miles from nowhere without much hope of rescue. "No one wished to stop for lunch. None of us were hungry; our thermos bottles of coffee sufficed for the moment."

Miraculously the oil lasted through their ordeal and subsequent getaway. With much relief, they arrived at the city of Gya at seven o'clock that evening. Upon reaching safety, Antonio explained to Harriet that they had narrowly escaped the hands of local highway robbers called brigands.

"Antonio had suspected this as soon as he had seen the way these savages were dressed and made up. He believed that the brigands had planned to imprison Maria and me, and I still tremble when I think of what might have become of my three faithful men in the hands of those savages," Harriet said. "We congratulated one another on having escaped with whole skins."

This experience would haunt Harriet for days. "Only then did I truly understand the anxiety of my friends in regard to my going through the wilds of India," she confided.

CHAPTER SIXTEEN

On the Road to Calcutta

Harold obtained oil and petrol in Gya, about three miles out of town, where a crew of locals helped him to carry these much needed supplies. The party settled into a *dak* bungalow and once again Albert worked his culinary magic, creating a meal for his tired and hungry travel companions from eggs and some potatoes Antonio had been able to gather.

The following morning, the skies opened. This was a welcome event as it was the first time Harriet's party had experienced rain since visiting India. It came down in torrents, making it impossible for them to depart.

The entire party placed their washbowls and buckets outside to capture rainwater as it came down in spouts, in anticipation of its cleansing potential. Harold entertained the natives by rigging a spout from a piece of hose he carried. He showed his curious audience how American's "caught" water.

"While in Gya, we made the acquaintance of a cigar-smoking missionary, a white man dressed in Indian garb. He inquired if we were Americans."

The man explained that he was an American expatriate, but had been living in India for over twenty years, and had no plans to return to the United States because he enjoyed the comforts of this exotic nation. The talk immediately turned to "donations" and he spoke of how difficult it was to procure funds and to convert Hindus and Mohammedans. In converting these people, he said, there was the potential of adding to his flock of "adherents." But as he spoke, puffing harder on his cigar, Harriet shrewdly observed that he neglected to state his exact purpose for these adherents.

"Here and there missionaries are doing good work in teaching the natives English," Harriet explained. "This enables these natives to obtain employment in the big cities and receive higher wages than they would otherwise."

Hungry for news of the states, the missionary left early the next morning, armed with every American newspaper Harriet could offer him.

An attendant had been paid to keep the open fireplace ablaze, which kept the chill from the interior of the bungalow. Maria, also up early, hung freshly washed clothes to dry from every available post, taking advantage of the heat of the fire.

Eager to begin the final lap of their Indian journey, Harriet and her companions set their sights on Calcutta. They set off, traveling along the Grand Trunk Road for approximately three hundred miles.

Along this route, large herds of black sheep and goats shared the road, making navigation tricky. With their long silky hair, they were beautiful to look at, but proved to have ferocious temperaments. "Honk Honk had his own troubles with them," Harriet recalled, laughing. "When he became too familiar with the goats, he was disciplined in short order and took no more liberties."

At times, it overwhelmed Harold just how far from civilization he actually was.

"During one particularly lonely stretch of road, Mr. Brooks spoke to me. 'Here there are no telegraph, or telephone poles, or wires.' Sometimes I think it was all too much for him to take in. 'No billboards, hotdog stands, or any advertisements whatsoever. How is it...' he wondered, '...that we don't see *any* homes or people, but when we stop for lunch in a shady spot along the Grand Trunk Road, people seemed to appear from nowhere?'"

At those times, curious natives quietly approached and crouched in semi-circle formations around these strange visitors. They pointed good-naturedly at Harriet and her party like they would animals at a zoo. By meal's end, these inquisitive but friendly natives enthusiastically accepted any morsel of food offered to them.

Here, as throughout much of her travels in India, Harriet was continually dismayed to meet so many half-starved elderly people, eager to grab up any crumb, even begging for the water Albert used to boil their potatoes.

In the Bengal district they traveled through miles of poppy fields with huts that displayed the title "Opium Inspector" and other words written in Hindi. Men, obviously under the influence of the drug, staggered into the path of the Locomobile. On several occasions, Harold narrowly avoided running them over.

On one such occasion, the Locomobile was rolling along at about twenty miles-an-hour. "We noticed two men coming toward us. The younger one was trying to control his elderly companion. Thankfully we slowed down, for the older man suddenly broke away and tried to fling himself in front of our car in an apparent intent to commit suicide. Mr. Brooks missed hitting him by only three feet."

In the city of Buhri, the Locomobile experienced a punctured tire and a blowout which depleted their supply of extra tires. But here they also had the good fortune to obtain chicken, eggs, potatoes, and good sweet bread from the commissary of an English barracks so they wouldn't have to raid their small supply of flour.

Harriet recalled that throughout India it was common to see old women grinding wheat between two round stones. "It reminded me of the biblical description of the two women grinding at the mill."

They were now two hundred and twenty-four miles from Calcutta.

They entered the city of Asenol with excitement. In this railroad center they would be able to obtain a supply of oil and petrol. But here they would also find it impossible to find a place that would take them in.

Their quest for lodging brought them to the courthouse and police station, but all they found here were buildings that looked like small prisons filled with occupants under the influence of opium.

Coal had been discovered in Asenol four years prior and English businessmen had invested heavily in the city's mines. But the residents did not understand the effects of the soft coal that was being extracted. When they stood over the open fires, handling their pots and pans, *everything* got blacker, even themselves, and they took on a most unusual hue. "The whites of their eyes against their coal-infused skin made them resemble the 'end men' in a minstrel show."

In this city the air was so blackened with smoke from train traffic and coal that Harriet wished not to set up their tent in the heart of the city. "We found a club house associated with the English engineers, and we bravely inquired if they would take us in."

But the caretaker shook his head and told them that the gentlemen could stay there, but not the women!

As they drove through town, rows of elegant homes sequestered behind gated fences taunted Harriet. "Surely, there must be someone who would let us set up camp on their property."

Desperate, Harold waved down an approaching motorcar. The occupants, Major F. S. Agabeg and his charming wife, listened intently to their plight. It just so happened that the major was the vice-president of the club that had turned them away. He immediately went to the club house and ordered the coolies to take their baggage, and further commanded that the amenities of the club be available to them at their disposal.

Major Agabeg helped them procure an Indian cook, and posted a notice in the club house reminding members that ladies were present, and to reconsider any amusement that might annoy their rare female guests.

"Only one or two of the gentlemen appeared that night," Harriet said, laughing.

The following day, Harold filled the Locomobile with a fresh supply of petrol and oil. Harriet dressed in a clean gown and readied herself for luncheon at the home of Major Agabeg.

"Mrs. Agabeg welcomed us as if we were old friends," Harriet recalled, smiling. "It was so nice to sit down and dine again in a civilized manner!"

Major Agabeg told how he had been sent to Asenol by an uncle who had invested a great deal of money in the local mining industry. But coal was difficult to sell, as many locals had no money with which to buy it. The local Maharaja had no use for coal as it was deemed too dirty. The major explained that most of the city's coal supply was shipped to Calcutta for use on the steamers and railroads.

"The major relayed that he believed that in a short time, this area would become a vast desert as no one was replanting all the trees that had been cut down, and of course I agreed with him."

Harriet so enjoyed the company of the major and his wife that their stay in Asenol was extended for a couple of days. Their next goal was to reach the city of Burdwan some sixty-six miles from Asenol, of which the first twenty or so were very hilly.

"Oh, Poor Maria," Harriet said. "I recall an error she made here."

"What happened?" I asked.

Harriet laughed, shaking her head. "When we got to Burdwan, Maria realized she had locked up all of our boxes with all of our supplies, and then left the keys at the club house in Asenol."

"What did you do?" I asked.

"Well, we settled into our *dak* bungalow, but we had no coverings for our beds as they were all locked up. I sent a telegraph to Major Agabeg informing him that I was sending Antonio by train to retrieve our keys."

The ever-dutiful Antonio returned to Burdwan at four o'clock in the morning. Harriet used the keys to take out whatever supplies they needed and everyone bundled themselves up and got as much sleep as possible during the night. They would need their rest, for their next stop would find them in the capital of this Indian nation.

CHAPTER SEVENTEEN

Bidding Namaste to India

In the parlor of Bella Vista, Harriet stood and walked to a window, staring out toward the road. She continued to speak about the final chapter of her voyage through India, a nation that obviously had exceeded her most exotic imaginings.

The Locomobile had rumbled into Calcutta at three o'clock in the afternoon with a cargo of weary passengers. "The excitement of the mislaid keys, and the proximity of our bungalow to the street and railroad, had made sleep the night before nearly impossible," Harriet recalled.

The car's entrance into this capital city elicited great excitement, but brought Harriet to the sad realization that they were nearing the end of the Indian portion of their journey.

"Checking in at the Grand Hotel, we attracted the attention of a dozen excited employees. 'Why, Madam, where did you come from?' the hotel clerk inquired. 'Bombay,' I answered."

"Yes, but how?"

"'In that motorcar,' I said, pointing to the Locomobile."

"'Do I understand you to say you came all the way from Bombay in a motorcar?' he persisted."

"I replied in the affirmative."

"But the clerk mistakenly assumed that I had stored the car onboard a train, only taking it out for short touring jaunts throughout my trip. To this doubting clerk, and anyone within hearing distance, I loudly proclaimed, 'I assure you that we drove through India every inch of the way without the use of *any* train.' Returning to the business of checking in, I addressed the desk clerk and said, 'I *do* hope your hotel allows pets, because my little dog has also made this journey and wishes to rest, too.'"

When she was told that they would welcome Honk Honk, a very dirty and tired party settled in to recover from their month-long ordeal.

I couldn't help but recall Harriet's encounter with the doubting men at the start of her Indian trek, who wagered against her reaching Calcutta. "Did you send a postcard to that hotel manager back in Bombay?" I asked.

Harriet turned to me and smiled. She settled into a parlor chair across from me, just offering a dismissive wave of her hand in response. "You know, I would like to stop to ask that you make it clear in your reportage that never once during my trip across India, a distance of twenty-three hundred miles, was my car, or anything in it, ever molested."

Harriet was anxious to emphasize that while the natives were very curious about her and the car, their manners were perfect and that with the exception of the incident with the brigands, the local people never put a hand on the car, something that she couldn't say for the people of her own country.

At the hotel there was a bit of sadness among the travel companions, for Antonio now had to bid farewell to Harriet and the others after serving them so well. "Antonio told me it had been his honor to accompany me on my great journey. He enjoyed the last of his duties by serving me a tray of tea with bread, butter, and orange marmalade before he retired from his role as my translator, protector and friend."

A happy, but weary Harriet rested and settled down to read and answer correspondence that had been forwarded to her. She quickly dispatched Albert to the office of the P & O Steamship Company to confirm that their sailing accommodations had been reserved and that they would embark in two weeks. But Albert returned with some bad news, informing Harriet that there were no reservations for their party and it would be four weeks time before they could sail for Ceylon.

Harriet was incensed. "I immediately put on my topee, and with a fan and umbrella I started for the office of the steamship company."

At the office, Harriet was greeted by a clerk with a round face. "He looked like a puffed raisin; his two eyes bulged and he had a little round mouth. I asked about my reservations. He said, 'Why yes, Mrs. Fisher. We *did* receive your letter, but everything had been taken up a month before your letter arrived and there was no possible way of getting state rooms for you and your party on that steamer.' I demanded to speak to the superintendent, at once."

Mr. Jenkins, the superintendent, received her after some time. "I explained to him that I could not miss the next steamer as we were due in Colombo, the capital city of Ceylon."

This accommodating gentleman, who greatly impressed her, immediately set about making special arrangements for her entourage to sail to Colombo on schedule.

"He asked me if I and my party would be agreeable to occupying a hospital room on board the ship. I assured him we would sleep just about anywhere, as long as we could leave on time."

These arrangements were made, but this presented another problem. "Once again, poor Honkie would not be able to sail with us."

Mr. Jenkins arranged for the dog to make a solo voyage on another ship sailing for Japan, arriving on time to rejoin his mistress when she arrived for that part of the journey.

In Calcutta, Harriet received a whirlwind of social invitations, more than she could possibly accept. She and Mr. Jenkins became fast friends, and Harriet spent a good deal of time dining with him and his sister-in-law, who was keeping house for his family while Mrs. Jenkins was away in England.

On March first, Harriet's party enjoyed a side trip to the breathtaking Darjeeling region. They left unescorted at five-thirty in the morning and traveled along on what they hoped was the correct road. Arriving at the foot of the mountain within three hours, Harriet was required to obtain special permission to ascend it in her car.

Surprised by this, she was informed that this was necessary as the Locomobile would be the first automobile *ever* to ascend the Himalayan Mountains! "If I recall, there seemed to be some concern that we would be killed or we would cause a train wreck."

The train traveled on a regular switchback, winding in and out of the Sonada forest, within close proximity of the road that the car would use, Harriet explained. "As the car followed the tracks through these very steep grades, it kept pace with a trainload of smiling faces that curiously peered at us from the train's windows. In some places we had to run right on the tracks!"

Harriet declared this drive though Darjeeling as being superior to a drive down Broadway or Fifth Avenue in New York City. Of this part of the trip she proclaimed, "At last I had found my dreams of India realized. There in the Himalaya Mountains, blessed with as beautiful a day as one could imagine, with the orioles singing, making one think of spring."

From the seats of the car, they enjoyed vantage points and scenes that could not be experienced as a passenger onboard a train.

Besides the train, they also shared the road with local people who were on foot. Some of these poor people were so startled by the sight of this "monstrous" sight climbing the hill that they failed to *salaam* in customary greeting!

Harriet observed that the facial features of the Darjeeling women were similar to the Native people of America. They wore rings in their ears and noses, and Harriet marveled at the strength of these women as they sawed and cut wood while carrying infants on their backs.

"I was told that these people practiced polyandry, which permitted women to have several husbands," Harriet relayed with amusement. "Finally, I had found one place in the world where women are permitted to legally enjoy the same privileges that men who are sometimes called gentlemen enjoy illegally elsewhere!"

At fifteen thousand feet above sea level, they arrived at the Hotel Darjeeling, a well-kept lodge with a crackling fire that offered them a cheery welcome.

"But the altitude had taken its toll on me. I had trouble breathing and experienced a smothered feeling," Harriet recalled. "'Signora is ill!' Maria called out upon looking at me. Mr. Brooks immediate called for a doctor."

"'Madame has a weak heart,' the doctor declared upon examining me. He gave me some medicine and bound me in strips of woolen sheets soaked in warm water for the duration of my episode, which lasted for about two hours."

But it was difficult to rest after she was informed that the Dalai Lama was expected to arrive at the hotel at any moment. Harriet donned a heavy fur coat and positioned herself in a wheelchair on the hotel's terrace. With Harold at her side, she witnessed the great spiritual leader coming down off the mountain.

"I explained to Mr. Brooks that the Dalai Lama was fleeing Tibet. Some of his people preferred a more youthful leader and so he had been forced to leave his post. He had to escape persecution for having dared to live too long."

The Dalai Lama was carried high above the ground on a *dandie* supported by dust-covered servants. He appeared dirty and tired, but Harriet noted that he was dressed in a magnificent red robe with jeweled chains about his neck. On his head, a small sailor-style hat sat crookedly, the result of the jostling he had received during his transport.

Even the Dalai Lama's pony appeared exhausted. As the loyal animal was led down the mountain, Darjeeling Indians threw themselves on the ground and caressed its mane and tail.

"This was quite an exciting time for these locals," Harriet relayed. "The Lama and our motorcar arriving at about the same time divided the honors on this occasion."

Despite all the man made pageantry and excitement, Harriet always took time to appreciate the spectacular scenes presented by Mother Nature. "From the balcony of my hotel room I marveled at the glorious sight of the sun rising above the ice-covered mountain range. The mountains glistened like beautiful iridescent jewels. On one such occasion, I had Mr. Brooks roused to experience this rare and breathtaking scene."

A rejuvenated and rested Harriet bid a reluctant farewell to this wondrous place, returning to Calcutta, where she was greeted like an old friend. The rooms of everyone in her party had been cleaned and filled with bouquets of flowers in honor of their return.

At this point of our interview, Harriet stood and walked over to her desk, where she rifled through a drawer to retrieve a newspaper. "Here is an article that appeared in the local Calcutta newspaper *The Empress*," she said. "Allow me the indulgence to read you a few bits from this superlative article."

"To our list of distinguished visitors this season, we have now to add Mrs. Clark Fisher, who in the course of her journey around the world in her motor-car arrived in Calcutta last week...This most remarkable lady is the widow of Lieutenant Clark Fisher, of the U.S. Navy...She is the first to accomplish this feat, which makes her of great interest to the people here in Calcutta."

Harriet paused to smile.

The article went on to say how in 1900, Harriet had been introduced to Queen Victoria at Windsor Castle, as well as other member of European royalty. The reporter wrote of how the party had fared well in their camping experiences and that Harriet had set an example for those who wished to have similar excursions.

Harriet seemed to especially appreciate the fact that her trip through India had impacted the nation in a way no woman had before. *"We are sorry more people of this sort are not tempted to visit India, for it is quite a new type of woman coming from over the sea. This American woman has set the example and shown the way."*

"Speaking of gender, I had observed that throughout my travels in India, I rarely caught sight of young girls in their teens. When I inquired about this, I was told that females were only allowed to be seen in public up to nine years of age or so, and when they were very old."

The final hours of Harriet's stay on this mysterious subcontinent found her party lavishly entertained everywhere they went.

"Mr. Brooks enjoyed these elaborate meals, but not the smoke from so many cigarettes. He complained about how much these people smoked."

The following day, after such a meal, Mr. Jenkins went out for a drive alone in the Locomobile with Harriet. "Mr. Brooks was quite protective of me, too. For example, he did not approve of my driving alone in the Locomobile with just Mr. Jenkins! Imagine that."

But the heat of the food and of the rush of activities during her two weeks in Calcutta had also taken its toll on Harriet. "My throat was being scorched by the spicy curry- and chili-infused dishes of that region. I was informed this 'hot stuff' was intended to ward off stomach ailments and disease. I remarked that I thought it was more likely to cause the very thing they desired to avoid. It may have killed germs, but I think it might have been responsible for the death of many humans as well!"

The task of cooling off in the region's intense heat also took some effort. With blinds closed to the scorching sun, Harriet reclined on a mattress made of grass. Above her, large fans whirred, kept in constant motion by native boys dressed in white outfits with red sashes. They worked for hours without resting. "I regretted leaving everything in India except the heat and the monotonous motion of those fans."

Before being shipped off for another solo journey Honkie received lots of petting and loving admiration from many in attendance. The little dog was granted the special privilege of playing in the beautiful private park in front of the Grand Hotel. "He enjoyed himself in independent American fashion," Harriet recalled happily.

It was time for Harriet to bid *namaste* to this place that had touched her soul and exceeded any of her preconceived imaginings. "The mystic quality of India, that wonderful magic of atmosphere and antiquity… is impressive," Harriet recalled with a sigh.

She became quiet for a few moments, resigning herself to this bittersweet recollection.

CHAPTER EIGHTEEN

Sir Thomas Lipton and Billikins the Monkey

Harriet continued to wax nostalgic about her departure from the friends she had made in India. "In the Far East one sees humanity under different aspects from those we observe at home."

"Mothers and fathers part with their children, husbands with their wives, oftentimes forever; here, too, the traveler feels the pang of parting with friends with whom one is beginning to wish for a closer friendship. But the parting hour seems to come to all, and so, like ships that pass in the night, we move on."

On March tenth, Harriet set sail for the Island of Ceylon.[1] She was pleased to find their ship accommodations to be comfortable.

Upon their arrival they went to the custom house, where Harold signed an agreement to have the car examined for the next five days before their tour of Ceylon could commence. The car would have to pass inspection, as would the humans. For the first three days in Ceylon, Harriet and her party were subjected to extensive health checks.

"All the inhabitants of, and visitors to, the island are carefully watched to prevent contagious diseases," Harriet said. "We had our pulses felt and our tongues checked and if the slightest symptom of fever presented, you were to be quarantined and sent off to the hospital."

In Colombo, they checked into the colonial-style Galle Face Hotel and spent their quarantine time exploring the local landscape that presented a multitude of charming and picturesque drives. "In many ways," Harriet said happily, "Parts of Colombo reminded me somewhat of India."

They familiarized themselves with the highly-regulated rules of the road for Ceylon. "We were informed that we were only permitted to travel ten days without a license, and that the tax for this would be forty rupees, which we thought was rather high."

---
1 Ceylon became known as Sri Lanka in 1972.

The Locomobile and its passengers received a clean bill of health and were now free to explore this English-ruled Crown Colony that covered 25,481 square miles and was inhabited by a diverse population comprised of Europeans, Sinhalese, Burghers, Tamils, Moors, Malays and others.

Harriet was encouraged to learn that most of the roads on the island were decent and the rest houses, at least those close to the larger cities, were far more comfortable than those in India.

Bidding farewell to their friends at the Galle Face Hotel, they headed west, intending to tour the entire island during the course of two weeks. The road on which they traveled was magnificently lined with coconut palms. "When we were thirsty, we would stop the car and call to the natives who where gathering coconuts," Harriet recalled. "Whereupon they would take a large knife and cut off the top of a green coconut and give us the most delicious and refreshing coconut water to drink."

They left with a supply of canned meats, cream and milk. They were informed that since game was plentiful and there was no limit on what they could hunt, their food supply would be plentiful.

Ten miles out of Colombo, the Locomobile proudly displayed its fourth American flag since its departure from New Jersey, the elements having taken their toll.

When Harold navigated a narrow road from behind a slower moving motorcar, Harriet demanded impatiently, "Toot the horn, Mr. Brooks! That car is moving much too slow."

Harold obeyed her orders, requesting permission to pass. As the Locomobile overtook the slower car and pulled ahead, its passengers—two men, two ladies, and their chauffeur—intently scrutinized Harriet and her crew.

This exotic island nation would present many surprises. Not too far into their trip, in a quest to escape the intense heat, they came upon an inviting spot in the cool of the jungle and decided to have luncheon and set up camp. "But this little camping party on these grounds led us to be very cautious from then on, for we soon found ourselves literally covered in wood ticks."

They packed up and headed along a road dotted with sugarcane fields, sparkling lakes, views of the sea beyond every turn, and a glimpse of some of the exotic inhabitants of this country.

Members of the Sinhalese tribe appeared first. "The Sinhalese men, dressed in white with their hair done up in a knot tied at the base of their heads, resembled women," Harriet recalled. "But it was almost impossible to view the skittish Sinhalese women because they scampered and fled in fear as the Locomobile approached. I could only catch a glimpse of their backsides with their long hair flowing behind them in the breeze!"

The first evening on the road, they took lodging at a small rest house at Puttalam which proved to be very dirty, and Harriet was glad that they were able to provide their own bedding.

Early the next morning they were eager to move on toward Anuradhapura. After a short time on this road they met up with members of the Rock Vedda tribe, a savage-looking people who wore no clothing at all. Upon sighting the Locomobile they too ran into the dense forest, emerging only to take furtive peeks at the motorcar and its curious occupants. Harriet had been told that these people were rarely seen.

"I advised Mr. Brooks to keep moving. I had heard that these people are well-known for their remarkable skill with the bow and arrow."

As promised, the jungles of Ceylon were abundant with wildlife and Harold took advantage of the abundance of fowl, somewhat to Harriet's dismay. Once again, Harold brought down a bird with exquisite green and gold plumage and a curved tail feather nearly a yard in length. "My heart sank," Harriet sadly recollected. "Such a beautiful jungle fowl, it was such a shame to see it like that."

But later that evening, Harriet appreciated Harold's skill as a hunter and Albert's as a cook. "Albert prepared this bird in an old-fashioned pot-pie, complete with dumplings. It was a very savory and tempting dish."

At the city of Anuradhapura, they passed a doctor's health inspection and were given free passport to continue their tour. Outside of this sacred city, they stopped to visit ancient sites and were told these were the remains of some of the world's oldest temples.

At her hotel that evening, Harriet was pleased to find herself dining in the company of Mr. James Gordon Bennett and his wife Baroness de Reuter. Mr. Bennett's father, the late James Gordon Bennett Senior, was the founder and publisher of the *New York Herald*. His son, better known to all as Gordon, had taken over the editorial reigns of the newspaper upon the passing of his father, and had made his fortune as the publisher of the Paris edition of the *Herald*.

At a later date, while researching a story, I would connect the name of this colorful editor to another of Harriet's renowned acquaintances. In 1909, Bennett had offered a trophy for the fastest speed on a closed circuit for airplanes. In an event held in Rheims, France, that trophy was won by none other than Glenn Curtiss.

"It was so nice to meet some old friends there," Harriet said. "The Bennetts had been guests of mine on Lake Como a couple of years prior. Ceylon was a favorite place for Mr. Bennett to winter, and nearly every year be brought a party over on his yacht, the *Namouna*, with a couple of motorcars with which to tour the island."

Mr. Bennett told Harriet that he and his wife were stopping at the city of Kandy, and imparted some useful information about the roads on which they would travel to Kandy, a sacred Buddhist site, built during the fourteenth century. A picturesque city, it is situated on the banks of an artificial lake with a road known as "Lady Horton's Walk" that winds through the lake's hilly landscape, overlooking the valley of Dumbera and the Mahaweli Ganga, the nation's longest river. "This view presented a majestic beauty that can scarcely be surpassed," Harriet said.

Harriet toured a temple that contained a tooth of the Buddha, then visited the Peredeniya Gardens, where she picked nutmeg, cloves, and cinnamon. They ended their day at the Queen Hotel, where they once again met up with the Bennett party.

But the next day brought an encounter of an unpleasant nature.

"The following morning, I was approached by a fine-looking man in a uniform," she recalled, frowning. "He asked if I was Mrs. Fisher. I told him I was and he introduced himself as the president of the Automobile Club. He said that he was very sorry, but he was there to inform me that I was going to be arrested for driving away from Colombo without the proper license for my car!"

Harriet explained to the man that she had been informed that as they were not going to be staying long, one had not been necessary. The officer phoned Colombo and after a brief discussion, the matter was dropped.

But Harold did not escape her wrath, since it was his job to take care of obtaining all necessary licenses. "I blamed this upsetting incident on Mr. Brooks and I recall it was one of those occasions when I was awfully upset and cross with him."

More enjoyable days found them visiting an elephant *kraal*, the pearl fisheries, rubber tree farms, and tea fields. But traveling at fifteen thousand feet above sea level once again affected Harriet's health. "This altitude was really starting to trouble my heart and I informed my party it was time to head back to Colombo."

They made the return trip, covering about seventy-five to eighty miles a day. Descending a road filled with sharp turns and curves, Harold honked the Locomobile's horn nearly incessantly to warn other motorists and bullock carts of their approach.

They stopped for only one more irresistible visit. "With Albert left in charge of the car, Mr. Brooks, Maria, and I went off for a long walk into the sapphire and ruby mines. I must say that there were so many of these precious gems that after awhile their novelty wore off, and one lost their desire to possess them."

But she did find something she wished to possess of quite a different nature, when Harriet noticed a baby monkey darting in and out of a stand of tea bushes. "'Stop the car, Mr. Brooks,' I yelled. I climbed out and followed this little monkey."

Harriet was informed that they were on the grounds of Sir Thomas Lipton's tea plantation, and the monkey belonged to the plantation's caretaker. Harriet tracked the monkey to the caretaker's hut.

"I made indications with my hands that I wished to possess the baby monkey, and after some negotiations, the man allowed me to purchase the animal. With some gentle coaxing, the monkey jumped into my hands and I had him in a firm grasp."

"How did the others react to the news that a monkey would now be joining your party?" I had to ask.

"Well, quite frankly, they appeared to be disgusted," she said. 'Just how do you plan to keep a monkey in a car with so much more traveling ahead of us?' they all demanded to know. 'And what about Honkie?' they further inquired. 'How will he feel about sharing his car with another creature?'"

But the little monkey proved to be a good travel companion. "To my delight, and their surprise, he curled up in my arms and seemed to enjoy the motoring, as though he had been used to it all of his life."

When they checked back into the Galle Face Hotel, he was well received, much to Harriet's relief. "'I shall christen this monkey Billikins," I announced shortly after he had joined our family, 'He is named after the good luck doll so popular back in America now. I expect that he will bring me good luck, too.'"

Not only had Harriet secured a pet from Sir Thomas Lipton's property, but she was about to discover she had made his acquaintance earlier in her tour of Ceylon.

After dinner one evening, an American consul by the name of Mr. Davis approached Harriet. "He said 'Mrs. Fisher, Sir Thomas Lipton would like to make your acquaintance.'"

Harriet jumped at the chance to meet this famous business mogul. But Harriet was surprised that upon their introduction, Sir Thomas laughed and playfully shook his finger at her.

"He said, 'Do you remember passing a motorcar about two weeks ago just outside of Colombo?' 'Yes.' I said. 'It was I who requested my driver to pass!'"

Sir Thomas explained that it had been his car that we had passed so unceremoniously. "'I was surprised to find a car even larger than mine on this island,' he explained. 'And I was even more amazed when this car, displaying an American flag no less, dared to pass me!'"

Harriet and Sir Thomas enjoyed a good laugh over the matter.

"Lipton suggested we should turn back and accompany his party to England to enjoy the races with him."

But Harriet regretfully declined, explaining her ambitious travel plans to the amazed businessman.

On March thirty-first, two days before leaving Ceylon, Harriet celebrated a birthday. While out picking up some new suits for himself, Harold purchased a bouquet of flowers for her.

But the day did not end well for this young man. "Mr. Brooks and I had another scene," Harriet recalled. "He dared to frown at someone who was smoking a cigarette on the hotel lawn. As I stated before, Harold did not care for the practice of smoking."

Harriet and her friends now prepared to set sail on the *Delta* from Colombo to China, where they would be motorless for a brief period of time. The Locomobile was shipped ahead to be retrieved in Japan.

This was also a time for another kind of celebration. Harriet was about to be rejoined by His Highness the Maharaja of Baroda, Her Highness the Maharani, their pretty daughter, Princess Indraraja, and their suite of attendants. They would tour China together.

"A jollier party never left any port," Harriet recalled of this time, with unabashed joy.

Reflecting on her adventures in Ceylon, Harriet observed that in this exotic land, "We found the highest civilization and also the most extreme degradation; and between these two extremes one could find almost everything the heart could desire."

Photo Section

The majority of the photographs in this section were taken by Harold Fisher Brooks

The Fisher and Norris Factory

Bella Vista, Ewing, New Jersey

The journey begins; Trenton, New Jersey 1909

Locomobile at 125 East Hanover Street, Trenton, New Jersey

The Locomobile receives 1st Prize for Floral Decoration at Contrexeville, France

The testing of the tent on the busy streets of Paris

Devil's Bridge, Switzerland

Villa Carlotta, Italy - Harriet's beloved Lake Como home

Harriet's yacht, the Carlotta, sailing on Lake Como

Glenn Curtiss and his prize-winning airplane in Brescia, Italy

Crating of the Locomobile in Genoa, Italy

A trip in the desert, Valley of the Kings, Thebes

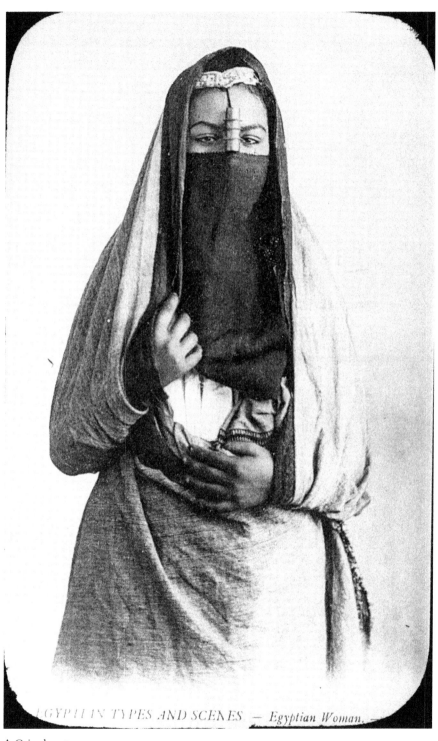

A Cairo beauty

At the Pyramids, West Bank of the Nile River

The Maharajah of Benares

On the road from Poona to Bombay with a friend, Mr. Cassie

Ferry at Thana

Fording the challenging Tapti River

An elephant ride in Allahabad

Judge Nehru's home in Allahabad

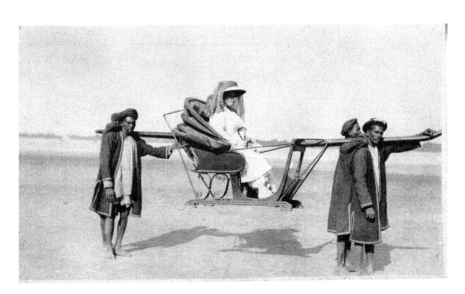

The Dandie of His Highness of Benares

The Burning Ghats in Benares

Boarding the ferry at Dehri-On-Sone

A Luncheon with friends in Calcutta

Train ride near the Sonada Forest in Darjeeling

The last stop at a däk bungalow before reaching Calcutta (Albert in front of car). Bengal, India

A rest for lunch in Ceylon (now Sri Lanka)

A Ceylonese beauty

Chinese "Rik shaw" and Sihk police in Shanghai

The Willow Pattern tea house, Old Shanghai

Departure from Kobe, Japan

Luncheon with the Maharajah of Baroda and his wife (seated on cushion making sandwiches) and his daughter (r). Also pictured, Miss West, an English governess, and Harriet W. Fisher.

In Nara, Japan, with High Highness's Fiat.

Princess of Baroda, daughter of His Highness of Baroda, on the road to Nagoya

Ferrying with a loaded motorcar on Hamana Bay

Preparing to cross Hamana Bay

Ditched!

Leaving Kyoto, March 1910

A curious Japanese crowd

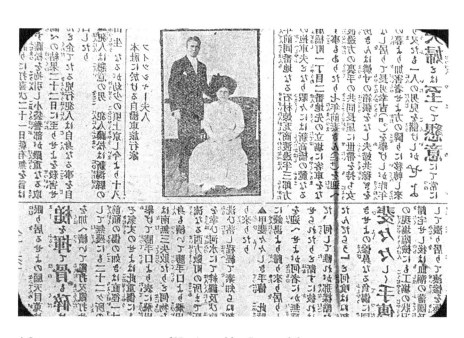

A Japanese newspaper account of Harriet and her Locomobile

"Death Camp" in the Hakone Mountain Pass, Japan, awaiting men and material to build a bridge

Resting up in Atami, Japan

A Japanese Beauty

On the famous Cryptomeria Road, Nikko

Horseback riding in Japan

Locomobile ready for shipment at Yokohama, on board *S.S. Siberia*

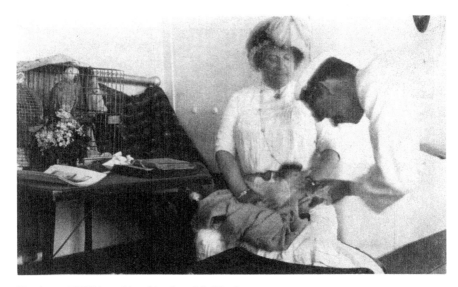

Harriet and Billikins with a friend on S.S. Siberia

U.S.A. Sailing vessel, Golden Gate Park. First to round Cape Horn

Banquet at Palace Hotel, San Francisco

Farewell luncheon with the Indrarajah, Maharini Baroda, Miss West and Harriet at Cliff House in San Francisco

Leaving San Francisco, escorted by members of an auto club

Mrs. Fisher and her party enjoying a mid-day rest at camp in California

Point of Rocks Hotel, Rock Springs, Wyoming

At Lake Tahoe, Nevada

Maria helps to make bridge over washout in American Desert in Bitter Creek, Wyoming

Honkie running outside cabin at Lake Tahoe, Nevada

Mr. McBluff's house in Medicine Bow, Wyoming

Camp near Evanston, Wyoming

Mormon Cathedral, Salt Lake City, Utah

"Held up" in Sandusky, Ohio

Honk Honk playing with Billikins

Honk Honk, the Locomobile mascot

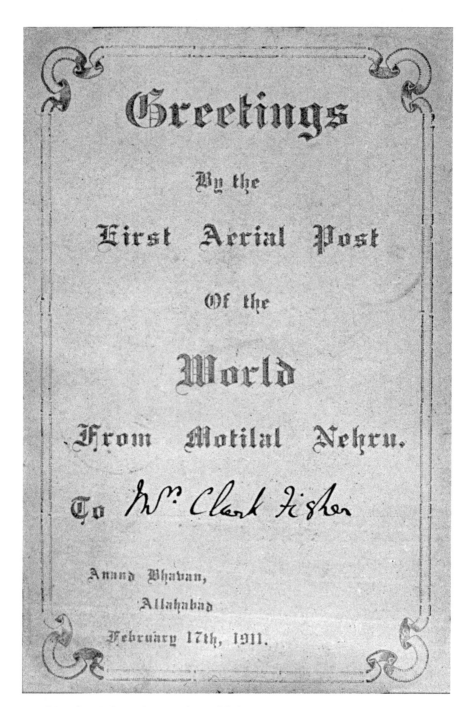

Aerial Post from Judge Nehru sent from Allahabad, India, to Harriet Fisher

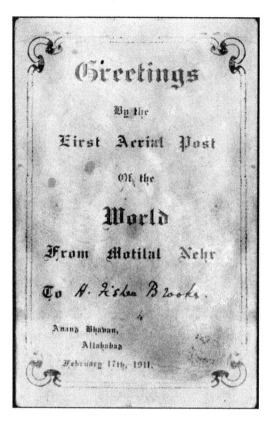

Greetings – Aerial Post from Nehru to Harold Brooks

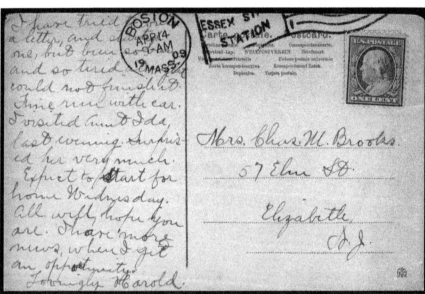

Postcard dated April 4, 1909 telling of purchase of Honk-Honk in Boston

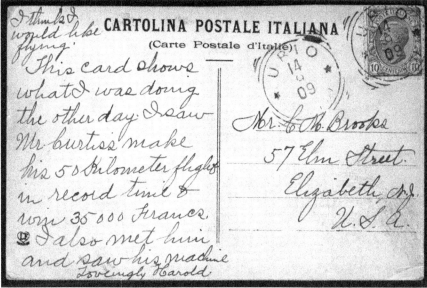

Postcard of Airplane Meet describing meeting Glenn Curtiss, September 12, 1909

Postcard of Airplane Meet with description of Glenn Curtiss's flight, September 14, 1909

Postcard depicting a group of natives in Hong Kong, 20 April, 1910

Postcard of O'Reilly Street in Havana, Cuba, February 21, 1911

Postcard of Jappy, Honk Honk and Harriet (undated)

Postcard showing back view of Villa Carlotta (undated)

LIST OF PASSENGERS
BY THE
S. S. "Somali"

Leaving Calcutta 10th March, Colombo about 15th March, Port Said 28th March, Marseilles 3rd April

FOR

LONDON.

CAPT. A. G. CUBITT, R. N. R.

Baird, Mr. L. W.
Baker, Mrs. G. H.
Batchelor, Mr. Albert E.
Battye, Captain C. W.
Bayley, Mrs. W. E. and Child.
Binning, Mr. F.
Borgia, Miss Marie.
Brand, Miss
Broom, Mrs.
Brymer, Mr. D.
Brooks, Mr Harold Fisher.
Candler. Mr. A. P.
Carter, Mr. J. J.
Carter, Mrs.
Cattanack, Mr.
Champness, Mr. G. E.
Cobb, Mr. W. H.
Cobb, Mrs.
Cobb, Miss
Cock, Mr. J. K. de
Cochrane, Lieutenant.
Collins, Mr. H. S.
Danby, Mr. C. J.
Danby, Mrs.
Daniell, Mr. J.
Duncan, Mr. R.
Duncan, Mrs.
Drummond, Mrs. R. G.
Edmondson, Mr. H. C.
Ekins, Mr. G. W.
Ekins, Mrs. and Infant.
Evans, Mr. L.
Evans, Mrs.
Evans, Miss
Ewan, Mr.
Ewan, Mr. J. B.
Fisher, Mrs. Clark.
Flint, Mr. A. M.
Frank, Mrs. Marshall.
Freeland, Miss
Furlonger, Mrs. M.
Gall, Mr. R. L. B.
Gall, Mrs. and Infant.
Gilbert, Mr. J. A.
Gilbert, Mr. H.
Gilbert, Mrs.
Giles, Lt.-Col., A.
Giles, Mrs.
Green, Mr. John.
Hanan, Mr. G. R.
Harry, Mrs. and Child.
Heinig, Mr. R. L.
Heinig, Mrs.
Heinig, Lt. W. H.
Hillman, Mrs.
Hind, Mr. F. P.
Hope, Mrs. W. H.
Hore, Mr. J. E. P.
Hudson, Mr.
Hudson, Mrs.
Human, Mr.
Human, Mrs. and Child.
Innes-Brodie, Mr. T. S.
Ingram, Mrs. and Infant.
Johnston, Mr. H.
Judah, Mr. E. S.
Judah, Mr. S. E.
Kempton, Mr. M. K.
Lafone, Mr. A. M.
Lawrie, Mr. William.
Lewis, Mr. E. A.
Linton. Mr.
Lomax, Mr. C. P.
Macdonald, Rev. J. I.
Macdonald, Mrs. and three Children.
McIntosh, Miss J.
Mackie, Mr. F.
Maguire, Mrs.
Malpas, Mrs. and Two Children of Mrs. Davis.
Matson, Miss
Miller, Mr. N.
Mitchell, Mr. W.
Miskin, Lt. W. L.
Murse, Mrs R. W.
Morton, Mr. R. H. A.
Morton, Mrs. and Child.
Nicolis, Miss
O'Farrell, Mr. F. M.
Parish, Mr. A. M
Parish, Mrs. and Child.
Payne, Two Misses D. and J.
Payne, Master C.
Peyton, Mr. Guy W.
Playfair, Mr. G. F.
Playfair, Mrs.
Porter, Mr. J. E.
Porter, Mrs.
Prescott, Mr. R.
Ravenhill, Captain A.
Reed, Miss C. A.
Rendle, Miss C.
Rhodes, Miss
Robson, Mr. E.
Robertson, Mr. A. C.
Rooke, Vice-Admiral E.
Rooke, Mrs.
Ruthven, Mr. J. L.
Sheean, Mr. W. J.
Simpson, Mrs. A. E.
Sinclair, Mr. Bruce.
Sinclair, Mrs. and Infant.
Sinclair, Miss C. C.
Smith, Lt. G. V. H.
Spier, Mrs. S. F.
Stuart, Mr. J. Gordon.
Stuart, Mrs.
Stuart, Miss K. B.
Stuart, Mrs. Villiers and Maid
Swart, Dr. B.
Thurley, Mr. R. P.
Watson, Mrs, E. A
Welman, Lt. W. H.
Williamson, Mrs. R. L., Nurse and Infant.
Wolf, Miss M.
Warren, Mr. V. B.
Walthew, Mr and Mrs.
Walthew, Mrs. Dorothy.
White, Mr.

Pennslar & Oriental Navigation Company ship manifest – *S. S. Somali*

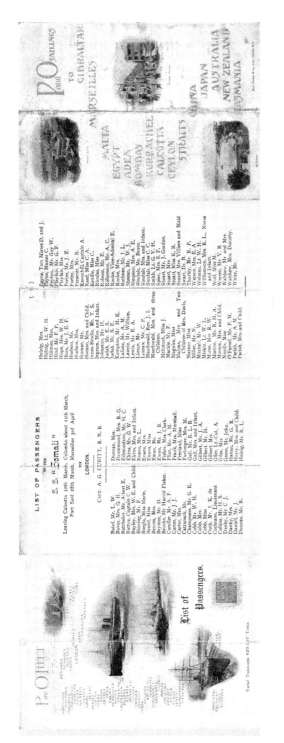

Above and next page: Article in "The Empress - An Illustrated Journal", March, 1910

Left: Pennslar & Oriental Navigation Company ship manifest – *S. S. Somali*

THE EMPRESS
AN ILLUSTRATED JOURNAL

Vol. XXIV.] CALCUTTA, No. 1, MARCH, 1910. [Price One Rupee.

HER 40 H.-P. LOCOMOBILE.

ON THE BOMBAY-CALCUTTA RUN.

adjourned to refresh themselves during the progress of the "First Aid" competition. The band played a pleasing selection of music throughout the afternoon. This annual event is looked forward to with the greatest interest.

ON the same afternoon Mrs. Molesworth Macpherson gave a very pleasant garden party, many people coming on after a short visit to the sports at the Light Horse Camp.

MRS. CLARK FISHER ON A TOUR ROUND THE WORLD

TO our list of distinguished visitors this season we have now to add Mrs. Clark Fisher, who, in the course of her journey round the world in a motor-car, arrived in Calcutta last week and left a few days ago for Colombo.

This most remarkable American lady is the widow of Lieutenant-Commander Fisher of the United States Navy. Since her husband's death she has managed the Eagle Anvil Works at Trenton, N. J., which he founded, and was admitted as the only woman member of the National Association of Manufacturers in the States. Mrs. Clark Fisher has a decidedly unique personality. Her knowledge of the world and its social problems is great. She is versed in all spheres of life and, although extremely practical, her sympathies are ideal. A few years ago she was one of the most prominent society women in the east of the United States. In 1900 she was presented to Her late Majesty Queen Victoria at Windsor Castle and has met various members of the Royal houses of Europe. For a person prominent in society and diplomatic circles, almost everywhere, to undergo the hardships of this present trip, is a thing which would not appeal to the average woman of position. It is somewhat of a contrast to 5 o'clock teas and an afternoon drive on the Strand.

She has always taken a deep interest in automobiles, and has made a study of their mechanism to such good purpose, that she is as well informed as any chauffeur.

The present trip is being performed in a 40-horse power Locomobile of the ordinary four-passenger stock roadster model. It has a 40-gallon tank, with a sufficient gasoline and oil capacity for a distance of 400 miles without refilling. Attached to the tonneau is a rack for trunks and the camping outfit. In the forepart of the car the Star-spangled Banner waves on the right, the pennant of the Automobile Club of America on the left.

Her entourage consists of a young American Engineer, Mr. Harold Fisher Brooks, a cosmopolitan valet, an Italian maid and an Indian servant. On their way from Bombay they have frequently camped out on the road and seemed to have thoroughly enjoyed it.

In course of a conversation, Mrs. Clark Fisher expressed her delight at her reception both by Europeans and Indians throughout her tour in this country, and mentioned in particular the hospitality of H. H. the Maharaja of Benares and Mr. Motilal Nehru at Allahabad.

THE news of the latest method of reading character may interest our fair readers, not by the lines of the hand, but by the lines in one's forehead. The new science is known as *metoposcopie*, and four centuries ago was in high favour. Cardan, the apostle of *metoposcopie*, was an expert at reading men's characters and dispositions by this method. It was he who said that if women concealed their wrinkles by means of pastes and ointments, it was in order the better to keep their secrets. Seven principal lines traverse the forehead, and, like the lines in the hand, they are influenced by Saturn, Jupiter, Mars, Venus, Mercury, the Sun, and the Moon. The lines signify by their contour certain characteristics. Thus, if a certain line takes the form of an "M," that signifies happiness; if, however, it is shaped like an "X" and is surmounted by a kind of "U," that means infidelity. Ladies, watch your husbands' foreheads!

MRS. CLARK FISHER.

FORDING A RIVER.

MR. WILLIE FREEAR.
(In one of his clever impersonations.)

SPECULATION over the Indian Viceroyalty may be set at rest. When Lord Minto retires, he will be succeeded by Earl Grey, who is now Governor-General of Canada. Lord Grey is Lady Minto's brother; and Lady Antrim, who has for so many years been Lady of the Bedchamber and personal friend of Queen Alexandra, and who is the sister of both Lady Minto and Earl Grey, has recently been in Calcutta arranging the matter on behalf of the Imperial authorities. Lady Antrim is now on her way home, and the official announcement re the Indian Viceroyalty may be expected a month hence.

MR. WILLIE FREEAR, who is here depicted in one of his numerous characters from his famous "Frivolities," appeared on the 25th and 28th ultimo at the Empire Theatre, Calcutta, to crowded houses. He has a unique reputation in all parts of the world as an entertainer *par excellence*, and is the possessor of credentials from Potentates and Princes innumerable, and there is hardly a country on the globe he has not visited, and his success here quite justifies all that has been said in his favour. We feel satisfied that, should he again visit Calcutta with his whimsical and exhilarating entertainment, he will meet with another gratifying reception equal to that which welcomed him here last week in his funniest of funny performances.

CHAPTER NINETEEN

A Guarded Tour of Shanghai

On the second of April, Harriet and her party boarded a steamer called the *Delta* sailing for Penang, in the Strait of Malacca. Five days later they reached this destination, and then boarded another boat to Singapore.

Harriet was grateful to be on land again. It had been a long, somewhat uncomfortable sea journey by Harriet's account. "Oh, the heat was just unbearable," she recalled. "I gave our agent a good dressing down for not supplying me with a fan."

Under these conditions, even the proper English travelers had no shame about darting about ship in their pajamas as confident as if they were dressed for a visit to the Strand. "I was told that when it is extremely hot, the ladies go around in their dressing gowns."

"The government officials met with His Highness, and we all accepted an invitation to take a drive around Singapore and to dine at the hotel."

Their visit here was brief, and Harriet was anxious to move on to Hong Kong, where they went ashore briefly to "peep" at the city. They arrived in Shanghai on April fourteenth. Its bustling harbor presented a waterfront crowded for miles with cotton mills, shipyards, wharves, and workshops. "They call Shanghai the Paris of the East," Harriet said.

In this busy harbor, Harriet and her party were glad to see a trim rowboat proudly displaying the American flag, with a score of brawny arms working the oars with clock-like precision. Their craft swiftly and steadily navigated the waters, in stark contrast to the garish and sluggish motion of the local watercraft.

"The square, ruffled, bat-wing sails of these boats, that might have been white at one time, were now stained a deep brown wherever the primal material had survived. Many displayed blue patches making them look like crazy-quilts."

Harriet was relieved to find that they were not harassed by officious customs inspectors as they were in Manila, New York, San Francisco, and in Continental Europe. Near the Garden Bridge, which spans the Soochow Creek, which serves as the dividing line between the old English and American Settlements, Harriet took in the attractions at the Public Gardens.

"The queer thing to me about the Public Gardens is that not one Chinaman is permitted to enter. Only the English and American residents, and the nurses who accompanied their children," a perplexed Harriet observed.

"But the Chinese pay the cost to maintain these parks, and the little Chinese tots, with their little kimonos, are an interesting sight as they stand peeping into the park through the rails of the gates. With wistful expressions on their small faces, it appeared that they wished to be allowed to scramble on the grass and enjoy some of the privileges of the white children."

Harriet was fascinated by the stories about women and their employment in these parts. "I was told that two of the nurses sent over by the English government notified the head doctor of the hospital that neither of them expected to stay any longer than to prepare for their weddings. It seems both had become engaged to men on board the ship that brought them to Shanghai!"

But these men had to pay the hospital three months of their fiancée's salaries, as this practice was becoming costly. Harriet was informed that in some of the larger shops, there was great difficulty in securing the services of English girls. "It seems like every woman or girl, with any pretension to looks at all, gets married either before or as soon as she reaches Shanghai!" Harriet said, laughing.

In many cases, these young women were required to sign a contract with the hiring shop guaranteeing their employment for six months, or they young woman would forfeit the equivalent amount of their salary.

"I heard that some of the shop owners have on each steamer, a party going out, expecting to make a profit on their time, and feel quite sure that they will meet some man who will prefer female companionship in the Far West to living there alone."

Amused by these stories, I told Harriet that if I should not find a suitable husband here in America, I might book passage to Shanghai.

Harriet smiled and continued. "The Chinese people loved Billikins and insisted on shaking hands with my little monkey."

Harriet desired to tour Old Shanghai in the native quarter, where the Willow Pattern Bungalow stood. "But this was the first time during our entire trip where it was required of us to bring a private detective or a guide provided by the hotel," Harriet said. In fact they were told that they could not enter this area without one. "We felt no fear, but we were told that many Western visitors who had entered that place were never heard from again. This was, of course, a great concern for the local government, and for us, so we took their advice."

Harriet was also advised to purchase five hundred coins for her party. These would be used to throw at approaching beggars to keep them at a distance. This would help to ward off assault and to prevent exposure to the diseases these people might carry. It was also recommended that her party wear raincoats to cover themselves, and to don short skirts so as not to carry disease back with them.

"We dismissed some of this advice," Harriet said. "We had already been through so much." But those coins did prove useful. "As we walked along, we simply tossed these coins at those who approached us, and those cunning faces of these coolies did not make one feel any too secure," she recalled with a slight shudder.

The beginning of their Shanghai tour was not auspicious. Harriet claimed that it was in this city that she witnessed some of the most dreadful scenes of the trip. The pond around the Willow Pattern Bungalow was filthy and they were greeted by the skeletal and diseased figures of men seated around the entrance to the city.

"These men were an awful sight. Some of their faces were horribly mutilated, with one side of the face entirely eaten away showing their teeth to the roots. Many were covered by flies, most undoubtedly carrying germs and horrible diseases."

Hundreds of men labored along the city streets, working with silver and gold and cutting gem stones, like turquoise, that had been sent from all over the world to be cut here. In this city, all kinds of items, from lamps, candlesticks, and incense burners, were manufactured, and one found a number of silk factories.

These merchants were a different sort from those Harriet had met in other places. "I learned that bargaining here was out of the question. When the Chinese merchant told you the price of his items, nothing could induce him to yield a half cent, and he offered me a look of disgust at the mere suggestion."

Harriet and her party pushed their way through the masses of people to reach the interior of the Bungalow. Once there, they were offered tea. Their guide advised them to purchase it, but not to drink it.

"I can't say for certain," Harriet said. "But as our guide often stayed behind to converse with the local businessmen, I suspected he got one-half of this money."

Entering into the Willow Bungalow, they were presented with the scene of throngs of people praying to idols and golden images. Others gambled and had their fortunes told while a variety of men, stupefied by opium, slept on stone benches.

"These are very superstitious people," Harriet said. "And they do nothing without first consulting with these men of mystery. These fortune tellers shake up a lot of sticks in a long tube, and those seeking news of their fates pay a small price before pulling out a stick with a number that signifies good or bad fortune."

Harriet marveled at how men placed singing birds on gambling tables to bring them good luck. "I wondered if these men ever won anything, and I presumed that if they did, they soon returned to spend it again, trying to win more money."

As they had witnessed in India, the effect of opium was also apparent here. "The opium fiends appeared to be harmless. They lay on stone benches with their kimonos wrapped around them and their long braids, called queues, tied up around their heads."

But there was also law to be found in this land. On another day Harriet and her party were invited to visit a police court. "Here I was told by the English judge that nearly all the cases were those of men brought before him on the charge of kidnapping!" Harriet was informed that some of the local people seized young boys and girls to sell them, or to make them work for them.

Harriet watched two criminals being marched into court with their queues used to tie them together. A policeman, who led them, held the end of a braid in one hand, and a short sword in the other as they were led up to the judge. "If the child kidnapped was a girl, and the evidence strong enough, this criminal would lose his head," Harriet recalled.

Harriet found the immorality of the local women deplorable. "These hags, on a nightly basis, walked the street with girls as young as nine or ten. They would not hesitate to sell even their own daughters to any purchaser who had the right amount of money, without any feeling of shame."

Speaking of other side trips here, Harriet advised travelers to China to skip a sojourn to Peking unless they planned a long stay in this city. She described her train trip there as tiresome and the awful stench of that metropolis a continual assault on the olfactory organs.

"Many of the people I had encountered in China were in stark contrast to the educated and well-travelled Chinamen I had previously met," Harriet observed. "Many of the Chinese people, especially the coolies, have no idea of order or cleanliness and the spreading of disease of all kinds."

But Harriet sensed that many of the people she met in her travels in China seemed to know better conditions existed elsewhere, and had heard something of America. Even her rickshaw drivers knew about opportunities in places like New York or Philadelphia. "'No money China, but wife and children here,' they would confide in me. 'Me go back to America some time.'"

But she also encountered individuals in China who were well-educated and well-travelled. "These people seemed to understand the conditions that their people face and I think they are trying, with the rest of the Eastern world, to become more westernized in their ideas of civilization."

Harriet observed that, "In them, I detected a desire to be more Western-thinking, fascinated with the opportunities offered in America."

"Like your friend, Wu Ting Fang?" I inquired. Wu Ting Fang was a Chinese diplomat and politician who served as Minister of Foreign Affairs and briefly as Acting Premier during the early years of the Republic of China. I recalled reading a newspaper article in the *New York Times* where Harriet spoke of their acquaintance. She had told the reporter that this Chinese luminary had been quite impressed with her, describing her as the most fascinating woman in the world.

"Yes," Harriet said. "It was such a disappointment that our itineraries prevented our meeting here again in China."

Among the crowded streets of Shanghai, a popular mode of transportation were the long, narrow, one-wheeled carts loaded with up to ten passengers. This form of transport required careful manipulation to keep the cart from tipping.

But in that ancient city, Harriet observed changes on the horizon. Trolley cars frequently encircled the city, and residents were becoming acquainted with the telegraph and the telephone. "They seemed to be fully awake to the necessity for all modern improvements," she noted.

She additionally observed that the unique local custom of tying up prisoners with their braids would also soon be a thing of the past. She had read that this practice would be discontinued for the "higher classes," and it would only be a matter of time before all Chinese criminals would be queueless.

"I wonder what the police in Shanghai and Peking will do with their prisoners now," she said. "Mere handcuffs are so unpicturesque!"

In reflecting on the westernization of this ancient land, a wistful Harriet remarked, "I felt that I was there none too soon to see a little of what had been in the past."

CHAPTER TWENTY

"I fear, Mrs. Fisher, you do not know what you are up against."

While heading toward Japan on April twenty-fifth aboard the German ship *Beulow*, the sea was rough and the wind brisk during the one day journey. Harriet did not fare well.
"I heard a concerned Mr. Brooks telling everyone in our party that Mrs. F. was quite seasick from all the ship's pitching."

It was their first sea journey on a German liner and Harriet and her party were surrounded by passengers speaking German or French. "It was entertaining to watch the expressions on the faces of my party as they expressed their dislike of the German food offered at luncheon."

They came ashore in Nagasaki the following day, accompanied by the Baroda party, and were greeted by the governor general of that city. Harriet and her party, along with the Baroda's, were invited to a traditional Japanese tea ceremony.

"We obtained our first views of Japan from the seats of rickshaws," Harriet recalled. Escorted to a little bungalow made of thin wood with rice paper windows, they removed their shoes and sat semi-circle on silk-covered cushions. They were immediately served tea in tiny cups, and rice cakes presented on diminutive trays.

The proprietor of the bungalow, a man dressed in an elegant kimono, entered the room. He smiled broadly and stretched his palms out toward Harriet, her companions and the Baroda family. Then, dropping to his knees, he tapped his forehead to the floor three times before each of them. "I thought he would surely knock himself out," Harriet said.

Five young girls appeared next, dressed in kimonos elegantly embroidered with wisteria and cherry blossoms, their hair arranged perfectly. Four Geisha dancers followed, bearing musical instruments. They twanged and banged in a noisy fashion. "I am quite sure some of our American boys would get more music out of an old tin can," Harriet remarked. "However, I must say that everything there was done in such a dignified way that one hardly dares suggest it is anything but music!"

The little girl dancers flitted their fans in time to the music. With their fans held to cover the lower halves of their faces, they peeped over them in an engaging manner.

"O-o-o-o-o," they chanted as they performed the Dance of the Four Seasons. "Next, they put on these perfectly hideous masks made out of some kind of plaster which was held in front of the faces by a stick. What a contrast to the pretty faces of these children as the peered from behind the sides of their grotesque masks."

This performance lasted for over an hour, and when the dance was complete the girls sat with their American and Indian guests, playfully examining the clothing and jewelry worn by Harriet and her party with typical childlike curiosity.

"Harold found the Japanese people, especially the girls and women, most amusing," Harriet said.

They were served a variety of delicious tea and fruit, but Harriet declined the offering of Japanese liquor called sake. "We told them 'No, thank you.' I had heard that this drink can be very dangerous if partaken of freely, and the effects felt the next day are worse than if one had imbibed half a case of champagne."

The Barodas also graciously refused, since they did not partake of alcoholic beverages. "The Hindus are very temperate," Harriet noted. "Not using liquor or tobacco in any form."

This warm and welcoming tea ceremony held in their honor ended in a flurry of bows, after which each young performer received a coin from Harriet.

They were then whisked away on rickshaws for a guided tour of the city's temples and magnificent gardens. "We came to rest on the grounds of a beautifully-landscaped cemetery and it seemed as if we were visiting the living, and not the city of the dead," Harriet recollected. "The flowers, in their brilliant colorings and gay dress, turned every thought toward life."

Harriet and the Maharini Baroda enjoyed a shopping trip while in Nagasaki, a city that was well known for its production of items made from tortoise shell. Harriet bought gifts for everyone, including a tortoise shell comb and brush set for Harold.

Harriet found Nagasaki a place well worth visiting, but could not imagine anyone wanting a lengthy stay. Harriet's party and the royal family boarded a steamer and ventured to the city of Kobe. Here, she and the Barodas bid each other a temporary farewell, as the Maharaja's party would travel by train to Tokyo. They looked forward to a reunion later on their route through Japan.

"In Kobe, it was my first priority to reclaim Honkie!" Harriet said. "I had not seen my little dog since leaving Calcutta." She quickly made her way to the office of Brown's Shipping Company. Upon her arrival she asked to see Mr. C. M. Birnie, whose family had been taking care of Honk Honk.

"I was informed by the hotel clerk that Honk Honk was well known in Kobe. He said that the Birnie family had become very attached to him, and he was afraid it would be very hard for them to part with the little dog. He asked if I was his mistress."

"I assured him that I was and asked if my dog was well. He told me that Honkie was fine, and gave me the home address of the Birnie family."

Fearing that her dog would not recall her, Harriet wasted no time. She summoned two rickshaws and took Harold with her to fetch Honkie.

The Birnie home sat high up on the side of a mountain. "That bungalow very much reminded me of a scene right out of Madame Butterfly," Harriet recalled.

"Just as Mr. Brooks and I approached the gate we encountered a man who said, 'I presume you are Mrs. Fisher, the owner of Honk Honk?' 'I am,' I said. 'And I've come to claim my beloved dog. I have missed him so.'"

"Mr. Birnie introduced himself and went to open the gate with a key. As he did, he called out to his children and asked, 'Where is Honkie?' He turned to me and announced, 'If Honk Honk fails to recognize his mistress, *I* will claim him for my children. They so dread losing him.'"

"'If my little dog does not recognize me I shall be glad to leave him to them.'"

But this matter was decided in short order.

"I rushed into the yard calling out, 'Honk Honk where are you?' The overjoyed dog rushed at me, running in tight little circles of excitement. He barked with happy recognition, jumping on top of me."

"'Honkie. Down boy!' I commanded. 'You will surely ruin my gloves and gown!'"

"'Our Honk Honk is looking fine and in good health,' Mr. Brooks said, petting the dog."

The dejected Birnie children came and slumped down next to Harriet. Fighting tears, they hugged the little terrier. "They asked me if I were really going to take Honkie away with me."

They told Harriet that he was the best hunter of cats and ducks they had ever seen. Mr. Birnie proudly showed Harriet and Harold a coconut shell that had been lovingly engraved with Honkie's initials and those of the captain of the *Catherine Apgar*, the ship upon which Honkie had sailed to Japan.

"He told me that this had been Honk Honk's ball aboard ship."

"They had no trouble getting a permit for bringing Honkie to land, Mr. Birnie reported to me. But the captain of the ship, and the entire crew, held a funeral march when they took Honkie away."

Harriet was also told that her letter to the crew and her slippers were preserved in the Captain's cabin of the *Catherine Apgar*, where it was intended they would remain as souvenirs of Honkie's time on board.

"Why, everyone who met my dog just fell in love with him."

Harriet, Harold, and Honk Honk prepared to depart the Birnie residence just as Mrs. Birnie arrived home. "She said 'Look at the tears in my children's eyes,' in her charming English accent. 'Mrs. Fisher, would you not come up again and bring Honkie to call before you leave Kobe?'"

"'Leave Kobe?' Mr. Birnie asked me. 'Just where is it that you are headed?'"

Upon hearing of Harriet's plans to cross the interior of Japan in a motorcar, Mr. Birnie became concerned. "He said to me, 'I fear, Mrs. Fisher, you do not know what you are up against. Japan is an old country, and has been slow in adopting new ideas, and the roads are narrow, in fact, nothing but paths in some places.'"

He cautioned her about dangerous rivers and the rickety bridges that would not withstand the weight of her Locomobile. "He said he did not think some of them were even strong enough to bear the weight of anything heavier than a rickshaw."

Harriet listened to his advisement with cool resolution. "I replied that I would take my chances, and would let him know how we made out."

Harriet promised the children they would return, but she would find out the concerns of Mr. Birnie were not in the least bit exaggerated.

CHAPTER TWENTY-ONE

Honkie meets Billikins

"We returned to the Mikado Hotel in Kobe to be greeted by scores of newspaper men," Harriet recalled. "As ours was the only car in the entire city, each reporter was anxious to snag the first interview with this bold lady motorist from the East!"

Harriet observed that they appeared to very concerned about how Harriet would portray their nation to her fellow countrymen back home, and they flattered her at every occasion.

"This was all quite different from what I had been led to expect from the Japanese people," Harriet said. "I was in a happy frame of mind by the kindness shown to my little dog, as well as my entire party."

A Mr. Yoshihiro Yamakawa introduced himself to Harriet. He told her he was representing the *Osaka Daily News* and was extremely anxious to accompany her party on their trip to Osaka as it would be the first large car to ever venture into that city.

"He said to me 'Mrs. Fisher, the Japanese people are so pleased that an American woman has so much confidence in our people, and country, as to make such a trip.'"

He told Harriet that he could help with translating, and explained to her with great dignity that the common people of Japan were terribly afraid of newspaper criticism, and therefore would be on their best behavior.

Harriet told the reporter that Harold had gone to the custom house to retrieve the Locomobile, and that he was welcome to join them.

Harriet was also relieved to find that Billikins was included in the local hospitality. "With his friendly, knowing look, and his little hand stretched in greeting to all wherever he went, he attracted attention and admiration."

Our talk returned to the interest the Japanese press had paid her, and the number of flattering articles that had appeared in the nation's newspapers during her visit.

"Mr. Brooks was particularly impressed by the reporter from the *Kobe Herald* and an article he published about our travels." With these words, Harriet again went to her desk and retrieved a newspaper story to share with me.

"*An Interesting Personality in Kobe*," Harriet read to me. The piece had appeared on April twenty-ninth, when the reporter wrote of how Harriet had not experienced any ill feelings or poor treatment during her journey due to the courtesy and consideration she provided to all she met while behind the wheel.

"I think Mr. Brooks was flattered, as this reporter had referred to him as a young American engineer," Harriet said, laughing.

"*Mrs. Fisher is enthusiastic about her trip, and takes more pleasure in chatting about the experiences she and her companions have had on the trip than the average lady does in discussing social problems, engagements, and triumphs.*"

"Average lady?!" she stopped to remark.

"*Mrs. Clark Fisher is looking forward with the keenest interest to her trip through Japan. As she naively puts it, she wants to catch a glimpse of this interesting country before all the picturesque features of its old history are lost in the dust of twentieth century-civilization.... She comes not to criticize, but to learn.*"

"Naively? I don't think so," she said. "But I *was* there to learn."

The reporter noted that Harriet was the widow of Clark Fisher, the man who had held the rank of Lieutenant Commander of the United States Navy at the time of his death and had been to Japan some forty years prior.

The article also stated that Harriet was the only female member of the National Association of Manufacturers and the only woman ever to be have been entertained by the Automobile Club of America at a banquet held in her honor just before departing for her worldwide drive.

Harriet looked up from the article and graced me with a sly smile. "Please indulge me for a moment," she said, before continuing to read the reporter's complimentary closing sentences.

"*We have said enough to show that we have in our midst just at the moment a lady of strikingly powerful personality, one versed in most of life's spheres, and who nevertheless retains the warm-hearted, sympathetic outlook on life that belongs pre-eminently to woman, and that charm of manner which is one of her truest gifts.*"

A clock chimed, informing us it was now three o'clock. Maria reappeared with some more tea, sherry, and little cakes.

"I think I can wrap up this tale of my world tour in a few hours if that is fine with you," she said to me. Without waiting for my answer, she again poured a little of the sweet liquid into our glasses and we proceeded to make a toast to Japan.

"Billikins had obviously won the hearts of friends and admirers in Japan, but how did Billikins and Honk Honk get along?" I asked.

"I arranged the introduction of Billikins to his brother with great tact," Harriet said. "And not without a palpitation of my heart, as Honkie had chased monkeys in the jungles of India and was decidedly ferocious toward anything possessing fur and a tail. I must say that we anticipated that there might be a funeral shortly after the two were introduced!"

She told me of how she had carefully concealed Billikins under her arm and then had called Honk Honk into the room.

"He sniffed about curiously until Billikin's head popped out to get a look at him," Harriet recalled. "Honk Honk became very excited about this strange animal, and his stubby tail waggled nonstop, but, as I have remarked before, Honk Honk has a superior mind and is open to reason."

She talked soothingly to her dog, and boxed the dog's ears at any of his attempts to become too familiar with Billikins. To her delight, the two animals became instant friends. "And as you have seen here at Bella Vista, they remain the best of companions to this very day!"

Harold and Albert returned to the hotel from the custom house with the good news that the Locomobile had passed inspection and the officials had not required a deposit or any duties, which were normally said to be very high.

But shortly after retrieving Honk Honk from the Birnie family, Harriet had received a letter from an anxious Mrs. Birnie with the news that Mr. Birnie was sick with typhoid fever, a disease that was prevalent in the region.

"Poor Mrs. Birnie asked if I would please come and help her care for her husband," Harriet said. "After all they had done for my dog, I went and remained with the family until she was able to get outside nursing assistance."

Harriet had been advised not to eat salad or green vegetables as the Japanese were sometimes not careful in the washing of them, and the germs that caused typhoid lurked in these foods.

But when it came to the cleaning of their homes, this was not the case. "One of the interesting things I witnessed on my journeys back and forth from the Birnie house to the hotel were the housecleaning operations of the Japanese," Harriet recalled.

"The reporter who was traveling with us explained that on these occasions, all of the home's furnishings were removed from the homes and placed outside. On entire streets, for many blocks, one witnessed men and women as they scrubbed and cleaned all day long. After the cleaning was complete, the furnishings and clothing were put back in place."

The reporter told Harriet this cleaning took place on a weekly basis. This made sense to Harriet as she observed that the Japanese always ate on the floor, and left their shoes outside their doors.

"These people sleep on padded quilts directly on the floor, own no more than two or three kimonos, and I was told that they were just beginning to wear stockings with the big toe separated from the others!"

Harriet noted that their diet was also filled with simplicity, confined mostly to rice, sugar-cane, and tea. "Their tea is what we would call hot water, for it is almost imperceptible to our Western taste."

Of her travels throughout Japan Harriet reflected that it pleased her that wherever she and her party went, they were greeted by cordial and friendly people. "I came to feel as if I had known these people for years. I forgot their quaint style of dress and their wooden shoes because they constantly made the effort to make me feel at home. There was no longer any sense of strangeness to me in this far-away land."

Harriet learned a little of the Japanese language, but not enough for her comfort, so the proprietor of the Mikado Hotel found a translator for hire.

"He was a young man called 'Frank' Uchiami," Harriet explained. "I was told he spoke fairly good English and had spent time in America. He also informed me that he had 'biked' through Osaka and Kyoto and thus was familiar with the roads."

But Harriet had some reservations about her new employee. "For the first time in Japan, I noticed in him what might be termed a little undue familiarity," Harriet said. "Having claimed to have been in America, in what capacity I was not told, he was inclined to think that Americans should be treated familiarly to make them feel at home!"

For his services, Frank was paid three yen a day, which was the equivalent of a little over a dollar. He was to take care of himself and to find his own sleeping accommodations.

"I hired him for a day," Harriet recalled, "so that in the event I did not find his services satisfactory, I could send him off at once. I took the precaution to have a written agreement drawn up to that effect, as Harold feared our Frank had exaggerated his knowledge of the remote Japanese roadways."

Frank accompanied them on a trial trip to Osaka to see if the Locomobile was too wide for the narrow roads that covered most of that nation. In

Osaka, Harriet hoped to acquire some good maps of the interior roads, to try to find any that might be passable.

Osaka was only one of two places in Japan where road maps could be obtained. "But even these were printed in Japanese and intended for military use," Harriet explained. "But I had Frank study them and they proved to be of great help to us and enabled us at least to know if we were driving in the right direction!"

They departed from Kobe to Osaka under the curious and watchful eyes of hundreds of local people. The first part of the trip found them rambling past endless rows of rice and paddy fields with ease.

In some of the little villages through which they drove, the streets grew so restricted that Harriet could reach out and touch the roofs of the houses they passed. But a poor attempt at modernization almost halted their entire trip.

"At one point the road became so constricted that the Locomobile's path was blocked by a telephone pole. There was not enough room for the car to pass and we had to obtain permission from the home owner to take down a side of his little house, and its shutters, to make way for us!"

After successfully navigating around the pole, Harriet's party returned to reassemble the home, as they had promised the owner. The next stage of the journey found the car carefully negotiating several tight and slippery bridges, and at times literally travelling through dwelling places.

But bridges, homes, and poles were not the only things impeding their progress.

"Long before we reached a turn in the road, the road would be black with human beings. They had heard the tooting of the car's horn, and the blowing of our whistle," Harriet explained. "I would have Frank go on ahead and plead with the crowd to let us pass."

In these remote regions of Japan, the local villagers had never seen a car or a white woman. Often the Locomobile was mobbed by these crowds of curiosity seekers and admirers, sometimes requiring police assistance to clear them away.

"Their curiosity was nearly startling," Harriet said. "The local boys would take to following us on foot and we could hear the clack-clacking of their wooden shoes on the stones."

Like Antonio had before him, Frank traveled standing on the baseboard of the car, but unlike Antonio, Frank often failed to earn his pay. On one such occasion, some of the little children thought it was great fun to hang on the sides of the Locomobile, much to Harold's irritation. It took much persuasion to keep them from boarding the motorcar.

"Frank made no effort to reprimand them, Mr. Brooks complained to me. And I had to agree, for those children were wild, and Frank *was* of little use."

On one leg of the trip to Osaka, the car rounded a sharp turn and Harold was alarmed to come upon a peasant and his two-wheeled horse drawn cart standing in the middle of the road. The peasant, in turn, was so startled at the sight of the Locomobile that he dropped the horse's reins. The cart and horse were left stranded in the road as the peasant fled into a muddy rice paddy field.

Frank once again proved to be useless, as he made no effort to remedy the situation and left Harriet to take command.

"The enthusiasm of the newspaper man, who had accompanied us, knew no bounds," Harriet recalled, laughing. "The idea of a lady taking the horse of an old coolie and leading him about delighted him. He called out in great disdain to the coolie. By the look on the expression on the reporter's face, I needed no interpretation. I knew he was calling the peasant an idiot!"

Harriet and her crew returned to Kobe after midnight. Although they had not ordered food or expected a meal at this hour, they were surprised to find themselves graciously served a nice steak, toast, potatoes, and a pot of delicious tea by the proprietor who had awaited their arrival.

They had been triumphant in meeting their goals of traveling to Osaka. However, a predicted continual string of torrential rainstorms was certain to present problems, creating slippery roads and dangerous turns as well as causing the flooding of small streams over which they would have to cross.

"In all honesty, I experienced much anxiety about our drive through Japan," Harriet reflected pensively. "My plan was to get across Japan by car, stopping in Kyoto, Nagoya, Shidgonka, Atami, Odowara, and Yokohama, thence to Tokyo and Nikko. The chauffeur of His Highness of Baroda was to follow our car upon reuniting with us in Kyoto."

But, it was ultimately decided that if the Locomobile had been able to reach Osaka, they could successfully complete their proposed route through the nation's interior. "I derived some confidence in the knowledge that the road to Kyoto was fairly wide and had been used in the past for the parades of floats for many festivals," Harriet said.

As a thank you to the proprietor of the Mikado Hotel, Harriet offered to take the man's father for a ride in the Locomobile. "He was an old man, and evidently desirous of being able to say he had gone for a ride in a motorcar. But he only remained for a short ride as he imagined that everybody we met on the road was going to be ground under our wheels, and flourished his stick at anyone who did not get out of our way, calling them all sorts of stupid things!"

Finally, after seven miles or so, the elderly man could take no more. He suddenly decided he had a brother he wanted very much to visit in the vicinity. He stepped out of the car and shuffled off by himself.

"Harriet," I said. "I receive so many questions about how you were always able to find enough petrol, even in the most remote regions of Japan."

She explained that as there was only one motorcar in the entire city of Kobe, special arrangements had been made for a supply of gasoline. "There were several factories in Kobe that used gasoline engines and we were able to obtain an adequate supply."

Harold, Albert, and Frank set to preparing the car for its Japanese voyage. They spent an entire day polishing and readying the car for the next stage of its historic venture.

While the car was being readied, Harriet went on another shopping spree with Her Highness Baroda. "Although I had exercised great discipline during my trip so far, I was now unable to resist the beautiful items displayed in the shops of Kobe."

She purchased a hand-carved cabinet and a writing desk, created by a world-renowned woodcarver, and a bronze lantern that was estimated to be over three hundred years old. "That lantern has a carved owl sitting on its top, looking wise enough to be very ancient indeed," she said. "I also purchased a magnificent bronze figure of a Japanese girl called, 'The Wood-gatherer,' and a hand-hammered bronze gong I was told had been used in temples. I could just imagine summoning my guests to dinner at my *Villa Carlotta* where most everything I purchased was dispatched. When struck, the gong vibrates for more than a minute with the sweetest tone I have ever heard!"

Harriet explained that the bronze figure called "The Wood-gatherer" had been intended for a Japanese art exhibit in England. "The poor artist failed to finish the figure in time for the exhibit and he was heartbroken at losing a chance to have his work seen or purchased," Harriet said. "But a lovely solution was achieved. And now I am happy in the possession of such a work of art, and he is happy in having created it."

"It was now time to say farewell to Kobe, and our baggage was once again loaded onto the car. To our amusement, Frank did not hide his excitement and self-importance at being chosen for this important honor, one of which no other guide could ever boast. One of his friends even loaned him a pair of leggings, thinking perhaps that this would make him look like a proper chauffeur. And another friend gave him a cap!" Harriet recalled.

But the chauffeur for His Highness of Boroda's thirty-horse-power Fiat appeared not to be as confident as Frank. "Fearing that he would get lost, or be murdered, the driver of the royal car insisted that two men accompany him."

Harriet and her party would come to realize that the challenge presented during the crossings of the Devil's Bridge, as well as the *ghats* and rivers of India, would pale in comparison to what they would encounter in the interior of Japan. The warnings of Mr. Birnie, and the fears of the Royal Chauffeur, were not unfounded.

CHAPTER TWENTY-TWO

Touring with the Emperor's Blessings

Everywhere Harriet and the Locomobile appeared in this land, eager news reporters trailed them, watching Harriet's every move, scribbling copious notes and taking countless photos. That Harriet was about to tour Japan accompanied by Indian Royalty made this extremely thrilling news to all.

"Noticing our little American flag displayed on the car, the Japanese press asked her if their nation's flag could also be flown," Harriet said. "I told them I would be happy to do it."

As they had experienced on their trial run, throngs of excited children and men waved and cheered as the Locomobile passed them, often chasing after the car on foot.

"I asked Frank 'What is the cause of all their curiosity?' 'Why Mrs. Fisher,' the translator replied. 'You are a great hero to our minds, and they are only showing their admiration for your enterprise.'"

They retraced the route of the trial run, but early on, Harriet and her party got the feeling that they were soon to experience the greatest challenges since their departure from New Jersey.

"We were getting along very well until we came to a bad turn in the road, and the soft mud made it impossible to turn. Our heavily loaded car just sank into the mud nearly up to our hubs!"

They managed to pull themselves out of the muck, making their way over hills, through valleys and paddy fields, passing miles of little huts that lined both sides of the road. They navigated narrow, slippery stone bridges with patience, guided by the steady hand of Harold as he guided the car to safety.

"It seemed almost impossible that Mr. Brooks could drive over some of the canal banks we encountered, but we had no choice. In some places the road was so narrow, we prayed that no other vehicle approached as the only solution would be for *that* vehicle to turn around, or meet with disaster."

But no such incident presented itself and the Locomobile finally reached the bridge that would take them into Osaka.

"We quickly found out that the newspaper reporters had informed everyone of our arrival and crowds again gathered, snapping away with their Kodaks at our car, and the one being transported by the Baroda's driver and his new companions."

Harriet's party and the Royal family's driver were waved at and cheered on as they made their way through the town square of Osaka, where a sharp left turn put them on a fairly good road to Kyoto.

"We thought we were on the right road, and glided along, until we found the car on what turned out to be the bed of a railroad," Harriet said. "No one seemed to know what to do; we had to reverse the car and go back the way we came."

Here again, Harriet came to the realization that while most of the roads on which they would travel had never actually experienced the tires of an automobile, most humans had not done so either, a situation that could present danger for all parties involved.

"An old man sat with his feet dangling over a derrick platform," Harriet recalled. "When he saw our car approach, he drew up his feet away from harm. But he failed to do so when Mr. Brooks put our car in reverse."

The man cried out, and Harriet exited the car. She discovered the man's bare foot had been scraped by the car's fender. She examined his injury and found that he was more frightened than anything. "It was just a scratch, and he was too ignorant to see his role in the incident. I gave him ten yen for his trouble and he ambled off smiling and clasping his money."

Harriet noted that it was at this point that the two local men who had been accompanying the Baroda's chauffeur chose to abandon that car to leave the driver to fend for himself.

They reached the Kyoto Hotel by five o'clock in the evening, when they were reunited with the Baroda party. "They were filled with inquiries about the roads and as we were so glad to see them again, we forgot all of our difficulties," Harriet said, smiling at her recollection. "I began to feel that I was really a member of His Highness's party!"

Having settled into their accommodations, Harriet and her new friends left for Nara, a city that had once served as the capital of Japan. "His Highness rode in my car with his secretary, Mr. Brooks, Frank, and Albert. Her Highness Princess Indraraja and myself followed in the royal Fiat."

In Nara, they received a cordial reception and Harriet was pleased to meet up again with her friends, the Atkinses. "A mutual friend, Mrs. Cummings, was delighted to be presented to Her Highness, and she gave Billikins a little gold elephant to wear around his neck!"

In Nara, they were received by the High Priest, who had a special dance performed by women he referred to as the "Holy Girls" in their honor. "These Holy Girls were what we might call nuns and I was told that they only dance for royalty," Harriet said. "This dance was like a mythological play, but after we squatted in a circle around the dancers for over an hour, it became quite monotonous."

In the evening, the guests were delighted to find that the two mile sacred walk that led to the temple was illuminated, a privilege also reserved for a grand occasion.

"Mr. Brooks very much liked our stop in Nara," Harriet said. "He found it a pretty place, set amongst the hills, and he especially enjoyed the special privilege we received that allowed us to go through the Deer Park. We saw hundreds of these deer that were as gentle as kittens and very tame, as they ate right from our hands. So unlike any of the creatures we had seen in the wilds of India."

In Nara, and throughout Japan, Harriet was impressed that the land was always under cultivation. No acre went to waste as every inch of it was needed to provide food for so many of Japan's citizens.

Harriet also detected a presence of detectives and law enforcement personnel wherever they roamed. She came to learn that the authorities would dispatch coolies the previous night to prepare the roadways for their arrivals.

"They made repairs where they thought there might be some danger for us, but for this I take no credit, for all of this was due to the fact that we were travelling with His Highness's party and the Japanese people simply thought of him as the King of India."

While visiting the city of Kyoto, Harriet's clumsy attempts to eat with chopsticks were so unsuccessful that she feared she would go hungry if she had to depend on them. "I could manage to hold them, but somehow the food never made it to my mouth."

She found her Japanese dinners enjoyable for the most part, although they did not always look inviting. But she was eager to learn about Japanese food and was willing to satisfy her curiosity. "I tried almost everything, but I drew the line at eating raw fish!"

Harriet was thrilled when she was extended a rare invitation to visit the secret and most sacred Mikado Palace, the home of Japan's emperor. Also referred to as the Mikado, the emperor would not be present during their tour. The Barodas' Fiat was out of commission after its two day journey, so Harriet offered the use of the Locomobile.

They approached the palace gates, expecting to enter the property on foot. "But we were surprised when we were allowed to drive through those gates," Harriet recalled. "I was told that no other car had ever driven on the grounds of the palace."

I inquired of the reason for this special permission," Harriet said. "And I was told that I had been given the respect and blessings from the emperor himself!"

This enormous structure was filled with magnificent rooms named for colors and flowers. Inside the Chrysanthemum Room, Harriet was stunned by a view of the grounds beyond the palace windows. "That was the most delightful little garden I have ever beheld," she exclaimed. "With its miniature lakes filled with small islands landscaped with tiny trees, it reminded me of a beautiful living painting. I was told that one tree, that stood only about two feet high, was over one thousand years old."

Harriet and her royal guests were among the very few outsiders to have ever been granted permission to enter many of these rooms. "Of this we considered ourselves very highly honored," she noted.

This special treatment had spoiled them. The Japanese, as well as Harriet's other gracious hosts, had been so generous and hospitable that Harriet and the Baroda party were surprised to see that they had been charged for their stay at the Kyoto Hotel. "Speaking for myself, I had been entertained so royally for so many months, that I began to take everything for granted."

It was on to Nagoya on the twelfth of May, a city noted for its cloisonné and china manufacturing. Harriet looked forward to visiting an exhibition of Japanese manufacturers in that city.

But the road to Nagoya presented its own challenges. "We were driving through the paddy fields when our heavily loaded car began to sink," Harriet said. "We tied two ropes to the car of His Highness and they were able to pull us out after much tedious work."

At a midday luncheon that day, Her Highness of Baroda was happy to make sandwiches for her travel companions. "We had a very jolly picnic party. There was no pretense, and the royal party sat on cushions scattered on the ground enjoying their food."

But not all of their accommodations in Japan were as clean and pleasant. "The Nagoya Hotel has to be one of the worst I have ever seen," Harriet recalled. "No attention was paid us and the place was inconceivably dirty and the meals impossible to eat." On this occasion Harriet and her party were happy to enjoy the contents of Albert's tea basket.

In Nagoya, Harriet toured one of the oldest palaces in Japan. "Again we were told by the local people that we were receiving privileges that they could never hope to possess."

This palace, constructed of solid oak, was now mostly in ruins, and great care was taken to prevent fires. Its caretakers touched the floor of the sacred palace and then kissed their fingers. "I detected in their eyes a desire to accompany our party as we walked through the palace's most sacred rooms."

In this city, Harriet and the Baroda party devoted considerable hours to shopping for cloisonné and lacquerware. "'In America I am aware of our large collections of Japanese-made bric-a-brac, or small decorative items,' I commented to a shop keeper. 'But here, I see very little. I think I know where all your bric-a-brac goes,' I told him. Those decorative little cups we in America sometimes use for cigar ashes are used in Japan as tea cups, and in Japan, I observed that they often drank their tea without sugar or milk."

On her second day in Nagoya, Harriet ventured to an exhibition she had greatly anticipated. "There we witnessed the wonderful ingenuity of the Japanese and their superb imitative faculty. The exhibition featured replicas of nearly every machine or small article one could imagine. With its exact replicas of items like the American cash register, one would have thought it was a small exhibition in America."

Wherever they went, Harriet and her party found themselves followed by small forms wrapped in kimonos. Despite the quality of the items displayed at this exhibition, Harriet observed that those attending the event seemed to find their American visitors more fascinating than any item displayed behind the glass cases.

It was time to drive onto Yokohama. "It was raining awfully hard, and fearing that his car would skid because its tires lacked chains, His Highness decided to ship his car and his entire party to Tokyo by train," Harriet said. "I had to confess, we had found our chains very useful on numerous occasions."

It would soon become apparent that the Baroda party had made a wise choice.

CHAPTER TWENTY-THREE

Crossing the Raging Rapids

On May 13, Harriet's party began their trek to Yokohama without the royal family.

The initial travel on the Old Takaido Road heading out of Nagoya presented good passage. In these parts, Harriet was aware that the standard means of travel was by foot, with members of the higher classes transported by *dandies* such as the ones that had transported her so often in India.

"I understand women were forbidden to travel alone on this road and had to be accompanied by men," Harriet said. "Furthermore, I was informed that other restrictions were put in place for all travelers, but while severe penalties were said to exist for not heeding travel regulations, most seemed not to be enforced."

The Japanese peasants followed the custom of giving those of wealth, or position, the right of way. "Coolies and workingmen would rush to one side of the road to make way for us. At times, this effort to be polite would upset their heavily loaded carts. But as we neared the city of Yokohama, we observed a great difference in the manners of the local people."

The Takaido Road was tree-lined, and easy to maneuver, and Harold was relaxed at the wheel, having become familiar with this course during side trips he had taken to Kobe. "The road ran along well for a distance, but then it suddenly disappeared," Harriet recalled.

They found themselves instead running along a constricted path, and negotiating sharp curves and very long and narrow bridges. As Mr. Birnie had warned, many of these bridges were so poorly constructed that on several occasions, all of their suitcases and cargo had to be removed from the car and carried over by hired help to lighten the weight of the Locomobile.

"At times we were obliged to get out of the car and use a hatchet to chop pieces off the bamboo stumps to allow the hubs of our car to pass without being jammed," Harriet said.

A few bridges swayed back and forth under the weight of the car. One bridge that spanned nearly seventy-five feet was only made up of poles and planks laid on frames, with only a couple of inches between them. "I doubted any other car had, or ever would, go over these streams until new bridges are built," Harriet recalled. "My heart was in my throat a good deal of the time. I expected that our car would surely drop to the bottom of a fast-moving stream and be sucked up in a mud hole. After this particular crossing Mr. Brooks had confided that he, too, had feared at any moment the Locomobile would surely go to the bottom."

Harriet declared that she doubted if motoring would be popular on this road for at least a decade, as she estimated that it would take millions of dollars to build bridges of substance, and there were just too many streams to cross.

"In fact, if I had been compelled to return over these very same bridges on a return trip, I would surely have chosen to travel by train," Harriet surprisingly declared. "Upon the crossing of each bridge, I thanked the rain storm that had prevented His Highness and his party from accompanying us."

Harriet claimed that this chapter of her trip had been the weirdest, and most challenging, so far. "We finally came through the pass and neared Shizuoka at around eleven o'clock that evening. My nerves had been tensed almost the entire time."

In the distance, lanterns flashed in the darkness. "Frank happily informed me, 'They are looking for us.'"

In due course, a large group of boys and men had gathered near Harriet and her party. They relayed to her that everyone feared the travelers had gone astray in the mountains. Guided by the acetylene lights of the Locomobile, the lanterns of the search party, and the soft glow of Japanese lanterns that illuminated the road into town, they were led to the Daitokwan Hotel. "We were weary and hungry and happy to be served a much-appreciated dinner of fried eggs, rice cakes, and potatoes, with a pot of hot tea."

After their meal, a couple of police officers approached Harriet and inquired whether she wanted them to remain and guard the hotel.

"I replied, 'But why? I am not a bit afraid!' Wishing to make myself clear, I asked Frank to inform the officers that I felt as safe as if I were staying at the Waldorf Astoria Hotel in New York City."

Frank apparently interpreted correctly, for upon hearing his words, the officers smiled at Harriet broadly. "You know, there are times when the Japanese smile is hardly less than gorgeous."

Around the World in 1909

The following morning brought hordes of photographers, police and representatives of the press to the hotel. Newsmen eagerly sent up pieces of pasteboard to Harriet's room begging for an interview.

"Because the Maharaja was not with us, I was informed that it was being reported that an American lady had been racing her car through Japan, against the King of India, and that the American lady had won! Apparently they thought the 'loser' had given up and gone home."

"'What has become of the Indian Prince?' one reporter asked me."

Harriet informed the press that this tale was simply not true. "I explained to them that we started out simply as a friendly party, and His Highness decided it would take much too long on account of the rainstorms, and the slippery roads would make conditions too hard for his car to pass, so he put it on a train for Tokyo while we traveled on in my Locomobile."

"They inquired of me, 'Will you end your trip, too? And ship your car by train to Tokyo like the Maharaja Baroda has?'"

"'No, no, no!' I quickly set the story right and told them under no uncertain terms, if anyone else had ever been over the road to Tokyo, on foot or on horseback, I was going."

The stunned crowd nodded their heads, murmuring something that Harriet thought sounded like the word, "Ohio."

It was time to relax and Harriet and her party visited the public baths. They were curiously amused to observe that the men and women bathed together indiscriminately. "We viewed this activity as people at home might view skaters upon visiting a rink," Harriet recalled. "But now, I do not think they allow Westerners to gaze upon this sight as they have begun to feel a little sensitive about it."

Harriet mentioned to a newspaperman that she would like to visit his home, and to see how he lived. "He told me that he feared that 'Madam' would find little to interest her and that he, like most Japanese, was poor. But he told me that he would take pleasure in showing his home to me if that was what I desired."

Harriet, Harold and the reporter arrived on foot to his small house made of bamboo with a roof she described as "artistic."

"We removed our shoes and stepped on a raised platform," she recalled. "We bowed our heads to enter inside the door and I was pleasantly surprised to see what I would call a 'Doll's Playhouse!'"

Harriet thought the reporter's wife looked like a teen-aged girl. She ran her hands down her own body and then clasped her hands together in front of her in an odd style of curtsy upon greeting Harriet. The reporter's two daughters also presented themselves to their guest, and performed the same greeting while his elderly mother sat in the corner of the room.

"The entire house was scrupulously clean and the tiny kitchen boasted one little charcoal stove. I was shown the content of the house's closets lined neatly with every item in its place," Harriet remarked.

They sat for tea and the reporter apologized for not having a chair to offer his Western guest. "I think he thought I would consider it a sin to sit on a floor."

"We drank from tiny cups and all the while the reporter's wife laughed and giggled, hiding her face behind the sleeve of her husband's coat, as though one of the funniest sights she had ever seen was Mr. Brooks and I sitting on the floor."

The reporter informed Harriet that the small pass over which they had just traveled was considered dangerous and most people had not thought it possible for an automobile to get through.

"I became inclined to think that our motor trip gave these people a great deal of excitement," Harriet said. "I think we kept them stirred up for days, and that was good, as we would find ourselves in more peril in the days to come."

At this point Harriet directed her attention to me. "Young lady, I want your readers to understand that I made this trip in the face of the caution and warnings from other travelers and guidebooks that advised us never to travel at night, and that our lives would be in jeopardy in the interior of Japan," she said thoughtfully.

"I tried my best to obtain information as to what lay ahead, but the only thing I learned was that we were going to ferry the rapids at the Fujikawa River to reach Atami. All we had were the maps we had obtained in Osaka, which by the way, I was under oath to return to the officials who had loaned them to us."

At five o'clock in the morning, Harriet's party was back on the road headed for Atami, a restful resort town famous for its hot springs. But first they had to endure arduous travel conditions much like the day before, replete with muddy washouts and perilous sharp turns, all the while with the crossing of those dreaded rapids weighing on their minds.

"We reached Fujikawa by noon, where we again found ourselves under police protection," Harriet recalled.

The Locomobile came to rest at the banks of the Fuji River, considered to be among one of the swiftest-moving bodies of water in Japan. The rapids raged before them and it was clear that a smooth crossing would be nearly impossible. Rain poured down on them, with only a small umbrella that was blown about by the gusting wind offering any protection. For a moment, it looked like Mr. Birnie's warnings might be coming true, and that their trip would come to its end by this powerful force of nature.

But even under these conditions, Harriet's spirit was not quenched. "Despite the uncertainty and our discomfort, we were of course obliged to cross, although did not know what lay before us. We had no thought of returning."

Harold sprang into action. He and a band of coolies began to assemble a large floating barge on which the vehicle and its passengers could be carried to the opposite side of the river. Members of the local police force rushed in to help, attaching their own boats with ropes to the hurriedly assembled watercraft.

With the car and passengers safely on board Harold's makeshift barge, they began their crossing under the curious gaze of hundreds of villagers. With all their strength, bands of coolies pushed the Locomobile away from the rocky coast with long bamboo poles. But the rapids had their own plans.

"We were about midstream when I heard the ropes holding our car to the police boats snap," Harriet said. "It sounded like a pistol shot. We were left to the mercy of the rapids with all of our hope placed in the men who tried to row us to safety."

But the current was too strong.

The guide raft carrying the Locomobile broke free, and like a tiny leaf in a whirlpool the barge carrying the motorcar hurtled toward the base of a railroad bridge.

"The car swayed from side to side with only a few inches of room to spare between its tires and the water. Fortunately our Mr. Brooks had lashed the front and rear wheels of the car securely to the planks that supported the car."

Harriet recalled the expressions of fear and anxiety on the faces of her party and those looking on from the river bank. All watched in horror as the coolies labored hard from the sides of the boat, their bamboo poles nearly bending in half as they tried to keep the boat off the rocks that seemed to rise from everywhere in the middle of the rapids.

With a ghastly tremor, the Locomobile landed on a large flat rock near the shoreline. This victory was followed by a collective shout from the exhausted coolies who had brought the car and its passengers to temporary safety.

It was a dubious victory, for the Locomobile was now anchored about fifty feet from shore and nearly five hundred feet below where they had intended to land. "But we were fortunate. If we had traveled only two hundred feet more," Harriet said, "we would have most certainly crashed into the buttress of the railroad bridge!"

They were drenched to the skin, but safe. Harold offered his boss his hand in silent congratulation. A number of coolies came onto the rock and Frank told Harriet that she would have to be carried to land on the backs of one of these men. She complied, with Billikins the monkey tightly clasped in her arms.

"But now we had more trouble to face," Harriet said, sighing. "We had to backtrack at least a half mile over the rocky river bottom to return to the main road."

But she remained optimistic. "Now I was ever more determined to push onward and overcome whatever difficulties might lie before us between here and Yokohama."

A crowd had gathered around the car and Harriet set about ordering the locals to clear the road of the big boulders that blocked their path. Harriet pointed to the boulders, and with just a few words got her message across. They seemed to understand her orders and went to work immediately.

"I glanced around and saw a line of men that must have gone on for a mile. They carried planks and bamboo sticks necessary to lift the car off the boat."

Harriet mapped a route for the car, but quickly found out that the other side of the river bank contained many more large, slippery boulders through which the car would have to navigate. She remained undeterred.

"'I will get out and move those boulders with my own hands if I have to,' I told everyone around me."

And she did. Using the largest boulders she could manage to carry, she joined the men as they built up a ramp on the lower side of the rocky bank, no more than two feet high, then selected a spot that presented the best opportunity of getting the Locomobile back onto its path.

They were back on the road, but the going was slow. Heavy rain continued to pelt them and it seemed that another huge boulder impeded their progress every few feet. It took four hours for Harold to bring the Locomobile to safety on the back side of the river bank.

While delighted onlookers congratulated them at their hard-won success in crossing the rapids safely, Harriet let herself relax. "For the first time I sank down, almost exhausted," she recalled.

Harriet and her crew took shelter in a small hut and refreshed themselves with sandwiches and cups of tea from their thermos bottles. "We were delighted to learn that two policemen would continue to accompany us," she said. "We were told that the road ahead was underwater in parts, and at times it would be hard to know just where the road actually was."

The policemen went ahead in a flat little boat with coolies pulling them. The Locomobile followed. "We never knew if at any moment we would sink. But we were led to safety finally, to a flat paddy field, at dusk. The people stared at us as if we had arisen from the interior of the earth, and in a way, we had."

But a brand new challenge loomed in the distance, one that would make all others pale in comparison. "My boy Frank pointed ahead to Mount Fuji, which rose in magnificent beauty, all capped with snow." Harriet said. "He announced that we needed to make the Hakone Pass before nightfall."

Harriet's sense of victory was to be short-lived.

CHAPTER TWENTY-FOUR

"The Female Napoleon"

On the seventeenth of May, the trek through the Hakone Range began. Without warning, the clouds reopened, and rain seemed to fall by the bucketful, making travel treacherous. "Mr. Brooks was obliged to put on our two rear chains," Harriet said. "We made hardly more than six or eight miles an hour at that rate."

The stunning views of this region, illuminated by breaks of intermittent sunshine, would ordinarily be cherished by Harriet, but nothing could distract her from the reality that at each moment they were plunging into unknown dangers.

At first they had found themselves enjoying a mile or so of good road, but like so many thoroughfares in Japan, this one soon turned into nothing but a rough path. Harriet was informed that where the government had fixed the road, repairs had been done correctly, but as these roads were kept up by farmers and local land owners, they were nothing but steps dug out of the side of the mountain in most cases.

"We had no way of knowing what the end would be," she reflected. "But 'never turn back' had become the motto of my life, and although at times it seemed impossible to travel over those roads, we kept on, occasionally using those military maps, and trying to reckon the distance between us and civilization."

As she surveyed the rock-strewn road that loomed ahead for what appeared to be miles, she realized that she would have to motivate an exhausted crew.

"I repeated out loud that I had made '*never turn back*' my motto!"

And she expected all those around her to adopt it too.

The car had to be literally lifted and turned many times by a team of hard-working local men led by Harold. These loyal local villagers had continued to escort Harriet's party, helping to navigate her car around an endless series of sharp turns leading up to the pass.

But as daylight faded, there was no relief in sight. If anything, the road conditions had worsened as the Locomobile approached a brand new challenge.

"We found ourselves approaching a narrow footbridge that spanned a precipice from two to three hundred feet deep," Harriet judged. "All about us immense mountains rose on both sides, covered with gigantic black rocks."

Harold, exhausted from the day's events, wearily and distractedly drove the Locomobile toward the entrance of the bridge.

"'Mr. Brooks, stop the car!' I commanded with urgency."

Harold saw the cause of his boss's concern, and braked just in time. "'That bridge is only about half as wide as our car,' he remarked to me."

They would come to learn that, at one time, a more substantial bridge had once stood here, but it had been burned, and the current bridge that had been hastily thrown up was only intended to be used as a temporary foot bridge.

"To be fair, no one ever dreamed that anyone would even attempt to cross this bridge on horseback, let alone drive a motorcar over it," Harriet said. "We got out of the car and when we looked over the sides of those mountains, we all shuddered at the thought of what would have become of us if we had gone only a couple of feet further."

There was nothing more that could be done. Harriet, having spotted a little cluster of huts huddled against the mountainside a few miles back, dispatched Frank to get help and instructed him to telegraph ahead to Atami to summon more assistance. She also asked him to gather some brush to make a fire.

The Locomobile was left standing at the brink of the abyss, and the weary team set to creating a makeshift campsite in the cold and damp evening. "We carefully searched for a good place to set up our tent, but the pass was so narrow that we had no choice but to erect it right over a small mountain stream, with the water running right through!"

But there was room for a cot and their baggage would remain dry. A small moment of relief was enjoyed by her party, but a cautious Harriet recalled, "We rejoiced at surviving the day, oblivious to the dangers of our present position."

Once settled into camp, hunger overcame them. "We realized we had no bread or baking powder," Harriet said. "But I had brought with us a bottle of fruit salts that we ascertained might have some rising properties."

The alcohol stove was lit and a mixture of flour, condensed cream, and some of the fruit salts were combined in a pan to make a concoction Harold called "Enos fruit sauce." Harriet ladled the mixture onto a hot plate, letting one side of the cake brown before flipping it over. "To our delight, it raised up and was the best biscuit I ever tasted, not unlike a muffin," she recalled, proud of her culinary accomplishment.

Harold especially enjoyed them and ate every last crumb as he waited for Frank to return with help. For good measure, Harriet gave everyone in her party a generous dose of quinine and something she called "stimulants."

They were just finishing their meal when Honkie started to bark furiously, announcing the arrival of Frank, who had returned with about a dozen coolies. They presented Harriet with a bag of charcoal, bundles of brush for fire, and some fresh eggs. About a half-dozen of the men carried planks and bamboo poles.

An excited Frank relayed that many villagers were out looking for Harriet and her party at the foot of the pass. "Most amazingly, Frank announced that a gang of Japanese engineers was on their way from Atami, and would meet us on the pass!"

But the villagers informed Harriet that there was great concern for their safety as the road on the other side of the bridge was as bad as the road taken to get up the mountain, and nearly impossible to pass.

From the moment she heard that the engineers were coming to meet them, Harriet was convinced that they would succeed in their passage. "'You will see whether we get through or not,' I told these men. 'And furthermore, we will do it if we have to build a road all around the mountain.'"

And build they would.

But first some rest was in order. "For all his hard work, I insisted that Mr. Brooks take the most comfortable bed for the night," Harriet said.

Harold retired on the cot in the tent. Maria spent the night with Harriet in the car and they took turns stoking charcoal and wood on the fire.

The mysterious coolies vanished in the rocks, wrapping themselves with their rainproof woven bamboo coverings that made them resemble huge porcupines. "Whenever one of these figures approached our car," Harriet recalled, "Billikins put up such a terrible row he proved himself as good a 'watch dog' as Honkie!"

Harriet had been informed that the Japanese disliked being out in the rain, or being wet. This was due to the fact that their houses were so small that they had no means of hanging their clothes to dry properly. Subsequently, this constant source of moist laundry caused homes to be so damp that their families were frequently exposed to colds and fevers, and illness was prevalent.

Early the next morning, Harriet awoke to the glorious reflection of the sun on the peaks of the mountains in the distance; a sighting of nature's magnificence from a vantage point that was witnessed by very few.

It was time to make a bold move.

"I suggested that Mr. Brooks and Frank take a walk over the bridge to find out what kinds of roads we would face once the bridge was successfully crossed. Despite what we were told, I was so hoping for good news on that front."

Harriet and the remainder of her party were left alone in the company of what she described as "wild-looking men of the mountains," which caused her some unrest.

"Albert kept pretty close to his rifle while he went about his business, arranging things after breakfast, but beside a few peeks of curiosity from these men, we were left alone," she noted.

But Harold and Frank returned with news that did not please Harriet. The conditions of the road on the other side of the bridge were indeed very similar to the ones over which they had just traversed.

The only good news came from Frank, who let Harriet know that ten men were willing to build up the bridge, clear the road and see her party to safety over the mountain and into the village of Atami.

After all the engineering details were confirmed, Harold got to work alongside the coolies, using the wooden planks to widen the narrow old bridge.

By noon that day the work on the bridge had been completed. Their luggage was removed from the car to make it as light as possible. Then, the inevitable process of crossing began.

"We offered up a prayer for Mr. Brooks' safety as he started the drive across the bridge, with less than three inches to spare on each side of the car's tires," Harriet said, with a visible shudder. "But he made sure that the car was lined up straight when getting it up on the bridge, and he moved very cautiously. When he landed the car on the other side of the pass, we were very much relieved."

The coolies who had transported the party's supplies and baggage over the bridge thought it best not to reload the car. Instead, they placed the belongings of the entire party on a small cart that followed the car.

The energy and endurance of these men impressed a curious Harriet. "I still do not know how these poor fellows ate or how they survived," she said. "It was a mystery to us, for these villagers were very shy about their eating habits. They did not like anyone to watch them eat, and while we were eating, they would turn their backs and smoke on their little pipes."

As Harold had reported, the roads on this side of the chasm were again extremely narrow, filled with hairpin turns, and clusters of rocks and boulders. In some spots, the road had to be built up, with the men cutting away at the mountain wall using pick axes and then physically lifting the car to get it around an endless series of sharp turns.

"In many instances, we were obliged to tie ropes to the rear of the Locomobile as it went around these sharp corners. The men would hold onto the car with all their strength to keep the car from rolling off the mountain."

Harold observed that these roads were as slippery as if they were covered in grease. He was glad to have packed chains for the tires, but in this rough terrain, they were almost useless.

"Mr. Brooks complained to me that they just kept snapping!"

"They reached the top of the Hakone Range Pass and in the distance we spotted a 'black speck' moving along the mountain side. 'It's the engineers!' Frank announced."

Their arrival came at a good time, for the Locomobile now stood directly in front of a boulder that Harriet described as the size of a small elephant. Frustrated and fatigued, Harriet threw her hands up in the air, in a rare public display of self-doubt.

"'Oh, why did I ever undertake this trip?!' I yelled."

But a few moments later, her spirits were lifted when she was presented with a card bearing congratulations from a member of the Japanese Corps of Engineers, who was accompanied by a police chief. Frank translated to her that these officials had feared that she and her party had fallen down the mountainside and that everyone was now relieved and excited by their safe passage.

"My boy, Frank, told me that the Japanese Press was calling me the Female Napoleon, and that news reporters were eagerly awaiting our arrival in Atami."

Harriet pointed to the enormous boulder that stood between her and her goal to reach Atami. "I made signs with my hands and eyes to get them busy getting it moved."

Through Frank's interpretation, Harold was told to back up the car, after which the coolies were directed to literally attack the stone, pushing it inch by inch toward the edge of the precipice. With one last push, the boulder went crashing over the edge and down the side of the mountain, making a thunderous sound.

"We stood and watched as the boulder gained momentum each moment of its descent, taking down trees and rocks as it went," Harriet recalled, warily. "I wondered afterward if any of those little huts that were built on the sides of that mountain might have been taken, or destroyed by this rock, and if I would be held responsible for the loss of several lives."

Ropes were once again fastened to the rear of the Locomobile, and scores of men held fast to them to prevent the car from going too fast as they began their descent of the mountain pass.

Harold continued to cautiously maneuver the motorcar over grades that were slick and at times straight up and down.

"Mr. Brooks later told me that if the brakes had given way, we should have plunged hopelessly down to death."

A universal attitude of gratefulness was experienced by all when they caught a glimpse of the sparkling waters surrounding the seaside village of Atami, a place known as the "Riviera of Japan."

Arriving into town, the locals greeted them with astonished expressions. They were truly incredulous that a motorcar had successfully made it through the treacherous mountain pass, something no other car had ever done.

CHAPTER TWENTY-FIVE

"The Talk of Tokyo"

It was time to recover.

In the wake of their exhausting ordeals, Albert nursed a strained knee and Harold a blistered foot. Even Billikins and Honkie needed some rest and recreation and a break from guard duty, and they played wherever they pleased in the welcoming village of Atami.

Harriet lounged in a kimono and received a massage, followed by a revitalizing bath in a hot sulfur spring.

"Massage is a fad of the Japanese," Harriet said. "They believe in the efficacy of massage, and seem to believe that every ill under the sun can be rubbed away."

But she learned that it was more than a fad. She was informed that in Japan schools had been established to train blind people in the practice of massage. Upon hearing this, she sent for blind women and enjoyed her very first massage.

She described her masseuse as plaintive with a "solemn little face" who did not utter a single word. "But she seemed to know every muscle and nerve in my body, from my toes to the crown of my head," Harriet recalled. "She worked me over until the perspiration streamed from my face, and I fell into a most refreshing slumber."

At her hotel, Harriet inquired as to the class of people who visited Atami and was informed that a few English people had discovered this relaxing spa resort and had come for the baths and the "rest cure."

The hotel *was* restful, and although the beds were comfortable, one had to furnish their own bedding. Harriet found the meals satisfactory, and she was served by "happy little Japanese girls" waiting on her as if they only lived to run about in their wooden shoes doing whatever she asked of them.

Harriet admired the Japanese people's fondness for animals, noting, "Billikins gave no end of entertainment and amusement to the crowds who came to visit him and he was allowed to run about wherever he pleased."

After her first good night's sleep in a long time, Harriet awakened to the scent of orange and lemon blossoms and the happy singing of children, and delighted in the magnificent view of the blue sea dancing in the sunlight.

"I had been warned to never leave my windows unlocked in Japan, as we were likely to be robbed," Harriet said. "But I generally left my windows open and never lost any valuables."

Harold had captured many intriguing images with his camera throughout the trip and now had two rolls of film to be developed. A Japanese photographer who did the honors was impressed with the young man's skill as a photographer and told Harold that his pictures were very good. Harold, thrilled to receive this compliment, had a set of three prints made and gave one to Harriet.

It was with sincere regret that Harriet and her companions said farewell to Atami. "Atami was far more beautiful than anything I had ever seen even on the coast of France," Harriet declared. "I was sorry I could not spend a month resting in this beautiful spot."

They left promptly at nine o'clock in the morning per the advisement of the president of the railway that ran from Yokohama to Atami. The railroad had been built on the main road and it was the only road from Atami to Yokohama. "We were told that if we began exactly at that hour, they would hold their car back, giving us the lead as we would be obliged to travel for a good distance on their tracks."

They continued on to Yokohama, but as happened so many times before, a stretch of good road would eventually dwindle to nothing more than a narrow path. They often had to drive up onto the railroad tracks, or to get out of the car and widen the road. "We had learned from wisdom, and carried pickaxes with us, as we found they were more useful to us than shovels."

But now the Locomobile itself was about to create a new kind of excitement when its front right tire blew out, making a loud "Bang!"

"'Shot! Shot! Prince Ito Shot' screamed Frank, responding to the loud pop of the burst tire. Paralyzed with fear, the young translator believed there had been a gun shot. 'Shot, Prince Ito!' he yelled repeatedly. I took him by the collar and shook him. 'Get a hold of yourself!' I commanded of him."

"Frank explained that we were situated in front of Prince Ito's house, and he had believed that someone had been shooting at me and my party."

Harriet was aware that seven months earlier, Prince Hirobumi Ito, regarded as one of the men most responsible for the modernization of Japan, had been assassinated by an un-wielding Korean nationalist. She assumed that Frank now believed that Harriet and her party might also be the target of an assassin.

The sound of the blown tire, accompanied by Frank's excited shouts, had attracted a crowd of startled people. Some of the villagers gathering around the Locomobile thought a dog had been shot.

"I explained to Frank that one of the car's tires had burst, and if he got off his seat and examined the car, he would see how much 'damage' had been done. For good measure, I lifted Honkie to show everyone that my dog was alive and well!"

As the tire was repaired, Harriet and her crew prepared to eat their lunch on the side of the road. "But Frank told me that one of the men in the crowd was the head gardener of the late prince's house and had suggested that it would be much more pleasant if we would accept his invitation to come and dine on the property of the Ito home."

Eager for a glimpse of another royal residence, Harriet accepted this invitation. The gates of the home opened wide, and the Locomobile rolled onto the grounds of the Ito's country house.

"Although we did not quite understand the reason for all of this hospitality, we allowed two attendants to carry our tea basket while we walked up to the house," Harriet recalled.

They were invited to recline in an open piazza overlooking the sea. On a small table, a beautiful cut-glass dish filled with immense strawberries, little sandwiches, sweets, and tea awaited them. Three Japanese men got busy tending to Harriet and her party.

After lunching, Harriet and her party were left to explore the grounds at their leisure. In comparison to other palatial homes she had visited, Harriet found the Ito country home to be relatively small. But it was surrounded by exquisite little flower gardens, and the grounds of the house were sprawling and perfectly maintained.

Harriet was awed by the perfectly-trimmed hedges that surrounded clusters of old-fashioned pinks, snowballs, and irises. As they took in this splendid sight, flocks of birds sang out from the branches of magnificent trees. Harriet called this place Paradise.

Once again Harriet's timing was fortuitous. "We were told that very few people had ever received this privilege, but that Princess Ito, on hearing that we were travelling in this region, had extended an open invitation to our party."

"What an extraordinary stroke of luck that we broke down where we did!"

Entering the interior of the home, the first thing that caught Harriet's eye was a photograph of William Jennings Bryan, signed by the celebrated American politician, that had been presented to the Prince on a visit by Bryan to this home.

"Then we were escorted to a small wooden pagoda where we observed four drawings done in India ink. One was of Prince Ito, and the others were of Japanese leaders who had paid with their lives for daring to open up Japan to the Western world, but are now regarded as saints and martyrs."

Harriet was intrigued by a small box that was shaped like a casket. Inside this box rested the mirror that had belonged to the prince. On each side of the box stood a huge bouquet of what had been his favorite flowers. "The mirror was carefully placed face down as the Japanese have a superstition that one is not to look into the mirror that had been owned by the deceased."

Harriet was so grateful for the hospitality extended her by the head gardener of the Ito residence that she informed Frank she wished to leave this man a tip. But Frank expressed some hesitancy, only consenting to relay her message when she insisted.

"When I offered the man a tip, I was surprised that in response he put his hands behind his back and said, 'Madam, this is Prince Ito's house, and no one in Prince Ito's service can accept a tip.'"

"I felt compelled to show my appreciation. I offered the gardener some postcards I had of the Locomobile parked outside of my villa in Lake Como," she said. "He appeared to be delighted with this and insisted that I inscribe my name in a big guest book he had brought me."

After lunch, Harriet happily departed with a beautiful bouquet of fresh-cut roses that had been left for her on the seat of the Locomobile, compliments of the royal gardener. With this lovely memory, Harriet resumed her trek to Yokohama, a bustling port city not far from Tokyo.

"We congratulated ourselves on all the good things that were happening to us," Harriet recalled. But like so many times before, this fine road ended abruptly, becoming no more than a constricted and narrow trail.

And other dangers lurked.

"At one point, we were going along at about ten miles an hour when I saw a little child running about," Harriet recalled. Without any warning, this child ran in front of the Locomobile and slipped right in front of its path. But the skill and instinct of Harold Brooks saved the day. "How Mr. Brooks ever did it, I do not know. But he turned the car so it ran into a fence to avoid striking the child!"

Harriet rushed to the aid of the youngster. "I took him in my arms to see if any bones had been broken, but this child, finding itself in the arms of such a foreign-looking stranger, gave out such a great cry that I concluded that no great harm had been done."

A woman came and took him from her. Harriet indicated as best she could that he should be taken to the well to wash away the dirt and dust that covered him to see if he had incurred any injury. "From what I could tell, the child just suffered from a little bump on the forehead," Harriet said.

But the accident had created a great deal of tension and anxiety among the gathering villagers. Many of them had witnessed the accident and believed the child had been killed by the motorcar.

"The fact that Harold had been able to stop the car from harming this child, at the risk of our own lives, was lost on these people."

The child had been spared, but a local homeowner did not fare as well. The nose of the Locomobile had ended up lodged well into his fence.

The curiosity of onlookers was turning into anger. "I told Frank to explain to the crowd how the accident had happened."

Frank did as she asked, and as he spoke to the villagers, Harriet and her crew got back into the car and slowly drove away.

They were more than relieved when they arrived at the Oriental Place Hotel in Yokohama, where they were again beset by hordes of newspaper men and photographers who surround them on all sides.

"I was settling into my room when I received a visit from a local policeman in regard to an accident and an injured child. I recounted the story to the officer and assumed this would put an end to this inopportune episode," Harriet recalled.

This incident caused her to be concerned that the people of Japan would unfairly view automobile travel as unsafe. "Before we headed for Tokyo the following day, I wished to show one of the reporters just how difficult it was to navigate the narrow roads of this nation."

However, something more pleasant than road safety, and the accident, now occupied Harriet's mind. She would soon be heading for Tokyo, where a special reunion would take place.

"Were you excited about meeting up with His Highness and Her Highness of Baroda again?" I inquired of Harriet.

Her eyes lit up with pleasure at this memory. "Oh yes! The Baroda party was delighted to see us again, and His Highness told me he regretted that he had not been able to enjoy such adventures that we had passed through!"

Harriet and the Baroda party rested in, and then toured the city of Yokohama together for two days. Her Highness invited Harriet to accompany her for some shopping and sightseeing. They would enjoy these activities while travelling in a special car provided by the Emperor of Japan himself.

But this fun outing soon took a serious turn. "Her Highness and I were lunching when Frank appeared to inform me that I was to go to the police station in regard to an incident that had occurred on the road from Prince Ito's house to Yokohama."

At the station, it was determined that the boy had not suffered any injuries, but Harriet received a fine for the damaged fence. "I wished to do right by this homeowner," Harriet said. "I paid the sixty yen to repair the man's fence."

However, upon hearing of the homeowner's pursuit of Harriet, a high-ranking government official scolded the accusers for being so rude to their honored visitors.

"Soon after, we had a pleasant visit with a Mr. O'Brien, the American Ambassador," Harriet recalled. "'Why, you seem to be the talk of Tokyo,' Mr. O'Brian informed me!"

But unfortunately, not all of the talk was good, as the back road incident continued to haunt her. Some of the Tokyo newspapers had published exaggerated accounts of the accident involving the child who had been knocked down by the Locomobile.

Despite this unflattering story, the Japanese press remained hospitable to their special guests, eager to show Harriet the many sights of their city, including trips to the theater, where they happily interpreted for her.

But no interpretation was needed on the night Harriet experienced the sight of Tokyo's "Painted Dolls." She recounted scenes of young girls sitting behind windows with bars while "barkers" extolled the attractions of each. "In this circus environment, the Japanese men could buy a wife when they wanted an especially pretty one," she recalled, shuddering.

"Men purchased these girls by taking a number, viewing a photograph, and by arranging a private meeting with one, each option having its own set price. These little women sat in their windows perfectly indifferent to everyone," Harriet said. "They painted and powdered their faces and made their toilette as if they were in a private dressing room, oblivious to passerbys!"

She described this practice as a "sad sight" that had been in existence for thousands of years. "We can only wonder if the light of the Western World can change all of this."

Judging from her Western standards, Harriet related that she thought the young girls of Japan were generally modest, gentle, and pleasant looking, but that in many instances, this changed with their marital status. "In some regions of Japan, the common custom was for married women to shave their eyebrows and blacken their teeth in a manner that gave them a soulless, inane and vacant expression."

Standing at about five feet on average, Harriet described these women as sporting rounded shoulders, hollow chests, narrow hips, and small feet and hands. Their scanty dress revealed physiques that were poorly nourished. "The girls looked as if they passed from girlhood to middle age almost at once when wedded."

A woman who headed the Girls' School in Tokyo invited Harriet to address her students. Despite her desire to exploit every opportunity to share her culture with the young women of this nation, Harriet regretfully declined due to time constraints.

Young people seemed to be everywhere Harriet looked. "All along the roads of Tokyo it was a mystery where all the children came from. The streets and bungalows were literally crowded with them, but we rarely saw an old woman."

Throughout most of her travels in this nation, the Japanese people showed a healthy degree of curiosity toward the Locomobile. But while travelling on the road from Yokohama to Tokyo, Harriet observed a change in attitude. "There we received the first impertinent looks from people on the streets, none of them seeming any too friendly toward the motorcar."

Harriet also made note of the lack of automobiles in Tokyo and Yokohama. "We saw three or four in Yokohama, and in that city, we observed for the first time a small garage."

As Japan was awakening to the potential of automobile travel, the Mikado seemed to be intrigued with the motorcars owned by Harriet and the Maharaja of Baroda.

He sent his chief engineer to examine both cars, who then took several rides and scribbled copious notes of the workings of the engines.

In Tokyo, Harold accompanied Harriet on rickshaws to the famous pearl manufacturer, Mikimoto, where she purchased some of their famous cultured items. At another stop, Harold bought himself a khaki suit for his trip homeward.

On May twenty-seventh, Harriet's party was given a royal dinner as the guests of the Mikado. In their honor, they were served special strawberries picked from the Imperial Garden.

The next day the Locomobile rambled smoothly along the Crytomeria Road. Of this well-traveled road lined with magnificent Japanese red cedar, Harriet remarked, "This was the most beautiful road I had ever seen."

Although she had made that declaration a few times throughout our talk, I had read that this road was particularly lovely. Harriet described how the treetops met overhead to form a shady canopy that offered an occasional glimpse of blue sky and stunning views along the thickly-wooded road. "Unfortunately, the Japanese have permitted telegraph poles to be placed so close together on this road that it was sometimes impossible to make our way."

Their destination this day was for Nikko, a beautiful city filled with hot springs and ancient shrines, whose very name meant "sunshine" in Japanese. "When we arrived in Nikko, we astonished the natives by climbing a steep hill with our car to arrive at our lodging, the Kanaya Hotel."

While in Nikko, Harold, who had fully recovered from his donkey riding experience in Egypt, took an enjoyable ride on horseback. "Mr. Brooks appeared to be thrilled as he galloped on his horse through green hills and valleys filled with immense boulders and waterfalls," Harriet recalled, smiling at the memory.

One of the most vivid impressions Harriet took away from her trek through Japan was the love its people had for flowers. "In Japan, the badges of the most celebrated houses, or families, are floral," she explained.

"An open chrysanthemum with sixteen petals was the Imperial badge of the Mikados of Japan, and the Mikado's private badge was represented by the blossoms and leaves of the *Paulowaia imperalis*," she shared.

"The Shoguns of the Tokugawa dynasty are represented by three leaves of a species of mallow. And no matter how simple the table arrangements, or how plainly furnished a room, in Japan, there was always a small bouquet of flowers, or a single flower in a beautiful vase to always give an artistic flair."

The Japanese people's great faith in the Shinto religion, their worship of nature and ancestors, and their abundance of gods and goddesses was not lost on Harriet. "The Japanese have gods for wind, the ocean, fire, food, pestilence, mountains, rivers, and temples."

Chief among these was the radiant Goddess of the Sun, Ama-Terasu, who the Japanese believed was born from the left eye of Izamage, the Guardian of Japan. "From his right eye was produced the God of the Moon, from his nose the violent God, Susa Moo."

Harriet shared that the Sun Goddess was the ancestress of the heaven-descended Mikados who had reigned in unbroken succession from the start of the world. They were accordingly looked upon as gods on earth.

"The fact that the Mikado, or Emperor, of Japan was so interested in my motor trip was most likely the reason why we were granted so much protection from the Japanese people," Harriet explained. "I am pleased to tell of my positive experiences, as most of the guidebooks one reads will tell you quite the contrary in regard to traveling in the interior of Japan."

Although she had not met the Mikado Emperor Meiji, or spent time with the royal family, Harriet and her entourage were extended every courtesy of this progressive leader.

Meiji the Great, as he was known, was the 122nd Emperor of Japan, according to the traditional order of succession, reigning from February 1867 until his death in 1912. Harriet's travels were timely; she was a watchful observer of what the emperor wanted the world to know about a new and progressive Japan, making her a perfect ambassador.

During the reign of this Mikado, a period of rapid change had engulfed Japan as the nation quickly evolved from a feudal state to a capitalist and imperial world power characterized by the nation's industrial revolution.

At the time of the emperor's birth, Japan was an isolated, preindustrial, feudal country. By the time of his death in 1912, however, Japan had emerged as one of the great powers on the world stage. The *New York Times* summed up this transformation, declaring, "The contrast between that which preceded the funeral car [of the Meiji the Great] and that which followed it was striking indeed. Before it went old Japan; after it came new Japan."

Harriet delved into her take on the moral teachings of the Shinto religion. "Shintoism encourages one to follow their natural impulses, and obey the Mikado's decree; such is the sum of its theory of human duty."

Harriet found it interesting that in this religion, preaching formed no part of its "instruction," nor were the rewards and punishments offered by a future life used as an incentive to shape conduct. "The Shintos believed in the continued existence of the dead, but noted that the condition of this afterlife, whether painful or joyous, was nowhere declared."

For twenty-seven days the Locomobile had navigated the impossibly rough terrain of Japan's most remote regions, and the challenging roadways of its cities. It would now be polished and prepped for its return to America.

Overall, Harriet had been impressed with the Japanese, who she described as "energetic little folk." She found them desirous of a good education and admired the schools she visited in Tokyo. "The students always greeted us with a pleasant smile, and would respond pleasantly to our greeting when we called out to them, saying "ohio," which meant good morning, or "arigato" for thank you."

But now it was time to bid *sayonara* to her Japanese friends, but not before Honk Honk and Billikins were introduced to a new four-legged family member.

"The Japanese Press presented me with a fluffy little black and white Japanese 'Chin' dog," Harriet said. "I couldn't refuse him. I was told his name was Jappy."

Although the worldwide portion of the voyage was coming to an end, Harriet and her party faced a long journey home, and this time with two extra animals on board!

CHAPTER TWENTY-SIX

Sailing Homeward

In Yokohama Harriet and her companions, along with the Baroda party, boarded the Pacific Mail Steamship *Siberia* to being their journey homeward. Once again the Locomobile was crated and shipped on the same ship as its owner.

Not surprisingly, hordes of newspaper men gathered at the pier to take parting photographs of Harriet and her entourage, as well as of the Royal Indian family.

This admiration followed them out to sea. On board the *Siberia*, Harriet reveled in the numerous bouquets she received from her Japanese admirers. One contained a note that stated, 'Thank you Mrs. Clark Fisher for opening up Japan to the motoring world." Harriet described this bouquet as one of the largest and most beautifully-arranged that she had ever seen.

Nearing Hawaii on the eighth of June, Harriet and her companions celebrated Antipodes Day. "'Today we will have two Tuesdays, and two eighths of June, because of crossing the 180th degree,' Mr. Brooks explained this special occasion to me. I told him that this reminded me of the story of Jules Verne when he won the wager after traveling around the world in eighty days on account of this extra day!"

Two days later, they went ashore and settled into the Moana Hotel in Honolulu. The Maharaja had cabled ahead and made arrangements to secure a motorcar, and he invited Harriet to tour the city with his party.

While Harriet had enjoyed traveling with the royal family, I sensed that at times she had been resigned to share the limelight in her traveling show. The glamorous royal family from India seemed to be getting their share of newspaper coverage and notoriety.

My suspicion was confirmed when Harriet again went to her desk to retrieve a newspaper article from the *Pacific Commercial Advertiser* published on the eleventh of June from which she proceeded to read an excerpt in dramatic fashion.

"No other man in the world is the possessor of so many jewels as the Indian Raja, and he is the owner of the only gold and silver artillery in the world. Posted to defend his gorgeous palace are four guns fashioned from gold and silver. They are the products of a native artisan, who worked five years in fashioning them. Each of the cannon weighs four hundred pounds, and two are of solid gold and two are of solid silver, save for the inner barrel, which is of steel.

Dazzling and magnificent is the apparel of the bullocks that haul this royal artillery. Forty-five thousand dollars is said to be the cost of the trappings. On the horns of the animals are golden caps, and on their legs are anklets of gold and silver. Ornaments of gold adorn their heads, and when the royal artillery is in motion the splendor of it dazzles the eyes. The guns are guarded day and night by picked men from the royal body guard."

And the guns weren't the only thing to impress this reporter. Harriet continued to read:

"The most famous diamond necklace of the world is the property of the Maharaja. It is composed of two hundred beautiful brilliants of marvelous purity, each as large as a hazelnut. This necklace is valued at $12,000,000. Then he has a famous collarette, made of five hundred diamonds. Hanging from this circle of light is the fifth largest diamond in the world, the Star of the South. Emeralds are strung between the diamonds."

Harriet paused and looked at me. "And here it says that even His Majesty's carpets are made of gems!"

"In one room of the palace is a rug with a surface of four square yards, made entirely of beautiful diamonds, pearls, and rubies. The gems have been woven into a regular carpet, with designs and margins clearly defined. His household expenses are borne by the people, so that he is enabled to invest his enormous income in gems, rare carvings, paintings, and rugs."

"And the lovely Princess, the Maharini, did not escape this reporter's eye," Harriet noted.

"The princess yesterday on landing wore two magnificent bracelets set with emeralds and diamonds, which drew all eyes as the beautiful young woman walked to the waiting automobile.

Traveling with the party is Mrs. Clark Fisher of New Jersey, a woman of wealth and social position, who is a close friend of the Gaekwars' family. On arrival in San Francisco, Mrs. Fisher will travel across the mainland by motor. Her machine is aboard the Siberia."

"Well, I did manage to rate a paragraph," Harriet said with an exaggerated sigh. "Referring to the Maharaja's jewelry, I wish to say that while this magnificent jewelry was worn by the Princess Indraraja, and Her Highness, it really belongs to the state of Baroda, and the royal family is responsible for every jewel carried away."

Harriet explained that if any of these jewels were to be lost, that loss would be covered by funds from His Highness's private account. It was also not surprising that the royal servants who watched over the jewel caskets kept very strict records of every item taken out and returned. If a jewel was lost through the negligence of a servant, that servant must work to pay back the loss to the estate.

The Royal family and their jewels, and Harriet and her crew, car, and pets prepared to journey to the mainland; their most challenging tests behind them as they anticipated the upcoming roads of America.

Or so they thought.

CHAPTER TWENTY-SEVEN

A Farewell to the Royal Family

"On the seventeenth of June, as we neared the coast of California, we were greeted by the sight of the beautiful Golden Gate Strait in all its splendor," Harriet exclaimed. "Feeling a bit homesick, I asked out loud, 'Is it not good to be at home again?'"

But Harriet's momentary case of homesickness was interrupted by the greetings of a gentleman who came looking for her as the ship docked in San Francisco. He asked to see Mrs. Fisher, and introduced himself as a representative of the Locomobile Company. "He wished to congratulate me," Harriet recalled. Then he informed her that an automobile was at her disposal during her stay in San Francisco.

With the warmth of this greeting still fresh, Harriet attempted to leave the ship with her pets tucked under her arms, only to be startled when told she could not go ashore with her animals.

"When I asked why, an officer informed me that I did not possess the required permits, and that no animals, even the world-famous Honkie, Jappy, and Billikins, were allowed to land on the Pacific Coast without them."

Harriet claimed that no one had told her of this law before she had left Japan, and was only now learning that she should have obtained these certificates from the American Consul at Yokohama.

"I was told I needed to have a doctor's certificate that proved my pets were in perfect health and condition when they boarded the ship. I told this officer that my animals had been kept in my bathroom during our entire time at sea and were just fine!"

But there was no use in arguing with this man, who was only carrying out his orders. A crestfallen Harriet asked Albert to remain on board with the animals while she took care of the situation as only she could. She finally managed to obtain the required permits later that day and by four o'clock in the afternoon they had settled into the Palace Hotel.

"This incident did not escape the eye of the local newspaper," Harriet said. "The following day's edition of the *San Francisco Call* featured the headline, WOMAN MAKES ROUND THE WORLD TOUR WITH PETS IN AUTOMOBILE!"

Harriet read from another pile of newspaper clippings that she seemed to have in every drawer of her desk. As she read this particular item, she found it hard to repress a smile.

"*Except where there were oceans to cross, Mrs. Clark Fisher, who arrived here yesterday on the liner* Siberia, *has made the journey from her summer home on Lake Como, Italy, in a big Locomobile touring-car, Mr. H. F. Brooks running the car.*"

"Harold liked that line, by the way," she paused to interject.

"*Accompanying her was her maid, a man servant, and Honk-Honk, a Boston bull terrier. In India a monkey was added to the entourage, and in Japan, a Cheen dog. The journey has occupied eleven months so far. The only hitch in her whole journey occurred yesterday, when Chief Officer Stevens refused to allow the dogs and the monkey to land, because Mrs. Fisher had neglected to acquire a health certificate for them before leaving Yokohama. Mrs. Fisher stormed and even threatened, and refused to be separated from her pets. Honk-Honk was a native born pup, the monkey her closest companion, and the Japanese dog too cute for anything.*"

"Yes, I most certainly did storm around!" Harriet confirmed.

"*Stevens remained obdurate to her pleadings and only smiled when she told him she would report the matter to Washington. 'All right,' she said; 'I will go back on board the ship with my pets, and will never, never, never leave unless they go ashore with me.'*"

"I meant it!" Harriet said, without looking up.

"*The Pacific Mail Company, however, was spared the burden of maintaining a permanent boarder and a menagerie, by the intervention of Chief Officer Trotter, who said he had no objection to the pets being landed. It transpired later that Mrs. Fisher had brought all her trouble upon herself. She smuggled the pets on board with her at Yokohama, and kept their presence in her stateroom a secret for two days. 'If she had taken them on board openly,' said the inspector, 'she would have been given a certificate which would have insured their landing here without difficulty.' Mrs. Fisher's home is in Trenton, New Jersey, and she said she valued her bull terrier more for his watchfulness, than as a pet. 'Honk-Honk stood guard at night,' declared Mrs. Fisher, 'and a native would have been extraordinarily clever to have got within ten feet of our bungalow or tent without Honk-Honk knowing it and giving the alarm. He rather disgraced himself in some of the native villages by chasing chickens, but he took such good care of us that we could not deny him a little diversion once in a while.'*"

I found it amusing that Harriet did not have anything to say about the reporter's comments about her being the cause of her own troubles. She simply placed the article back in the desk drawer and said, "That was very true. Honkie was very loyal to us all."

Once this pet issue was resolved, Harriet enjoyed a spirit of entertaining wherever she ventured. Each day she was an honored guest at some luncheon or dinner. "So here again, where I had expected to be among strangers, I was at once made to feel at home," Harriet recalled. "And many old acquaintances called on me. Some people I had not heard from or seen in many years."

One of her callers was the wife of an officer stationed in that city. The women traveled together visiting the government reservation and enjoyed tea in the officer' quarters.

But the time spent in San Francisco was also bittersweet. "It was time to say farewell to His Highness of Baroda, my dear friend Her Highness, and her daughter, the Princess Indraraja, at a special luncheon given for us at the Cliff House."

Harriet explained that the Baroda party was headed north for Canada before traveling on to New York.

While Harriet socialized and met with officials, Harold spent his time readying the Locomobile for the final leg of its voyage. "Mr. Brooks examined every part of the car to see how the engine had withstood the strain after the thousands of miles it had covered by land and sea."

She was happy when Harold reported that he had gotten the engine together and running. He replaced the tires, adjusted the steering gear, replaced springs and put on a new 1910 foot brake. He also relayed that some of the main bearings were loose and he was adding a small air-pump to the side of the car for the gasoline tank.

"Going up the high grades overseas, we had discovered that this addition would be necessary on our trip homeward," Harriet noted. "Without that pump, the gas would have to be forced up, or the engine would stop now and then."

And this was a very good thing for Albert, for the process of "forcing gas up" required him to put his mouth to the gasoline tank and blow!

"This was the first time Mr. Brooks had ground any valves or cleaned out carbon since we had left India," Harriet declared with obvious satisfaction.

On June twenty-second Harriet and Harold were invited to speak at a banquet sponsored by the Locomobile Company that was given in their honor at the Palace Hotel. Harriet was asked to give a speech and to answer any questions about her travels through India and Japan in particular. "You can imagine the Michelin people bestowed us with much attention, also."

Four days later the party's baggage was once again packed onto the motorcar and they departed for their long journey toward New York.

"On the first thirty miles or so, we were accompanied by about ten automobiles filled with our friends from San Francisco. After a farewell luncheon, we were wished a *bon voyage* and left to our own powers."

"We drove from San Francisco to Stockton and then to Sacramento, a long hard run, with several stretches of sand, and very rough roads in many places. The weather was extremely warm." Along this route, Harriet was thrilled to see that Billikins and his two little dog companions were always extended their full share of attention wherever they stopped.

"Billikins won friends with his sad face and by extending his hand in friendly greeting to all he met," Harriet said with a big smile. "I am so happy to say that he had behaved very well, never giving his mistress any trouble whatsoever. And all three were such good comrades. In the wide open spaces of the American West, they enjoyed grand romps without fighting or hurting one another whenever we rested by the wayside."

But after being treated so royally, and having been so revered in the exotic lands in which they had toured, Harriet and her party learned quickly that here in their native land, this special treatment was now a thing of the past.

At a stop in Placerville, California, Harriet declared she had one of the worst luncheons of the entire trip. "We shall never stop there again," she declared. "The meat was tough, the milk sour, the tea cold, and the waitress impertinent."

The waitress was grievously insulted when asked to pour a second cup of tea. With an insolent toss of her head, she informed Harriet that they only provided one cup of tea for forty cents. "It was only when I assured her we had the ability to pay for a second cup that we succeeded in getting it."

The next step of the California journey took a turn for the better in Sugar Loaf. They obtained lodging in a small mountain house run by a German woman and her two daughters, who Harriet said made them feel right at home. "They told me that few people visited the area, and those were mostly school teachers from San Francisco who spent their summer vacations in this restful spot."

The waters of a trout-filled river were clear and cold; and the fresh air infused with the scent of pine. Harriet and her party lingered there for several peaceful days.

They departed Sugar Loaf on the morning of June thirtieth and arrived at Lake Tahoe by noon time, but not before experiencing some car troubles. "Going to the summit of the mountain, the car's engine got too hot and the water boiled over," she recalled. Harold took care of this by opening the sides of the car's hood and allowing the hot air of the afternoon to "play around" the cylinders. "We also learned that we would need to use heavier oil at this altitude."

Harriet described Lake Tahoe as a beautiful sheet of water surrounded by invigorating mountain air. They settled into one of the cottages, equipped with three rooms and a bath. The cottages had been built in a manner that allowed all guests a view of the lake. "We drove our motorcar alongside and made ourselves quite at home."

But this idyllic setting would also become a place of convalescence for Harriet when she was stricken with ptomaine poisoning. She had been suffering bouts of this illness since landing in San Francisco. Fortunately, in Lake Tahoe, she received the care of a Doctor Kelsey, who was vacationing with his wife and children in a neighboring cottage. "This doctor saw me safely through this illness, thankfully."

While she recovered, Harold equipped the Locomobile with a new Klaxon horn.

Honkie, Jappy, and Billikins enjoyed this western setting. "My little animal family enjoyed the freedom from restraint here, and romped merrily."

A rested and now-recuperated Harriet and her party resumed their travel on the third of July. "We wished to avoid the crowds of people who were pushing, riding, crawling; any way to get to Reno to see the Johnson-Jeffries fight."

To accomplish this, they ventured at least one hundred miles out of their planned route.

Jack Johnson would win this epic battle called by many "The Battle of the Century" that took place on the Fourth of July. This historic fight between Johnson and Jeffries sparked nation-wide response, from celebrations to riots, as Johnson became the first African American Heavyweight Champion of the World.

During this arduous leg of their western passage, the Locomobile traversed countless miles of desolate and barren land covered with sage brush. As they rolled along, wild horses grazed, rabbits hopped, and little yips emitted by Honkie warned of approaching coyotes.

On the road from Kingsbury, Nevada heading east, the roads grew thinner and the grades steep and long, somewhat reminiscent of the roads of Japan. The road leading to Wally Springs meandered on for about eight miles, challenging the car with short, sharp turns before reaching the town. They continued on, cutting across the open fields to Grangerville and then on to Wellington.

On one stopover, a group of gun-toting cowboys came into town with cattle and entertained Harriet with an exhibition that showed off their technique with lassos.

From Wellington, they rambled to Hawthorne for over seventy-three miles. "We passed through the most desolate, barren county, the earth was parched and brown, and filled with sagebrush and rocks," Harriet recalled. "We passed by a place called Lucky Boy Camp, and finally got to Hawthorne, logging one hundred and twenty-four miles since leaving Lake Tahoe."

They stopped for the night in this town, obtaining a supply of gasoline and oil for the car before reaching the town of Mina, where they lunched.

Unlike many of the quaint scenic views they enjoyed on the roads overseas, in this part of the American West, the roads *and* the scenery seemed to leave something to be desired no matter where Harriet looked. "I am certain there had to be two thousand whiskey bottles lining the roads through which we passed."

The Locomobile rolled by the carcasses of all kinds of animals—horses, cows, and sheep—which had succumbed to thirst and heat. And the live farm animals they encountered were also in poor health. "We met one stagecoach drawn by four poor-looking horses that were so emaciated one could count their ribs."

Coyotes and rabbits were plentiful, but the former kept their distance thanks to the little cries of warning given by Billikins, who seemed to sense them long before they could be seen by humans.

They passed automobiles that had been abandoned by owners who had been picked up by another car, or had continued their journey on foot. In these parts, a variety of curious automobiles shared the road with the elegant Locomobile.

"A very amusing sight was of an old automobile coach that was being used in place of the stagecoach of earlier times," she recalled. "I was told that this automobile made two trips a day, carrying the mail and passengers between Placerville and Lake Tahoe."

"This battered vehicle was dirty and greasy-looking, but the proud passengers looked as if they enjoyed riding in this motorcar as much as if it had been the finest-looking car ever to be put on the road!"

Another car attracted her attention. "This car contained a party of men who had started out from San Francisco in high spirits," Harriet relayed. "They had travelled the same route as we had, but had run into another car ahead of them, breaking the car's water cooler."

Harriet admired the ingenuity of these men. In this case, mind overcame matter as they told Harriet that they had purchased an old milk can they were using as a water cooler by running some pipes in some manner.

"The next morning, off they started with that old milk can standing on the running board of their car, evidently answering every purpose."

From Mina, they continued on to the towns of Miller's Siding and afterwards to Tonopah. Nearing Tonopah, they spotted a water trough and took the opportunity to fill their bottles. "This was not a pleasant part of our trip. We were constantly thirsty, and with the desert heat beating our faces at all times, we filled our water bottles whenever possible."

As they replenished their water supply, they were approached by some men. One carried a gun, giving Harriet some concern for their safety. "At first I assumed we were in for a real holdup, but they entered into a friendly conversation."

The men were eager for the latest news out of Reno. They had heard that Jeffries had been knocked out in the fifth round of the epic boxing match Harriet had avoided so carefully. "We told these men that we did not care if they knocked each other's heads off," Harriet recalled, laughing. "One of them told us that it was easy to see that we were not from the West, and asked in which direction we were headed, to which we replied we were off for Tonopah."

She was informed by these men that the mail coach had just gone through the area. Its intoxicated driver had carelessly dropped a bag filled with mail off the coach about two miles down the road in the direction she was headed, and had not bothered to come back for it.

They asked Harriet if she wouldn't mind picking it up and dropping it off at the next camp. "We found the mailbag just where they said it would be, but the first camp we reached was twenty miles farther on down the road."

At this camp they handed the bag over to the proprietor, who seemed very amused by this event. "He told us that he believed that the coach driver, a man named Bill, was likely to have dropped *something* before reaching his destination," Harriet recalled with a hint of disdain. "It seemed to me that this was a place where a little government oversight might be called for."

Just outside of Tonopah, the landscape grew more desolate. For several miles, the Locomobile rolled over roads littered with empty tin cans, bottles, and glass, which took their toll on the car's tires and required Harold to perform many repairs.

The roads were also scarred by holes that had been dug by prospectors in search of fortunes buried in the arid earth. Nearby, abandoned axes, hammers and shovels rusted in the hot sun.

"One could see the smokestacks of the mines, pouring out back smoke," Harriet recalled. "There was not a garden to be seen, or even an attempt at one. It appeared that everyone there lived on canned goods."

But there were occasions of fun to be had in the West. "We arrived in Toponah just in time to experience the continuing celebration of the Fourth of July observed in regular mining town style!" Harriet recalled.

One of the day's activities featured a water fight with men standing on opposite sides of the street. They wore rubber suits and were armed with a huge fire hose with which they sprayed water at the party on the opposite side of the road. The side that caused the other to retreat in surrender was declared the winner.

In this town, Harold obtained ample gasoline. "We supplied ourselves with a pocket compass, a pair of two-and-a-half gallon water skins, a long-handled shovel, and five-gallon can to hold the gasoline."

The lodging here was very clean, but expensive. They enjoyed a fine supper and Harriet indulged in a sulfur bath.

Their departure from Tonopah once again found them rolling through parched desert land, scattered with springs of water bubbling out of the ground. Finally a welcoming oasis presented itself late that afternoon. "At about four o'clock, to our great astonishment, out of this barren country, we came to a house that looked as if it had slipped out of some country suburb!"

This home, called "Hot Creek Ranch," presented a well-kept yard and to Harriet's delight, everything was as neat as a pin, offering the promise of comfort.

"We stopped here and asked for a drink of cold water," Harriet said. "But a sweet-faced woman named Mrs. Williams asked if we wouldn't prefer a glass of milk instead."

In short order, a little girl came from the house bearing a large glass pitcher filled with milk, and four glasses. As they refreshed themselves with this sweetly delicious offering, Mrs. Williams asked them many questions about Harriet's past and planned travels. "After giving a good account of ourselves, our new friend insisted on our spending the night at the ranch."

Their hostess explained that for as much as six weeks at a time, they did not see anyone other than a family member, and that mail was sent and delivered only once a week. "She told us that she and her family were looking forward to a new railroad that was to be built nearby. She explained that there was plenty of copper and lead to be mined, but it had been too costly to haul it to Tonopah by mule."

Harriet was impressed with this refined, comfortable home so way off in what she described as desolate country, and sensitive to this woman's need for companionship. She accepted their hostess's invitation. After a good night's rest, Mrs. Williams spoke to Harriet as they dined in an area Harriet described as a "pleasant piazza."

"I listened to her account of how she and her husband had come to settle in that place many years earlier, and she introduced me to her two daughters, who had married lawyers and gone to live in Chicago and New York. They were spending the summer with their mother."

Harriet was grateful for this civil respite, but it was time to move on. Hot Creek and Ely were the next destinations, and once again, the road remained rough, harsh and barren. On several occasions, they would come upon a rancher's fence, forced to travel several miles out of their way before returning to a road. Many of these enclosed areas were posted with signs warning trespassers that they would be shot without further notice. "You can bet we never attempted to disregard those warnings," Harriet said.

Taking the advice of some local ranchers, Harriet took a short cut from Ely to Currant Creek, but came to regret this decision. "I would not advise this way to other motorists," she warned. "For this shortcut was one of those instances when the farthest way around is the shortest way to the place you desire to reach."

Passing what Harriet described as an extinct volcano, the right rear tire of the Locomobile blew out. Harold remedied the situation, but it was an extremely hot and dangerous place to be so inconvenienced.

"While Mr. Brooks and Albert worked on the tire, Maria and I took the dogs for a little walk. We came upon a little spring bubbling up from the ground, but not knowing if it was one of the arsenic springs found around those parts, we did not dare to drink from it, but took some water for the motor."

I asked Harriet if she or any the animals had had any close encounters with snakes, which were said to be prevalent in that part of the country.

"Yes, snakes do abound in those parts, but they are mostly of the harmless variety," Harriet explained. "We ran over several of them on those western trails, but the most odd-looking snakes we saw were those called 'Blow Snakes.' They would lie right across the road and puff themselves up like adders. We were told they were harmless, thankfully, and I suggested that in their inflated state, they might not make bad inner tubes!"

In the town of Cherry Creek, they set up camp for a night. Harriet met a curious miner who came to look at the Locomobile. He returned at five o'clock the next morning bearing pieces of hard stone that he offered her. "I've had those rocks cut and polished and they formed beautiful turquoises with little veins of gold running through them," Harriet said.

From Cherry Creek they rambled on to Cobra, Montello and the town of Lucin, where they stayed in a place that Harriet described as no more than a small dugout, but more than sufficient and reasonably priced. "For two rooms, with the privilege of the use of a cot, supper, one quart of coffee and breakfast for all us we were charged a total of $6.15!"

Harriet was informed that this was a stopping place for motorists who had been through these parts, at least up until reaching this location. "I should have known we were in for quite a ride when I was told that at this point, mostly every motorist stopped to send their motors on by rail car to the nearest repair shop."

This account reminded me of His Highness's wise decision to have his car shipped by rail to Tokyo, but I kept that observation to myself.

Despite what other motorists had chosen to do, and the advisement of others, early the next morning the Locomobile was bravely navigated toward the town of Ogden, Utah, where their luck changed for the worse. "This was one of the worst trips we had made since we started out from New Jersey," Harriet grimly related with disgust. "And the first time we got lost!"

At Terrace, Utah, Harold tried running the car on the railroad ties. But this was deemed too uncomfortable and hard on the car's tires. "We went down the bank and struck what we at first thought was the road, only to discover it was nothing more than a sheep trail on which we proceeded to lose our way."

The only directions in their possession advised them to follow the old Union Pacific Railroad. They took for granted this meant for them to follow the tracks. "So we tried that route and stuck to those tracks all right, but when we reached a place that was just about impassable, we spied what we believed to be a fairly good road on the other side of the track. After a lively debate, we decided to try to reach it. You can't imagine how hot, dusty and tired we were at this point."

They commenced the crossing of the railroad track, but amid the cinders and dust, the front wheels of the Locomobile did not land on the ties, but instead slipped between them. They found themselves hopelessly stuck!

Unlike their travels in Japan and India, Harriet and her crew did not have the help of anyone. Here, in their own nation, they were on their own.

But being stuck was the least of their troubles. "I suddenly noticed oil pouring from beneath the car," Harriet recalled. "And we soon discovered that the petcock, a valve mounted on the fuel tank to control the supply of gasoline, had broken. Thus began the liveliest work our little party had performed since we left our comfortable quarters in America on July sixteenth of the previous year!"

The car's location on the tracks put them in a precarious position. No one had any idea when a train might be due, and they had no lumber to work with except for some old railroad ties that appeared to be lying about at some distance.

Some backbreaking work was about to begin.

"The old railroad material was retrieved and carried back to the car, along with some rocks we had found. With all of our strength, we used them to jack up the car so as to get it off, and then over the tracks."

Hot sun scorched their heads, and beads of perspiration streamed down their faces. But Harriet was impressed with how her team worked like beavers, and in doing so finally managed to successfully jack up the rear of the car while Harriet stood guard. "While my party continued to work, I took my station some distance away from the car to warn of any approaching trains."

With a great sigh of collective relief on behalf of the entire party, the Locomobile was safely transported over and off the track. "Afterward, we all slumped down to the ground, nearly exhausted," Harriet declared. "But we would find that our fears of oncoming trains were unfounded. When we later arrived in Kelton we were told that a freight train only ran over that track once a week!"

But damages to the Locomobile demanded immediate attention. "We had to figure out how to mend that broken petcock," Harriet said. "Our oil supply was getting lower by the minute."

Harold found some canvas patches in his repair kit which Harriet referred to as "porous plasters" that were placed over the hole in the broken part, securing the patch with twine. Once in place, he held a hand over the patched area to prevent oil from pouring out until the plastering was complete.

"We worked in the heat of the day for nearly three hours with our mouths and throats parched with the alkali dust we breathed. We did not eat but occasionally took swallows of water to replenish ourselves."

Harriet looked over to where Harold and Albert spoke in quiet consultation. She did not like the expressions on their faces, and anticipated what would come next.

"My men informed me that they thought I was being too rash in keeping on," Harriet said, quickly shaking her head to and fro, still in disbelief at this thought. "They were in tacit agreement that the road seemed to be getting worse instead of better, and were put off by the deep washouts that appeared before us every fifty to seventy-five feet."

These washouts gave pause to car and driver, for each time the Locomobile had to pass through one something on the car would break or give way.

But Harriet, in true form, remained obstinate. "I was determined to keep on," she declared. "However, as I was confident that we were traveling in the right direction, and to prevent any mutiny, I gathered up what I needed, the two dogs, my monkey, and my maid, and we started out on foot down the road."

Harold and Albert had no choice but to make all necessary repairs and follow, lest they lose sight of their boss. But the damages kept adding up.

The men found a ravine that ran under a portion of the tracks and decided to descend the embankment and then go under the tracks, instead of crossing over them. But this put such a strain on the Locomobile that its driving chain slipped off its right wheel. Harold was able to quickly replace the chain and then maneuver the car up a slippery bank. The men then proceeded to follow the rest of their party.

At this point, Harriet discovered a trail of footprints that lead to an empty gasoline can, and a part of an inner tube. "We were getting close to a road, and evidently a car had been here before," she said. "I picked up the inner tube and swung it around my head in delight, for I knew that in this case, what man had done woman could do!"

Harold, in catching up to her, made his peace. "Mr. Brooks told me that although he did believe that we should have turned back, he was glad to see we were nearing a road. He also told me he thought that this was the most awful day he'd had since leaving Trenton."

Within a half mile or so, they struck the main road and headed toward Kelton, arriving in that town on the tenth of July. Unfortunately the lodging left much to be desired. "Our quarters provided for one mirror in four rooms, one wash bowl with a broken pitcher, and a piece of a tea towel cut up into squares they called towels."

And the meal was not much better. "For our Sunday night supper we were served tough beef with greasy fried potatoes, canned peaches which were sour, and tea which was no more than hot water!"

No doubt happy to leave Kelton, they got an early Monday morning start for Ogden, then Harriet's party was met by a Mr. Karr, who escorted them to Salt Lake City. They checked into the Knutsford Hotel for a two day stay, and once again, Harriet was less than pleased with the hotel's amenities. "We were charged twelve dollars for miserable rooms," she recalled. "The meals were also expensive. It must have been 120 degrees in the sun in Salt Lake City, the thermometer seeming to soar with the prices!"

At this stopover, Harold patched up the car's crank case and fitted a rear wheel tire with new bearings.

And Harriet had a bit of social research to perform of a somewhat curious nature. "While in Salt Lake City, I was anxious to see a real Mormon. Several of them were pointed out to me, but I could find no marks of identification that made them any different from other men in the East!"

The road out of Salt Lake City was especially challenging. Crews were putting down a new road, and in doing so, had torn up the old road, leaving the dirt dangerously soft. "Our Locomobile pulled through," Harriet noted triumphantly. "But others did not fare as well, as we passed four cars all stuck in the dirt, waiting for teams to come and haul them out."

In the town of Evanston, Wyoming, a Mr. Spaulding provided them with good directions on how to reach Cheyenne. "This local man told us he was familiar with the road we were to travel, and around thirty miles from Evanston, we would find a beautiful spring where we could set up camp."

This sounded promising, but upon starting out for Evanston on the fifteenth of July, they found themselves coping with torrential downpours, causing the clay roads to become extremely slippery. Reminiscent of their trip over the Devil's Gulch, once again their Victor chains kept the car on the road and saved the day.

But not everyone was on the side of the Locomobile, or any automobile, and their hapless passengers. "We rolled on much to the chagrin of some farmers who stood watching us, making remarks on the possibility of our having to give up!"

And in what seemed to be an unfortunate pattern, the lodging in Evanston was not restful in the least. "In Evanston, like in many of the other towns in the western part of the country, there was a more or less 'wonderful' hotel," Harriet stated with a sigh. "At least, they called it a hotel."

That evening she insisted that Maria sleep on a folding bed that was in the room they shared. Harriet chose to sleep on a sofa. "That sofa, if possible, looked more inviting than the bed."

But after a hard day on the road Harriet chose not to scrutinize her accommodations too carefully. "After about an hour after I retired, and with both dogs fast asleep at the foot of my couch, I dreamed that I had fallen asleep on the back of a bucking bronco," Harriet recounted. "It happens that I had gotten onto the wrong side of this couch, and in doing so, had caused the bed to double up. The dogs and I were thrown into a heap on to the floor. Mercifully, the sofa had not trapped us all in."

The next day found them in Granger, fording a river, and then passing through Green River before making a grueling drive through long stretches of "deep sand with high centers" to reach Rock Springs for another overnight stay.

"And how were the accommodations in Rock Springs, may I dare to ask?"

Harriet shot me a droll look before describing Rock Springs as no more than a town consisting of a railroad station, a hotel, and a pool room, with the restaurant containing three rooms—a kitchen, a dining room, and a bedroom.

"On a bench outside this restaurant sat an Italian and an Irishman," Harriet recalled. "To the right of the hotel and pool room, we spotted a couple of mules kept in an enclosure. When we inquired about them, we were told that men here made their livings by waiting to be called to pull heavy caravans and automobiles through the sand with these mules, as even horses alone were not able to pull this heavy cargo. These men appeared to be disappointed that we did not require their services."

Happy to move along, their route found them traveling next through Point of Rocks and then on to Bitter Creek, where they experienced another round of very disagreeable road. "We were forced to use sagebrush to fill in the washouts we came upon every few miles in what was called the Red Desert,"

Harriet said. "We crept carefully through the soft mud without a sign of life to be seen anywhere, only desert as far as the eye could see that seemed to go on endlessly for miles."

It was then on to Rawlins, where they got off the road and rambled through a field for about twenty miles to reach the town of Hanna. "The land was sandy and pocked with the burrows made by squirrels, making things very dangerous for motorists."

It was a bumpy ride and the party found themselves thrown from their seats each time the car's rear tires fell victim to one of these holes.

And things only got more difficult. "We reached Medicine Bow from Hanna only with a great deal of hard pulling," Harriet recalled. "During that trek, it was necessary for the chains to remain on the car."

They rolled up to the town's only hotel, but were informed that there was no vacancy. The proprietor recommended that they go see a Mr. McBluff, who lived around the corner and sometimes permitted people to take rooms in his home.

"We searched for a location to set up camp, but finding no inviting place, we decided to pay a visit to Mr. McBluff," Harriet said. After a knock at his door, he appeared on his front porch dressed in what Harriet described as his "Sunday best."

"'Yes, yez can have rooms,'" he spoke with a drawl. "But he also told us his wife was ill."

At this hour, having no other options, Harriet and the rest of the party accepted his offer even at the risk of imposing on Mrs. McBluff.

But the man's wife wasn't the only issue here. "From Mr. McBluff's unsteady walk and loose tongue, I deemed he was intoxicated."

They took the rooms he offered, and after washing, went over to the restaurant to get some dinner. While there, Harold and Albert called on the saloon keeper, a Mr. Gus Grimm, to obtain directions to Cheyenne.

"Later, when we got on to the road to Cheyenne, the name of 'Gus Grimm' would appear on signs scattered about on sheep trails and roads," Harriet recalled. "And each sign always pointed toward Mr. Grimm's place of business, where travelers could obtain fine whiskey."

Leaving the restaurant, Harriet and Maria headed back to the McBluff residence where they were startled by the cries of a woman coming from the home. "The cries of 'Help! Murder!' reached our ears as two little girls ran out of the house telling Harriet that their mother was being killed by their father."

"I rushed into the house to find Mr. McBluff wrestling with a young man while a woman clad in her night clothes, with her hair streaming down her back, tried to grab hold of Mr. McBluff while screaming for help!"

Harriet's sudden appearance on the scene managed to quiet things down. She was told that the young man was Mr. McBluff's own son who had come to the rescue when his father had threatened to strike his mother. This intervention had brought about the wrath of a drunken and abusive husband. Harriet assumed the role of mediator.

"I took Mr. McBluff by the arm and led him from the room," Harriet explained. "I asked him what the trouble was all about and he told me he had been to Denver for three days and had spent three hundred dollars."

He told Harriet that one hundred dollars spent a day was not bad for a blacksmith, to which she replied that she thought it was pretty good. He told her that he had earned that money by himself, and believed he had the right to spend it as he pleased, and that his wife could not tell him how he should spend his earnings.

"We spoke quietly for a bit," Harriet said. "Then he asked me if I was a Salvation Army Girl!"

Harriet informed him that she was not and he was curious to know what she was doing travelling around with her "caravan" in these parts.

"He asked me if my car needed any repairs and when I replied to the negative, he told me that we were the first 'autoists' that had been through town," Harriet said. "I think he was a bit confused, or a bad repairman, because although he said that he had seen hundreds of cars, none had come to him for any repairs."

Harriet drew his attention back to his row with his wife and son, and he relayed the "sad" story of his life. "Here was a man who would work for months, and then take his hard-earned money and recklessly spend it all in Denver in just a few short days," Harriet relayed. "It was if he just thought all he had to do was sign a check to get more money. If men like Mr. McBluff worked harder, and earned less money, they might not throw it away so carelessly."

On the twentieth of July they left Medicine Bow and headed to Laramie, another long trek over land that was dug up and filled with prairie dog holes. "All the way over, we saw Gus Grimm's signs pointing in the opposite direction. But we were actually grateful for their guidance, for without their presence, the mirages we encountered often lead us to believe we were coming to the edge of a mountain, or a cliff, when we were merely rolling over land."

They passed bodies of alkali lakes which from a distance appeared to be filled with water, but on closer inspections were merely nothing but hot beds of sand. "About fifty-four miles out of Laramie, we happened upon a fine spring of fresh water and decided to set up camp for the night. We reached Cheyenne for dinner."

Cheyenne was a place she described as "not unbearably interesting." They obtained a new supply of tires and hurried out of town.

Harriet's assessment of the landscape through which they currently traveled was apparent. "The alleged crops, wheat and oats, in Wyoming and Nevada were what I call poor. The farmers cut their oats, and make no attempt to thresh them."

But the sweet odor from the wheat and cornfields were described as delicious. "Their scent contrasted greatly with the odors of the flowers that had filled the air of most other countries through which we had journeyed," she noted.

From Wyoming until they reached Colorado, the farmers used the land until it had almost been worn out. "Evidently, they never returned any of their crops, or any part of them, for fertilizer."

Harriet was perplexed that this material, which she thought would make perfect fertilizer, was being used instead to fill in bad parts of the roads. "When I saw how poor the crops were here, I could not help but wonder why that material had not been used in the fields instead of the roads!" She felt certain that with this practice, combined with an ongoing drought, the local corn crops would not amount to anything that year.

But her appraisal of the local landscape improved as they traveled toward Nebraska and the upper portion of Colorado. "Here, we looked for miles about the countryside," Harriet recalled. "It was interesting to see tremendous farming machines at work, threshing the grain and stacking the straw, using binders, then piling it up ready for shipment. Those machines seemed almost human in what they could accomplish."

Bilikins managed to survive the activities of the Nebraskan farmers, but Harriet joked that if anything had happened to her monkey, there was certain to be a plague of grasshoppers without his fierce appetite. "Grasshoppers were tender morsels for him. Whenever we stopped along the way here, and he got the opportunity, he happily went to work devouring all of those little pests that he could."

I recalled Albert's story of Billkins up a tree in Nebraska, from earlier that day. "Is this where Billikins was almost left behind in that apple tree? I asked. "I wonder if the Western plains reminded him of his native home in Ceylon."

"Oh yes!" Harriet said. "But I think that he was probably as happy as we were to arrive in the city of Denver, a place where the roads finally proved to be easier to navigate."

CHAPTER TWENTY-EIGHT

Officer Ketchum and the Corruption in Cleveland

The city of Denver presented Harriet's weary eyes with a refreshing view of row upon row of beautiful homes. She was told that only a few years earlier log huts had stood in their place.

She welcomed the improved road conditions and change of scenery this city appeared to offer. "Here we had magnificent roads," she happily recalled. "After all the hardships of navigating the desert, my old car appeared to shake off her laboring. She darted along at the brisk rate of thirty-five miles an hour. It was as if she had never done anything but roll through parks on the smoothest of roads."

On the twenty-first of July, Harriet put the Locomobile in the care of the Sanford Motor Company, and its proprietor, Mr. Sanford, entertained her and the rest of her party. "We spent the evening at the White City, a most interesting lakeside resort."

Located on Lake Rhoda, the resort of White City had only been in operation for two years at the time of Harriet's visit. She shared that White City got its name from, and was famous for, its glittering display of 100,000 lights that made the resort sparkle.

"Afterward we dined at one of the clubs just outside of Denver. We headed out of that city three days later, reaching Sterling, Colorado by seven-thirty in the evening, having run one hundred and fifty miles that day."

In Sterling, they filled up the car with gasoline and oil and set on roads Harriet described as fairly good all the way to North Platte, Nebraska, with only some tricky stretches of sand to navigate near Ogallala. They ran on to Grand Island, Nebraska, where the Democratic State Convention was in full swing, and once again obtaining decent accommodations became an issue.

"We scouted places just outside of Grand Island for twenty miles around, but the open areas were surrounded by ugly wire fences, and we could not find a campsite that offered water or wood for a camp fire."

A man they spoke to in town told them they could get rooms over a garage. They were so hot and exhausted, and glad to get any room they could.

"The woman who ran this so-called lodging required twenty dollars for two miserable rooms in the rear of her house which were over a garage," Harriet said with disdain. "It offered the most forlorn and generally dilapidated views I have ever witnessed! Scattered about were old baskets, bottles, rags, and garbage of every kind."

Harriet refused the woman's requested price. They settled on ten dollars, which Harriet still deemed exorbitant.

On the twenty-seventh of July, soon after departing Grand Island, the tires of the Locomobile rolled across a milestone. "We were half way between Boston and San Francisco," Harriet noted. "The roads at first were bad, until we were about twenty-five miles out of Omaha, Nebraska, at which point we found them in fine condition."

Stopping at the Henshaw Hotel in Omaha, Harriet received a pleasant surprise. "I learned that Mr. Curtiss had been giving an exhibition here that day with his airplane!"

At nine o'clock that evening, he sent his card up to her room to arrange for their visit. "I had not seen him since his historic flight in Brescia!" They enjoyed a pleasant chat and he told Harriet that he had been sure that they would meet again somewhere on the globe during her "around the world" tour.

On the thirtieth of July, in Des Moines, Iowa, they were met and entertained at a luncheon given in their honor by the manager of the Iowa Auto Supply Company. "The president of that club presented me with a little gold badge!"

Except for a tire blowout in the town of Newton, the following day found them enjoying excellent roads with good guideposts all the way to Davenport, Iowa, where they garaged the car for the evening.

As they neared Chicago, Harriet was surprised to find the roads to be rough, but she was happy when, thirty miles from this city, two men were dispatched to escort them to this bustling destination.

"The strain of all the rough roads and heavy cargo began to take its toll on my motorcar," Harriet recalled. "It was necessary to have two new front springs installed."

In Chicago, a Mr. Banta presented Harriet to prominent citizens at an impressive banquet presented in her honor. She was given a set of beautifully-bound Automobile Blue Books, standard road guides written for motoring travelers in the United States and Canada, a concept developed by businessman and automobile enthusiast Charles Howard Gillette.

"These books included photographs of myself and my party, taken at points of travel along our route that had been taken by the press." At this banquet Harriet made a speech, and received many accolades and congratulations. On the fourteenth of August they departed Chicago with American Beauty roses adorning the sides of the Locomobile.

Near Valparaiso, the car struck a severe washout, breaking one of the new springs. They proceeded slowly until reaching the town of La Porte to make repairs.

They reached the city of Waterloo, Indiana, and remained there for two days. "We rested and enjoyed some good home cooking served up to us at the Waterloo Hotel, a small, but very comfortable place. I enjoyed my first taste of green corn since leaving America!"

After an evening in Toledo, Harriet was looking forward to enjoying her trip through Ohio. But on the tenth of August, while traveling through Sandusky in the late afternoon, they experienced an unpleasant encounter.

"We were rolling along, looking for the corner at which we were to turn, according to our directions," Harriet recalled. "We were going no more than twelve miles an hour when a man on a motorcycle pulled up alongside of the car and told us we were under arrest for speeding!"

Harold inquired of the man as to what the speed limit was, to which he replied that it was eighteen miles an hour. "Mr. Brooks pointed to our speedometer and showed him that he had been driving at the rate of only twelve to fifteen miles an hour."

The officer proceeded to imply that for a slight remuneration, he would permit them go on without incident. But Harriet declined his shady offer, at which point they were instructed to follow him back to an official office.

Harold turned the car around as directed by the officer. But as he did, residents from private homes along the avenue followed to inquire if this man had indeed arrested them.

"Upon learning that he had, these citizens were outraged and offered to come to our assistance. They wanted to know what I was planning to do," Harriet recalled. "I told them I would see the official and explain to him how slowly we had actually been traveling, and of course I would let him know who *I* was and that would settle this matter."

But Harriet's simple plan was no match for the crooked bureaucracy she faced. The officer who had pulled them over, a man she learned went by the name of Ketchum, had gone to see the official first, before she could make her appeal.

I couldn't help smiling because under the circumstances, his name of "Ketchum" was humorously appropriate.

"When I reached the office of this official, I found him tilted back in his chair with his feet up on his desk," she recalled. "A cigar hung from his mouth and on his face he wore a not very pleasant expression."

Harriet inquired if he was the official she was to see about this incident. "He grunted something that sounded like 'yes.' I relayed to him how my car had been stopped at the railroad crossing for speeding. I told him that this was not right and that there had to be something wrong with the officer's speedometer as I knew mine was absolutely correct!"

She further informed him that she had been told that if she returned and explained the matter to the proper officials, the matter would be dropped and she could be on her way.

"And do you know what he said?" she asked me, leaning toward me. "He told me that I must put up a hundred dollars, and if I did not, they would take our car."

Harriet refused and the official ordered her car to be seized.

Not wishing further troubles or additional delays, Harriet relented and agreed to appear the following morning with a check for one hundred dollars.

"Albert later told me that Officer Ketchum, and another policeman, had tried to start the car, but it had been futile," Harriet said, smiling at this recollection. "The car might still be standing there today, or perhaps they would have had it hauled off by a horse!"

I told Harriet I thought it was interesting how Harold had somehow evaded the task of starting the car, to which she just shrugged nonchalantly.

"I had never been subjected to such an outrage of this nature, and I had no intention of doing it then," Harriet recalled, defiance still evident in her voice.

The respectable citizens of Sandusky had offered to come to her assistance if she needed, and they did not disappoint her. At ten o'clock the following morning, Harriet reappeared at the office slightly earlier than required to be what she described as "on hand in good time." Not surprisingly, the office was packed with people who had heard about Harriet's troubles.

"I shall never forget the kindness of two women in particular. They had been sitting on their porch and had seen us pass. They were excited to see a motorcar filled with people that looked like they were having such a good time."

These women told Harriet that they had been impressed by the way her party had respected the streets and pedestrians of Sandusky by not tearing about in their car.

"All of this they relayed to the town official," Harriet said.

"But, after giving the officials my check, I was informed that our hearing had been postponed for two weeks, or I could pay a fine of $13.60 and be on my way!"

A man in the crowd offered to "go on" Harriet's bond for the one hundred dollars, but she demanded her check be returned to her and that the fine be dropped. After much negotiation and consultation with officials, she learned that her check would be returned to her; however, she would have to pay the $13.60 fine.

Harriet had the final word. "I turned to that Mr. Ketchum and said, 'For swearing to a lie and giving false evidence, I hope someday you will have a tumble from your motorcycle and will be laid up long enough to give you time to consider what an outrage you have done to me.'"

She exited the room amid the congratulations of the townspeople for her reclaiming of her one hundred dollars.

Harriet later learned that Officer Ketchum had been discharged from duty two weeks after this incident, and shortly afterward had fallen off his motorcycle, breaking his leg, and was at risk of losing his foot.

"Do you know that this was the first time we had been treated in this manner during our entire trip around the world, and the first time I was compelled to pay a fine, or be subjected to any such harassment?" Harriet reflected. "And it hurt all the more after having been treated with so much courtesy in the foreign places to which we had been."

I recalled the incident in Japan, but figured Harriet considered that a fine she had honestly deserved.

CHAPTER TWENTY-NINE

The Extra Lap

I took a furtive glance toward the parlor window. The sun had begun its arc to the west, infusing the landscape of Bella Vista in a golden glow. I knew our meeting would soon be over, and I was reluctant to bring our time together in this enchanting place to an end.

Harriet must have sensed my thoughts. "Let's finish up our chat with a walk," she said, heading first to her desk.

I gathered up my belongings and notes and got ready to leave. At her desk, Harriet was rummaging for yet another article I knew she would read to me. She looked up to find me peering at the image of the young, dark-haired man framed up on the wall, but said nothing.

We headed outside, as she spoke to me of the final days of her journey.

"On the twelfth of August, on a stopover in Cleveland, I had declared that our trip around the world was really finished."

Having made it to this city during the Locomobile's trial run the previous July, and with her time there spent as a student, Harriet regarded the ride home from Cleveland as a non-event. "For me, every mile from Cleveland to New York was just an extra lap."

The next morning, Harriet and her party were escorted by a cavalcade of motorcars from Cleveland to Painesville, Ohio. "It was a charming ride, with the lake on our left and beautiful homes lining the road. The air was dry and fresh, filled with the odor of vineyards."

On August thirteenth, Harold remarked to Harriet that it was three years ago, to the very day, when he had taken his first sail to Europe from New York with her.

"The next day, we rolled out of Erie, Pennsylvania, and headed for Rochester, New York. Allow me to read from *The Rochester Herald* of August fourteenth," she began.

"*WOMAN IN WORLD MOTOR TRIP HERE. Arrives in Rochester, Ending Remarkable Journey – 20,000 Miles in Her Touring Car. Intrepid New Jersey Woman, Factory Owner and Operator, Visits Europe, India, Asia, and Japan.*

There arrived in Rochester last night, quietly and unannounced, a woman who has just finished accomplishing a feat that for a man would deserve universal applause, and for a member of the gentler sex almost stagger belief. This woman was Mrs. Clark Fisher of Trenton, N.J., and the feat a tour around the world, traversing more than twenty thousand miles of actual travel by motor through Europe, Asia, India, Japan, and the United States. Mrs. Fisher is a woman of wealth and of unusual enterprise. For ten years, since the death of her husband, Clark Fisher, she has by her intrepid work and executive ability personally carried on a manufacturing plant, making anvils, vises, and rail-joints. She employs more than three hundred men and boys who belong to no union, many of whom have been in the service of the company for years. Since the business has been in her hands, she has increased its capacity about four times.

So it is little wonder that when she started on a tour around the world a year ago it was one that had to be carried through. And it has been carried through, all but the few remaining miles that lie between Rochester and New York City.

Mrs. Fisher sailed for France with a Locomobile forty horse-power machine among her baggage, on July 19th last…Mrs. Fisher, with her companions, has practically lived in the automobile since leaving this country. Only once has she had recourse to a railroad train, and the mere mention of one causes her to throw up her hands. 'Don't mention the stuffy things,' she said last night. 'Of course, I know that they are necessary, but the thought of them stifles me after travel by motor in the open air.'"

The article went on to chart their itinerary from Paris to Egypt, picking up with her travels through India.

"*From thence the party sailed to India and motored from Bombay to Calcutta, hundreds of miles through the jungle. In reality, this was the most remarkable strip of the journey. The thought of a woman rolling over the sands of India and skirting the terrors of the jungle in an automobile is enough to catch the breath. Yet this is what this daring New Jersey woman did, and she now owns the distinction of being the only person who has attempted this feat. The Indians were so astonished when they saw this intrepid American woman buzzing along in a 'devil wagon,' they fell prone to the earth as the party passed, and salaamed her as a magic princess from the land of marvels.*"

"I especially like that description," Harriet said with a big smile.

"Devil Wagon?" I asked.

"No, 'Magic Princess from the Land of Marvels!'"

"*From India the party sailed for Japan, and here once more took up the journey to the throbbing music of the motor-car. Here it was that the most untraversable roads were found.*

Around the World in 1909

The Emperor of Japan, who learned that an American woman was touring his dominions in an auto, sent his chief engineer to escort the party over the perilous mountain trails…

Mrs. Fisher comes back from her trip filled with enthusiasm for the things she has seen and heard from her car on the remarkable journey, and she describes them with a picturesque charm. She has taken the time to study the people, both high and low, whom she has met, and her description of them is human and sympathetic. She has the greatest praise for her usage at the hands of the great wide world."

The article's conclusion summed up Harriet's observations about her treatment and her feelings about returning home to friends and relatives.

"'*Everywhere I went,*' she said, '*I was met with the utmost courtesy and consideration. I did not ask it. It came to me to such a surprising extent that sometimes my breath was almost taken away by it.*'"

Harriet folded the newspaper. An occasional cluck of a hen or moo of a cow completed the living farmland portrait of our stroll.

"Ah, smell that fresh air. I love the scent of hay!" Harriet said. "I guess I have always been a farm girl. You know, I once lived in a gracious home in Flushing, New York, and I do enjoy time spent at my *Villa Carlotta*, but it is at this farm where I feel most at home."

She shared the history of the house with me. "This home was once called Reed Manor. It was built by Joshua Reed at the turn of the last century, no more than a home of four rooms and a hallway. Sometime in the 1860s, a library, dining room and two bedrooms were added, and a tower, with an elevated stage, and a third floor were added at the end of that century."

She told me that the last of the Reed family to own this property was Judge Alfred Reed. He had practiced law in New Jersey and New York, and was elected as the mayor of Trenton in 1867. He later became a justice of the New Jersey Supreme Court.

Silvano and she had renamed the property Bella Vista Farm when they had purchased it a year earlier.

"Sounds like you found a way to have a little bit of Italy in New Jersey," I said.

"Yes, you could say that." she nodded.

"Tell me about your welcome back to New Jersey after being away from home for so long."

"We were escorted home by representatives of the Automobile Club of America, and then Edward C. Bullock of Trenton's City Council made a resolution that I was to be officially congratulated after having completed my world tour during which I spread the name of Trenton, and its products, in so many foreign places."

"Arriving home, I was received by my financial adviser, Mr. Austin B. Snider, and the manager of my factory, Franklin Hendrickson," she recalled, telling also of how all of her employees from the Fisher & Norris Anvil Works had shown up to welcome her back. "My home was filled with great bunches of American Beauty roses, received from all kinds of prominent business concerns and individuals!"

"Were you glad to be home, or did you feel a bit let down after having experienced such an adventure?" I asked.

"After all the factory workers had departed, I sat down to have supper with my feet under my own table for the first time in over a year! It was a relief to be home safe and sound, and as I told that reporter from the *Daily Gazette*, I think there is no place like America. I love it!" she replied. "And I must confess that I really looked forward to getting back to work as soon as I had my bags unpacked."

The matter of home shifted our conversation. "Speaking of home," Harriet said. "How is it you are planning to return to your own home today?"

Her inquiry took me by surprise. I stuttered as I tried to explain how I had figured I would hitch a ride home with a farm laborer. "It's just a few miles down the road, and there is still plenty of light," I stated.

"Oh. So you *do* have a bit of the spirit of an adventurer!" she exclaimed. "Young lady, I do believe you will do very well in your work as a reporter. And you deserve to cover more than fluffy columns dedicated to ladies fashions and society gatherings."

I couldn't hide my joy at being so complimented; I felt myself beaming in the sunshine of her words. We continued to walk until we came to stand outside a large outer building with a double front door, the kind one saw on a barn. Two young men appeared, both with their shirtsleeves rolled up. Each opened a side of the building's door, pulling them wide open to reveal the shape of an automobile sitting idle in darkness.

"Is that…?" I said.

"Yes. It is *the* Locomobile," Harriet said.

After a short time, the sound of the car's engine filled the air as it rolled out into the light. The gray vehicle stood the worse for wear. Some of its paint had rubbed off in parts, its sides were scratched, badges from its battles in the jungle and with bullock carts. The leather parts of the car's interior showed much abrasion in spots.

Harriet walked to the driver's side. Without hesitating, one of the farm hands opened the driver's side door for his boss. She took the place of the young man who had been sitting behind the wheel while he hopped into the back seat.

On the other side of the car, I stood motionless, so astounded by this surprising turn of events. "Come join us," she spoke to me, pointing to the passenger seat beside her. "I so love Sunday drives."

The car's motor had attracted the attention of Honkie, Jappy, and Billikins. They came running toward us. It was clear they still enjoyed automobile travel despite all the time they had spent cooped up in one, day after long day.

"Old habits die hard," Harriet spoke to her pets, laughing. "Come along. Hop in!"

Honk Honk took a front seat, right on my lap. Billikins and Jappy joined the young workman in the back seat. What a sight this made, and I wished that someone I knew would happen by to witness this scene.

The Locombile rumbled down a path that soon brought us out onto the main road. It took off at a good clip; none of its power or speed seemed to have been diminished by its epic journey.

I could barely contain my excitement and viewed the familiar countryside with brand new eyes, just like Harriet must have seen Paris and her *Villa Carlotta* from these seats for the very first time.

Harriet glanced at my attaché, which contained my notes from the day's talk. "I hope you took good notes," she spoke above the noise of the car's engine.

I massaged my weary fingers and looked at Harriet, nodding my assurance that I would convey her message to the world in a satisfactory manner. It was clear she desired her rightful place in history, and she had earned it, I believed.

"You know, not all journeys have a happy ending," she said, slowing the pace of the car.

I remained silent, not knowing where the conversation was headed.

"Take Edgar Samuel Andrew, for instance. The dark-haired young man in the photo on my parlor wall."

I sensed she knew I had wanted to ask about him. "I know a little of that tragedy," I ventured. "The circumstances of his passing must have been so hard on you all."

"Yes, it was, especially when his occasion for coming to America was supposed to have been such a happy one."

Harriet relayed how she and Silvano had made plans to be wed in New York City. It hadn't been an easy decision, however. "There were so many things for us to take into consideration before we married; the differences in our ages, my fortune, his career in the Navy, and his ties to family and friends in his native Argentina," she recollected.

"Silvano was also homesick for his native land; he had been away for four years at that point. But I convinced him to stay in America, and run the anvil factory and settle here at Bella Vista."

She had offered him the position of manager at the anvil factory, although she knew he had dreams of a loftier lifestyle complete with rounds of golf, concert-going, and personal drivers.

With her eyes firmly placed on the road ahead, Harriet smiled wistfully and nodded as if speaking to herself, "But Silvano was a worker at heart, so I think the role of business manager finally appealed to him. It was a good partnership."

Their union was to be kept quiet; the only person to know of their engagement was Maria. "I convinced him that it was best for us to be quietly married at Grace Church in New York City. I knew the rector and loved how that church always seemed so European with its fabulous stained glass windows."

But Silvano had a special request. He asked that his younger brother Edgar be invited to sail from England to attend their wedding.

"Edgar had visited us once, but was now in Europe, living with his cousins, and attending to his studies," Harriet said. "Silvano invited him to our wedding, and wanted Edgar to stay on as an employee at the factory."

Harriet kept on. "But it seems that Edgar had become fond of a girl named Josfinia, or Josey, as he called her. This girl was planning to visit him in England, and had been looking forward to it, we've been told. But he had no choice. He heeded Silvano's wishes, and booked passage to sail to America on what we believed was the *Oceanic*. This would give him a few days to spend with Josey in England."

I listened, not daring to move. Honkie stretched and made a little twirl on my lap in an effort to nest more comfortably. In the back seat of the car, Jappy and Billikins remained quiet, as if they were hanging on their mistress's every word.

"But unbeknownst to us at the time, Edgar got some disappointing news from his uncle. Due to a coal strike, his passage on the *Oceanic* had been cancelled. He was now to sail on a new ship," Harriet said. "That ship was the *Titanic*."

I had heard rumors of these circumstances, but hearing this confirmed account from such a personal perspective was quite another matter. Her words attached themselves to my chest like weights, and I found myself holding my breath involuntarily, so mesmerized by them that we could be crossing the Devil's Bridge, or the Hakone Pass, and I may not have noticed.

"We didn't even know he was on board the *Titanic*," Harriet continued. "Before long, however, we received word from a young woman of about twenty-six named Edwina Troutt. She had come to know Edgar on their ocean voyage. She had survived her terrible ordeal at sea, but not without many emotional scars. She wanted to tell us of the tragedy and was able to give us details of Edgar's last minutes in a way we would otherwise never have known."

Winnie, as she was called, told Harriet and Silvano that when the ship's passengers received the announcement that they were in danger, Edgar had gone to warn a family of young women travelers. As they only spoke Spanish, he worried they would not understand the announcement of danger and wanted to make sure they understood. They were the very few Latin passengers on board that could translate.

"That was the last she saw of him," Harriet said. She spoke in a subdued manner, quite unlike any other time in our conversation that day.

"Yes, poor Edgar. Perhaps we should have just let him be to live his life in England. He was a little wild, but it seemed like he might have been maturing."

"You were only trying to do what was best for everyone," I said.

"Perhaps I take too many liberties," Harriet said. "Look what a chance I took by asking three inexperienced travelers like Mr. Brooks, Maria, and Albert to go out gallivanting through such dangerous lands in a motorcar. Things could have turned out so differently with all that we went through. I took a great chance."

"But they gained so much, and you did so much for women."

This statement brought the fire back to her voice. "Oh, no! Please don't paint me as someone who is, or was, trying to promote women's causes. Why I do not even think women should have the right to vote!"

"I don't believe in unionism, suffrage, or too much education! Well, maybe just women who pay taxes should be allowed to vote," she continued. "I believe that we are having too much education now, too much of the mind and too little of the morals and on the practical side of life."

I looked at her askance.

"Yes, I know that everyone seems to think that just because I run a factory, and drove around the world, I am all for the suffragettes. And the women's right to vote movement!" she exclaimed. "I think we have made progress quite nicely without having that right, although many of my opponents on this matter see things quite differently and voice their opinion quite strongly."

This subject matter ushered in a welcome distraction for her, for the topic of those rebellious suffragettes lead us away from our rather sad discussion of Edgar.

"Yes, during my first years of marriage to Clark Fisher, who was over thirty years my senior, in case you did not know, I had indeed lived a charmed country club life in the traditional role of wife," she stated. "But I did not regret this, for it taught me the emptiness of it all. I came to consider myself of the highest nobility—a princess of manufacturing. I still believe in the dignity of labor and take no shame that I work alongside honest men who live by the sweat of their brows."

The front left tire of the Locomobile caught a rut in the road. I clung to the seat beneath me as we swayed to and fro. Harriet continued unfazed. "When I inherited my husband's company, I was able to give my all to it. I learned how to temper, chisel the face of an anvil, mold vises, and make rail joints, and really grew to love working with iron and steel, and to hear the whir of machinery and the sound of the forge."

Harriet proudly related how she introduced new machinery to the anvil factory, increased the anvil output, and established a large foreign trade. "I am wagering that the United States government doesn't know that a woman makes the anvils used on the Panama Canal," she stated with pride.

She then addressed me. "So what about you?" she asked, putting the focus on me again. "You can do what you please. There are no limits; you are young, unmarried, and free to roam."

She reiterated what she had said about my reporting on matters of importance. "You appear to appreciate the advances made in the automobile travel. Are you aware of something called the Lincoln Highway?"

I told her that I had read several newspaper accounts of how the construction of that roadway had just recently gotten underway. "I have heard there is a man by the name of Fisher who is improving those so-called roads you and your companions navigated," I said. "He is building a gravel-covered road running straight through from New York to California. I believe it is being called the Coast-to-Coast Rock Highway."

"Yes, rock indeed," Harriet replied. "I think travelers like myself, and a few others, have shown the world that the automobile is a thing of the future, and our roads will have to somehow catch up. I like that Carl Fisher. He is a man who sees the big picture. "

"Is he a relative of yours by any chance?" I inquired.

Harriet let out a laugh. "It does appear that the names of Fisher and Brooks do seem to follow me around," she said. "No, he is not related to me, but I just had an idea for *you*."

I shot her a puzzled look.

"You are a good reporter, and I detect you have a desire to see the world." she said. "How about if I see to it that you go on the road at some point to tell the story of the development of that coast-to-coast road to California?"

"Could you really do that?" I implored.

"I will talk to the people at the Automobile Association on your behalf," she said. "You will recall how they threw a luncheon in my honor just before my worldwide tour."

The sun began its slow descent behind a hill in the distance, and the local landscape took on a hue I had never seen before, filled with the red, yellow and oranges of possibilities. I was speechless. The idea of her proposal fully occupied my mind.

"Aren't sunsets even more glorious when viewed from the seat of a motorcar?" Harriet asked, as if she read my mind.

I nodded yes, still too absorbed in the moment to speak. Despite the stillness of the late summer New Jersey air, the world buzzed with all the exciting and mysteriousness of far off lands that had filled my head for the entire day.

A tire of the car took on another rut and the vehicle bucked and rocked. "We do need those better roads, and sooner rather than later," Harriet declared. "It still surprises me that the American portion of our trip was the most difficult in many ways, and I am not just speaking about the roads."

Harriet again lamented about the hotel proprietors of the American West who offered such shoddy service, and the derisive onlookers who offered no support when the Locomobile succumbed to obstacles on the road, or worse, wished to profit from their troubles, not to mention the corrupt officers she encountered in Ohio.

"And even here in my home state, I've encountered similar treatment. I recall just a few months ago a trip to Lakewood, a town near the shoreline. We noticed some men whom we thought were repairing the roadway. Upon our return home, we were happy to see that the area where those workers had stood was smooth and looked perfectly sound, but it wasn't so. Our car sunk into the mud at that precise spot. Quite suspiciously, a dozen or so people appeared, and they were not very helpful with their comments at all."

These men inferred that shovels and planks would be used to help them out in return for some monetary compensation.

"I heard someone remark proudly that we were the fourth victim of the day," Harriet said. "It required great effort to free our car. By the time this was accomplished it was late in the evening and no lantern was placed by us to warn other motorists. I fear a serious accident is bound to happen there."

Harriet had relayed this story to a reporter from the *New York Times*, warning drivers that she believed these men had set a deliberate trap for motorists. "I asked readers if there was no redress for this type of conduct. Why is it necessary for me to pay an automobile tax and then ruin my clothes, strain my car, and delay my trip when the rest of the road between Trenton and Lakewood is good?"

I listened to her words, but my mind wandered far from New Jersey, its familiar landscape, pitted roads, and petty highway robbers.

She had changed subjects, now talking about the matter of motoring fashion. She spoke about the lower part of a Japanese men's costume with a plaited, divided skirt which she had borrowed and adapted for motoring. "It looks just like a regular skirt without its inconveniences," I heard her say.

I made a mental note of it, picturing her wearing such an efficient item. Even the feminine matter of fashion took on a practical side with Harriet!

But my mind was drifting like the sands of far-off hot deserts glowing in magnificent sunsets. Somewhere on distant continents, turbaned men charmed snakes, and whirled like dervishes in temples. Diligent dutiful coolies carried dignitaries on *dandies* to bathe in the sacred waters of the Ganges with the smoke of smoldering fires illuminating steep and ghastly *ghats*, Maharajas and Maharinis lounged on jewel-encrusted cushions in posh palaces while horrifying brigands readied for their next raid on their unsuspecting victims.

Exotic spices in Ceylon perfumed the air, the members of the royal family of the Japanese Mikado sipped tea among perfectly-tended gardens, powerful currents of Japanese rapids furiously churned and crooked narrow paths wove along majestic mountains daring men to pass.

And somewhere, I was certain, astounded natives of these remote lands shared the legend of the time a mysterious white woman and her "monster" had appeared out of nowhere, passing through their villages, never to be seen or heard from again.

And I knew of all these far-away splendid lands, and the people who dwelled there, because I was driving with the worldwide adventurer, Harriet White Fisher Andrew; The Anvil Queen, The Lady Iron Master, The Female Napoleon, The Talk of Tokyo, A Lady of Great Consequence, but perhaps the most deserving title of all…The Princess from the Land of Promise.

EPILOGUE

Harriet White Fisher, with Harold Brooks by her side, were not the first people to use the automobile to traverse unchartered territory in the United States or abroad.

For instance, in 2004 the Public Broadcasting System (PBS) presented *Horatio's Drive*, a documentary written and directed by Ken Burns and narrated by Tom Hanks. It told the story of Dr. Horatio Nelson Jackson, who, in 1903, became the first man to drive an automobile across the United States.

Others have made their mark on automotive history, claiming their unique place in the competitive timeline of the pioneering motorized traveler: George A. Wyman, first human to cross the continent on a motor-driven vehicle called the "California Motorcycle" in 1903; E. Thomas Fetch with Marius C. Krarup, besting Horatio Jackson's record by two days in their cross-country trek in a Packard, also in 1903; and of course there was George Schuster, who in 1908 left New York City, and by land and sea raced a Thomas Flyer, Model "35," around the world in forty-one days with crew members Montague Roberts, C.A. Coey, E.L. Mathewson, and Hans Hansen.

It has been noted that Harold Brooks, upon hearing of George Schuster's accomplishment, was disappointed to learn that he had not been the first man to have driven around the world. One can make the distinction, however, that while Schuster raced around the world, Harold leisurely toured it as he captured exotic people and places on film like never before.

During the early portion of the Twentieth Century, American women were blazing their own trails from the seat of motorcars. Around the time that Harriet Fisher and her crew were returning eastward on the last leg of their tour, a group of women, also from New Jersey, were making their own automotive history.

But unlike Harriet, who shared her Locomobile with a man, two servants, and pets, Alice Huyler Ramsey was heading from New York City to San

Francisco in a Maxwell Brisco, with three female companions. Just twenty-two years old, Alice, the wife of a United States Congressman, would become the first woman to actually drive a car across the United States with no man by her side.

Like Harriet, Alice turned to motor travel at a time when it was deemed an activity primarily for men. Harriet may have done as she pleased, unencumbered by familial ties, while Alice, on the other hand, felt she had to receive approbation from her husband to forge ahead on her own, and in doing so could have easily sworn off cars as a dangerous trend. But her husband appears to have been quite progressive, and Alice quite determined.

In 1961, Alice wrote in her autobiography, "I had always been fond of horses and hoped I would someday have one of my own.... Today I had the urge to drive Duke, the family horse, so I plucked up the courage and broached the subject hopefully."

On a warm spring day in 1908, she took the family horse and carriage for a solo trip. All went well until a noisy encounter with a Pierce Arrow automobile. Flying by at the startling speed of thirty miles-per-hour, the car spooked poor Duke.

"'Whoa, Duke, whoa!' I coaxed, as we flew up the empty street," Alice wrote. After she recounted the incident to her husband, he perceptively suggested that a car was a better alternative for her travels, and promptly purchased a brand new red Maxwell Runabout for her.

This was a turning point for Alice, who proved to be a natural behind the wheel. With the coaching of a professional tutor, she soon covered 6,000 miles and became an accomplished driver. Within a year's time she had begun participating in local racing events.

At one of those races she captured the attention of Cadwallader "Karl" Washburn Kelsey, a Swiss-born inventor, automobile manufacturer, and pioneer in the rototiller industry.

A sales manager for the Maxwell-Briscoe Car Company, Kelsey was a public relations genius. He took note of Alice's natural confidence at the wheel and her plucky personality, and proposed a spectacular publicity stunt that would change automotive history.

His plan called for Alice to venture cross country by car, as a number of men had already done. Traveling with Alice would be her two sisters-in-law, and a sixteen-year-old woman friend. Each participant received mechanical training, but Alice was the only trained driver.

Around the World in 1909

The four women traveled in a forest-green 30-horsepower Maxwell-Briscoe touring car provided by their sponsor. Equipped with a four cylinder engine, and fabric-covered tires, the vehicle had to be crank started and could go no faster than forty miles-per-hour.

On a rainy June 9, 1909, just a little more than a month before Harriet began her return drive home in the opposite direction, Ramsey and her crew departed from the Maxwell showroom located on Broadway, in midtown New York, in a section known as "Hell's Gate."

While both Alice and Harriet were woman of means who could have easily enjoyed the typically comfortable lifestyle of their social circles, both possessed a desire to challenge themselves by seeking excitement, adventure and learning on their own terms.

Each woman made their mark in history by fully developing their innate abilities and pursuing their dreams, mastering tasks that were normally associated with men.

In one area they differed, however. Alice was educated about the workings of an automobile, and did all of her own driving during her trek, writing in her autobiography, "I was a born mechanic, an inheritance from my father.... [He] had magic in his fingers, understood my interests, and encouraged me."

Alice Ramsey and her automotive companions drove approximately 3,800 miles in sixty days, and successfully completed their trip.

As cars improved, and their production increased, the poor excuses for roads on which they traveled had to co-evolve.

In 1912 America, the few miles of navigable or "improved" roads were found primarily in the outlying areas of large towns and cities. A road was regarded as "improved" or graded if it was covered in gravel or brick. These roads were bumpy and dusty in dry weather, and slick and nearly impassable during wet spells. Most frustrating to those who maneuvered over them, they often spread out from urban centers, ultimately leading motorists nowhere.

This predicament caught the problem-solving mind of Indianapolis businessman Carl G. Fisher, who had become intrigued with automotive advances while racing cars in France at the turn of the Twentieth Century. He observed that the Europeans were ahead of Americans in the development of innovative automobile design and craftsmanship, and devised an improved method of testing cars for the increasing number of automotive consumers.

Fisher also envisioned a dedicated track for racing cars, and became one of the architects and founders of the brick-covered Indianapolis Motor Speedway. With his idea now a reality, the Indianapolis 500 was initiated in 1909.

But Fisher was a restless visionary, and his views took him outside the confines of a race track to those of more practical matters. He set his sights on another grand idea that would tap into America's growing fascination with automobile travel. He introduced a plan for a highway which would offer one continuous route connecting the east and west coasts of the United States.

He called this project the Coast-to-Coast Rock Highway, a gravel-covered roadway that would cost approximately ten million dollars to complete, a relatively low figure even in 1912.

Fisher's plan called for communities along the route to provide the necessary building supplies for which they would receive the privilege of being a community situated along America's first transcontinental highway. Fisher also requested cash donations from American auto manufacturers and the industries that supplied accessories for them.

Despite several attempts, Fisher could not secure the support of Henry Ford, who did not believe that private industry should subsidize the development of the nation's roadways. This setback threatened to jeopardize Fisher's goal of having his highway built in time for the 1915 Panama-Pacific Exposition.

Undeterred, Fisher was energized by a nation that had become enthralled with the idea of this roadway, and ultimately found allies and financial support in the likes of Frank Seiberling, the president of Goodyear, and Henry Joy, president of the Packard Motor Company.

Upon learning that $1.7 million dollars had been slated to build a marble memorial to Abraham Lincoln, Joy campaigned to name the highway in Lincoln's honor and convinced those involved that a better tribute to Lincoln's legacy would be their support for a good quality road to serve a growing nation.

On July 1, 1913, the roadway was officially renamed the Lincoln Highway, with Henry Joy elected as President of its association. Carl Fisher, its Vice-President, wasted no time departing on a westward journey dubbed the "Hoosier Tour," to explore potential routes for the highway, one that at first included Colorado and Kansas.

Fisher was discrete about his plans because he wanted the nation as a whole to support the highway, not just the states through which it would pass. In actuality, even Fisher did not know the layout of the route, and no decision was to be made until after his tour.

Joy believed that directness was the crucial factor for the route, and supported the idea of bypassing scenic sights and large cities if necessary to avoid congestion and those awful narrow paths Harriet's Locomobile had endured.

He presented a road that included the states of New Jersey, Pennsylvania, Ohio, Indiana, Illinois, Iowa, Nebraska, Wyoming, Utah, Nevada, and California, many of the same states that had been included on Harriet's trip home. This was bad news for Colorado and Kansas, however, whose governors had greatly supported the Hoosier Tour and Fisher's intentions to include them.

The appeal from Colorado's governor was strong and persuasive, and the Highway Association conceded to his wishes and agreed to build a "dogleg" running from Big Springs, Nebraska southwest to Denver, and then back to the main highway at Cheyenne. But this compromise would prove to be unwise.

The problems that this dogleg allowance created for motorists became quickly apparent. Almost immediately, the Highway Association received letters trying to change the route. Its founders eventually dropped Denver from maps and travel guides, with a warning to motorists that signs posted in Big Springs pointing them to Denver were not to be heeded. Judging from Harriet's experiences on those trails, she probably would have advised motorists to steer clear too.

Apart from her role as roadway pioneer and anvil industrialist, what makes Harriet especially fascinating are the personal views which she espoused so vocally about what she believed were the roles of women in society.

Some might find it contradictory that she was quick to admonish some groups of women for wanting the very things she enjoyed. She had no problem with hardworking women, but she reasoned that if a woman was married, her primary role was to support her husband so that he could work from a solid home base.

Harriet believed that woman best served their country by being, "an able and competent helpmate," in their roles of wives and mothers, comparing a well-run household to a well-run business. In this sense, she believed that a woman "could be domestic and yet business-like."

She believed that moving away from this "model" was eroding the American family, and that even simple hobbies like needlework were being abandoned by farm women who preferred taking automobile trips!

Furthermore, Harriet did not support the women's right to vote, and shared her views freely, despite the opinions of her outspoken opponents.

This is illustrated in her participation in a public hearing conducted in March of 1912 by the Joint Judiciary Committee on a resolution to amend the New Jersey State Constitution to give the ballot to women. Harriet was one of many women who had converged in the Assembly Chamber of the State House to quickly fill the gallery seats before a delegation of suffragettes, who upon arriving later would find limited seating.

Finding these gallery seats occupied by their opponents, the suffragettes were not deterred. They squatted on the steps of the lower floor, filling the floor of the Assembly Chamber to full capacity.

Among those who spoke in favor of a woman's right to vote were the Chairwoman of the State Suffrage Association, Mrs. George T. Vickers, Mrs. Clara Schlee Laddey, President of the New Jersey Woman's Suffrage Association, representing the Joint Legislative Committee of all the women's clubs, and Miss Melinda Scott, an organizer for the American Federation of Labor. Scott argued that women needed the vote to improve their working conditions and to press for the enactment of pure food laws.

Fanny Garrison Villard, wife of railroad baron and publisher Henry Villard, promised political and social reforms if women got the ballot. The noted woman writer, Charlotte Anna Perkins Stetson Gilman, of San Diego, California, was next called upon to testify. She enumerated the states and countries where women could vote, asserting, "We have not as yet a democracy" until equal suffrage was the law of the land. "Women need votes just as much as men would if women had been making laws for men," she declared. Society would benefit because of women's ability to resolve issues and challenges that might arise.

Assistant Prosecutor George T. Vickers, of Hudson County, was the first male speaker. He asserted, "It was a delightful experience to be trotted forth by his wife to speak for suffrage." He noted that "...women have the inherent right to vote in New Jersey."

"No state had ever taken from women the right to vote once it had been given them, excepting New Jersey." "Equal suffrage," he maintained, "is inevitable because it stands for the highest civilization, including worldwide arbitration of great questions."

Harriet verbally attacked those suffragists for coming to the meeting with pennants, as the "antis" did not bring any. "They come carrying orange pennants bearing the motto 'Votes for Women,'" Harriet declared with derision. Her remark was met with mockery from her opponents, followed by a waving sea of swirling pennants to taunt her.

To these women, Harriet explained that she would introduce a speaker named Minnie Bronson who would reveal how they were being deceived by the promises made to them under the ballot. Miss Bronson, the editor of the *Woman Patriot*, an anti-suffrage newspaper, and a self-described "working woman," stated that she had investigated child labor conditions for the government and posed the question, "What was the discrimination against women in New Jersey, which was not overbalanced by rights in their favor?"

Bronson pointed out that workingmen were obligated "to pay the debts of their extravagant wives." She claimed laws protecting wage-earning women in the United States were better than those protecting wage-earning men and spoke of investigating strikes that involved women, where she asserted having the right to vote would not have aided their cause. Arguments to the contrary, she warned, were easily advanced by suffragists without having to substantiate them.

She went on to state the greatest changes ever made in English common law were for the benefit of women, despite the fact that they could not vote. "Votes for women are not needed to bring about better conditions for the females."

Despite her lack of faith in the promised societal reforms touted by those who supported the woman's vote, Harriet was a symbol of independence to those she met in her foreign voyages.

Her travel exploits may have captured the imagination of the world, but it was Harriet's business acumen and manufacturing leadership that earned her the respect of Victorian businessmen and political leaders. Wu Ting Fang, the Chinese diplomat who served as Chinese Ambassador to the United States, Minister of Foreign Affairs and, briefly, as Premier during the early years of the Republic of China, reportedly called her the most wonderful woman in America.

In discussing her worldwide associations, Harriet casually bandied about their titles without explaining exactly with whom she was lounging and dining. Many of these individuals were movers and shakers and social reformers in their own right; activists and leaders for social change, and in some cases, like the Maharaja of Benares, eager to impress a female American industrialist from America with his own iron-made creation.

The reigning Maharaja at the time of Harriet's visit to Benares was Prabhu Narayan Singh, whose reign lasted for forty-two years. He was knighted and later became an honorary colonel in the Indian Army. In 1911, he became the first Maharaja of the newly created princely state of Benares.

Judge Nehru, of whom Harriet spoke so glowingly, was Motilal Nehru, the quick-witted visionary who was much admired and respected by his supporters and his detractors alike. As illustrated in Harriet's fascinating accounts of her time spent with Judge Nehru and his family, Moltilal was an aficionado of good food, wine, and conversation.

Among his British and Indian friends and colleagues, he was renowned for his generous hospitality and lavish entertainment in his opulent home, Anand Bjiawn, which translates to Abode of Happiness. In 1900, Judge Nehru, a prominent lawyer, had purchased this palatial residence at 1 Church Road, Allahabad, for a sum of 19,000 rupees.

The house was in complete disrepair, but the estate was huge. Extensive renovation work was carried out over the next decade. Motilal also used his frequent visits to Europe to buy the choicest furniture and china, turning the mansion into a veritable palace resembling an elaborate replica of an English country estate. This was not lost on Harriet.

The palatial structure would ultimately become the cradle of the Indian Freedom Struggle which was to destroy British rule in India.

Motilal Nehru was a prominent member of the Indian National Congress Party, so a multitude of noted leaders and party activists visited the "Nehru House." This mansion became the virtual center of the Indian independence movement. It was informally the headquarters of the All India Congress Committee in the 1920s before it was donated by Motilal Nehru to the Indian National Congress in 1930 to serve as the party's official headquarters in the region.

The Nehrus built another house next to the old one and named it Anand Bhavan; the old house was renamed Swaraj Bhavan, which meant Abode of Freedom.

Indira Gandhi, India's former Prime Minister, donated Anand Bhavan to the nation in 1970 and it was transformed into a museum housing the books and memorabilia of her father and grandfather. Harriet would be pleased to know that it is now a place where classes are offered to teach arts and crafts to children.

Motilal, who was not born into wealth, is recalled by many who study Indian politics as second only to Gandhi in his legacy of reform. He was also the father of Jawaharlal Nehru.

Recognized as the architect of the modern Indian-state, Jawaharlal Nehru was the first Prime Minister of India and a central figure in Indian politics for much of the Twentieth Century. Gandhi referred to the love Motilal held for his son as "divine," and the story lines of father and son eventually merged into one vital story, that of the Indian Freedom Movement.

Under the tutelage of Mohandas Karamchand Gandhi, Jawaharlal would emerge as the principal leader of the Indian independence movement, ruling India from its establishment as an independent nation in 1947 until his death in office in 1964.

Jawaharlal's only daughter was Indira Gandhi, a ruthless social reformist who served as the chief of staff of her father's highly-centralized administration between 1947 and 1964, wielding considerable, but unofficial, influence in government. In 1966, she became India's third prime minister, and remained in that position until her assassination in 1984.

And what of the legacy of Harriet's favorite traveling royal family, His and Her Highness of Baroda, who also introduced social reform to India in their own manner? His Highness, whose full Indian name was Sayajirao Gaekwad III, was known as a "prince among the educators and an educator among the princes." He was instrumental in the banning of child marriage, the legislation of divorce, the removal of untouchability, the development of Sanskrit and ideological studies, and the encouragement of fine arts. He became the first ruler of his nation to introduce compulsory and free primary education for the citizens of his Indian state. His personal library became the core of the modern Central Library of Baroda, feeding a network of libraries in the towns and villages of his region.

With a striking resemblance to the Library of Congress in Washington D.C., the Central Library of Baroda was born in the Laxmi Vilas Palace, the residence of His Highness of Baroda, who seeded the library with a donation of 20,000 books from his own collection, much like Thomas Jefferson had seeded the Library of Congress with his collection.

During his tour of America in 1910, the one that began after his arrival in California with Harriet and her party, the Maharaja found his way to the East Coast, where he met William Alanson Borden, the librarian at the Young Men's Institute of New Haven in New Jersey. By the winter of that year, Borden had been summoned to Baroda by the Maharaja to help plan the new library.

Harriet was very impressed with Her Highness of Baroda, and considered it an honor to be her traveling companion. She was taken with the Maharini's observance of western customs and forward way of thinking. But interestingly, there appeared an article in a fall issue of *East West Magazine* where Her Highness had less than kind things to say about her experience with American women. One can only hope that Harriet was not offended, or did not feel she was the subject of the comments of the "Indian Queen," as she was referred to by the reporter in their interview.

Of the women she met in America, the Maharini reportedly stated, "They [American women] are tactless, which is only another way of saying 'unkind.' They are ignorant. Else why should they ask me, as many did, 'Are you an East Indian, a West Indian, or an American Indian?'" She went on to say that they [American women] were vulgar. "Why else should they stare at me on the streets as they do at the tigers in a circus parade, merely because I wear different and more reasonable garments than their own?"

Harriet's daring passing of business tycoon Sir Thomas Lipton's car, her subsequent acquisition of Billikins on his tea plantation, and his personally extended invitation for her to return to London for some automotive adventures also illustrate Harriet's penchant for attracting the attention of members of elite circles wherever she ventured.

Sir Thomas Lipton was one of Scotland's most famous and successful sons. An accomplished yachtsman, by the age of twenty-one Lipton had opened his first shop in Glasgow. His unique, brightly-illuminated store resembled those he had seen in his travels to America, and like his parents had, Lipton purchased eggs, meat, butter, and dairy directly from local farmers. Lipton set his sight on the tea trade, since it had become an increasingly popular beverage in the latter part of the 1880s, despite its prohibitive cost. Like he had done with the farmers, Lipton eliminated the middleman, and within a year was selling large quantities of tea in a number of packaging sizes in a variety of blends.

Over a period of time, Lipton quietly purchased several tea plantations on the island nation of Ceylon at distressed prices, enabling him to take control of the entire manufacturing process. Through his business acumen, Lipton became the trademark of a national commodity, and "Lipton's" became a widespread household brand.

Despite his considerable wealth and social standing, he never forgot his humble origins, and similar to Harriet, always showed compassion for the poor and unemployed.

Harriet was flattered that she had been given credit for opening the roadways of Japan. As her visit coincided with Japan's budding automotive industry, it is not surprising that the Mikado and his team of engineers were very curious about the inner workings of the cars owned by Harriet and the Raj from Baroda.

Around the World in 1909

Against the backdrop of the Japanese victory in the Russo-Japanese War in 1904, and the annexation of Korea by the Empire of Japan in 1910, the nation's automotive industry was heating up.

A brief timeline of the history of Japanese automotive history illustrates this. In 1898 a French Panhard-Levassor car is believed to have been the first car introduced in Japan. In 1904, Torao Yamaba produced the first domestically manufactured bus to transport his large family. The ten-seat, twenty-five horsepower, steam-powered "Yamaba" is often cited as possibly the first car made in Japan. One report indicates that a total of four Yamaba cars were made.

In 1907 the Automobile Trading Company produced the first entirely Japanese-made gasoline engine car, a 1.85 litre, petrol-powered vehicle of which twelve were produced. In 1910 the Kunisue Automobile Works produced a two cylinder, five horsepower Touring car and the following year manufactured a car named the "Tokyo," in cooperation with Tokyo Motor Vehicles, Ltd.

Even in the serene bucolic setting of rural New Jersey, Harriet appeared to somehow find herself ensconced in events of epic proportions. One may wonder how the circumstances surrounding the loss of Edgar Andrew might have affected Harriet and Silvano. Imagine how they would have felt if they had been able to read the letter written by Edgar that had been discovered in July of 2000 by British explorer Dick Burton. Burton, while exploring an area near the remains of the *Titanic*, had discovered Edgar's suitcase and pried it from its muddy bed. Amid several personal items recovered were books, postcards and letters.

On April 8, 1912, Edgar had written a letter to his friend Josey Cowan, who was in Argentina at the time, about his disappointment of not being able to see her. Its content is chilling:

You figure Josey I had to leave on the 17th this (month) aboard the "Oceanic", but due to the coal strike that steamer cannot depart, so I have to go one week earlier on board the "Titanic." It really seems unbelievable that I have to leave a few days before your arrival, but there's no help for it, I've got to go. You figure, Josey, I am boarding the greatest steamship in the world, but I don't really feel proud of it at all, right now I wish the "Titanic" were lying at the bottom of the ocean.

After posting the connection between Harriet and the Titanic online, I was contacted by Don Lynch, an expert and author on the subject. He happened to have known Edwina Celia Troutt. She told him that six months after contacting Harriet and Silvano, she had accepted the couple's invitation to visit Bella Vista Farm. In entries from her diary, it is clear how her experience on the *Titanic* had affected her, and gives a window into her impressions of Harriet, Silvano, and Harold Brooks.

Nov. 8th – Brother made enquiries at the South Station as to trains to Trenton, which he discovered were best to travel on Federal express all night. Had to get a waggle on to get already. Left Boston 8 p.m. on Express to Trenton. Said Good Bye to Elsie. Elsie promised to send telegram. Just after leaving Back Bay a sudden noise like an explosion caused me quite a little anxiety. I began to wonder if the xpress [sic] would deliver me safe & sound. No Titanic troubles.

Nov. 9th – Reached Trenton after a somewhat tiresome journey, but greatly enjoyed the lunch Elsie had fixed for me. To my very great surprise no one to meet me. I hailed a Cabby. He knew not the time. Finally I telephoned then cabbed to the office. Fisher & Norris. As I arrived the secretary ushered me into the office awaiting the arrival of Mrs. Andrew.

...Mrs. Andrew arrived with Mr. Brookes. My, what a different woman to what I had pictured. Anyhow I was very warmly greeted & after a little chatting was in the Auto en route for home. Reached home, an Ideal Farm house.

From Nov. 10th Sunday - ... *Monday* – Breakfast in bed. Got down about 10 o'c. Everything so quiet. Miss Fisher [most likely Harold's sister] & I went for quite a little country walk. Mrs. Andrew returned from the plant & joined us in conversing, also Mr. B. Mrs. Andrew is a very humorous person & kept us roaring althrough [sic]) lunch. After lunch we visited the farm, cows & horses, etc.

Tuesday – Mrs. Andrew stayed home with us & discovered that Mr. B. had been marching around with two letters in pocket for 10 days, mine being included. So that accounts for my arrival unannounced. Miss Fisher departs for home after lunch, Dear old lady. I did like her. Mrs. Andrew had a serious talk with me which I thought rather personal, but which ended in her saying she would like to convert her empty Stone cottage into an old fashioned English Tea house & put me in the commission but that causes for a lot of consideration.

It is safe to say that Harriet lead a life that was not typical by any standard. She also had the ability to surround herself with those on which she could rely, including the incomparable Harold Brooks. Of him, she paid the highest compliment when she discussed their travels in the American West.

"Our greatest annoyances occurred after our return to our own country. I don't believe that any other car could have stood a stronger test, and I want Mr. Brooks to have all the credit for taking the car over its remarkable journey, for he certainly used rare judgment in handling the machine and getting us out of uncomfortable situations."

The experiences of his trip around the world had a lasting effect on Harold. In his role of driver, mechanic and general overseer of the trip, Harold was thorough and dependable. This was evident in the numerous detailed entries in the journal he kept during the trip.

These entries relay in detail his role in the handling of financial transactions, licensing, and the concern he shared for keeping the Locomobile in top shape. It was a major responsibility for a young man with a limited education.

Harold was very close to his family, often sending money home and constantly and loyally writing long letters or postcards to his family members.

Throughout his travels, he thoughtfully purchased gifts for everyone. He would buy puppy biscuits for Honkie or a bouquet of flowers for Harriet on her birthday. In Darjeeling he compiled an incomplete list of the presents he had acquired for his parents and five siblings back home.

Father
Mother   *Shawl - Egypt*
Mabelle   *Buckle – Kandy*
Anna   *Buckle – Kandy*
Helen   *Scarf – Benares*
Oliver   *Scarf-pin – Egypt*
Marion

He was matter-of-fact in his depiction of events, and did not embellish his experiences, as witnessed in his final diary entry made the evening of his return home, when this practical and unassuming man simply wrote, "Unpacked and cleared things away. Wrote several letters. Had car washed."

Harold married in 1915, and with the help of Harriet, opened an automobile dealership with his brother, selling car parts and tires. By 1920, he owned three shops, but he lost everything during the stock market crash of 1929, never to fully recover.

Albert and Maria's relationship presented the love affair of the trip. Despite sharing a backseat with "baggage and boxes and baskets and everything piled in front of them and between them" a relationship eventually blossomed. Shortly after the party returned home, they became husband and wife, and remained faithful employees of Harriet's until her passing.

Honkie, Billikens and Jappy lived out their lives comfortably on the grounds of Bella Vista, no doubt enjoying the run of the house and grounds, much to the delight of Harriet and her visitors.

During difficult economic times, Harriet found it rewarding to see that Bella Vista functioned as a model of cooperative farming, providing employment opportunities for local men.

Harriet passed away at Bella Vista on November 17, 1939. Her obituary in the *New York Times* praised her for having been the only woman in the nation who had "actively engaged in the anvil and iron working industry." It was also noted how she responded immediately to those in need in the aftermath of the Johnstown Flood in Pennsylvania and reported that Harriet's beloved *Villa Carlotta* and her yacht had been seized by the Italian Government during war time.

The *Trenton Evening Times* lauded her for being the first female member of the National Association of Manufacturers and credited her for not only authoring *A Woman's World Tour in a Motor*, but also other works such as *Christmas Abroad*, *My Four Acre Farm* and *School Life in Germany*. Listed among her social and political affiliations were the Elna Royal Yacht Club, the Professional Women's League of New York, the New York Women's Republican Club, the National Authors' Club and the Ohio Daughters' Club of New York.

Silvano retired from the Argentine Navy in 1917. He became an American citizen and assumed executive responsibilities at the Anvil Works, successfully modernizing and expanding operations. He remarried in 1940, and continued to run the anvil factory. However, the following year he took ill, and despite his physician's advisement he continued to direct the affairs of the anvil business that was at the time completely engaged in war production. He continued in this capacity until his death in August of 1942.

BIBLIOGRAPHY

BOOKS

<u>Viel, Duster and Tire Iron,</u> Ramsey, Alice Huyler, Castle Press,1961
<u>A Woman's World-Tour in a Motor,</u> Fisher, Harriet White; Lippincott, 1911
<u>Who's Who in America</u>, Vol. 7, 1913, edited by Leonard, John, William and Marquis, Albert Nelson
<u>The Locomobile Book: The Car of 1911</u>, The Original Owner's Manual for the Locomobile, The Locomobile Company, 1911
<u>A Suitcase from the Titanic: Translated from the original by Marilyn Myerscrough</u>, Dick, Rodolfo Enrique, WIT Press, 2002

NEWSPAPERS

"Fisher-White," Wedding Announcement, July 30, 1898
"Badly Hurt by Motor Car," *The New York Times,* April 7, 1906
"Hard Times Over, Say Manufacturers," *The New York Times*, May 21, 1908
"Woman to Tour the World in an Automobile," *The New York Times*, June 27, 1908
"Woman Meets Adventure in Motor Tour of the World," *The New York Times*, 1910
"Woman Tells Men How to Boss Men," *The New York Times*, January 28, 1913
"Trenton Woman is Industrial Success," *Trenton Sunday Times Advertiser*, July 11, 1926
"Burial Tomorrow For Mrs. Andrew: Woman Anvil Maker Long Famous As Traveler and Author," *The Trenton Evening Times*, November 17, 1939
Mrs. H.F. Andrew, 72, Owned Anvil Works: Trenton Woman Was Only One of Sex in the Iron Industry," *The New York Times*, November 17, 1939
"Was Head of Fisher and Norris Anvil Works," *The Trenton Times*, August 25, 1942

Bibliography

Other Sources

Document: "History of Fisher & Norris Anvil Works"- a version of an article that appeared in the *Trenton Sunday Times Advertiser*, September 26, 1951, corrected and supplemented by Harold Fisher Brooks.

Harold Fisher Brooks' Diary of the Trip around the World January 1, 1910 – August 16 1910 [1908-1909]

Harold Fisher Brooks' Talk of his World Tour, 1909-1910 (Given October 24 and 26, 1956)

E-mail correspondences with author Don Lynch

Letters written by Harold Brooks

Interviews

Calgano, Ellie; Site Manager at the Benjamin Temple House, Ewing Township Historical Preservation Society – November 9, 2010 at Ewing Township Historical Society

Andrew, Fred - Son of Silvano Andrew, husband of Harriet Fisher Andrew at the time of her death, November 9, 2010 at Ewing Township Historical Society

Mello, Tara Baukus; Auto Writer - 2004 (via telephone)

Urban, Rebecca -Granddaughter of Harold Fisher Brooks - ongoing; 2010- to present

Internet

http://timestraveler.blogs.nytimes.com/2009/10/26/prince-ito-japanese-statesman-is-assassinated/?_php=true&_type=blogs&_r=0

Dr. Horatio Nelson Jackson http://www.pbs.org/horation/wheel

http://en.wikipedia.org/wiki/George_Schuster_(driver)

http://en.wikipedia.org/wiki/Lincoln_Highway

http://query.nytimes.com/gst/abstract.html?res=F40814F93D5B13738DDDA10A94D9405B838DF1D3 Wright, Kevin; Blog Post, February 25, 2012

http://astrological-thoughts.blogspot.com/2012/09/maharaja-of-benaras-sir-prabhu-narayan.html MAHARAJA of BENARAS - Sir Prabhu Narayan Singh (KASHI NARESH), Blog Post, September 29, 1912

Bibliography

http://www.biography.com/people/motilal-nehru-9421272#awesm=~oFABFJUQOiVqZb

http://en.wikipedia.org/wiki/Jawaharlal_Nehru

http://www.bbc.co.uk/history/historic_figures/gandhi_mohandas.shtml

http://www.msubaroda.ac.in/page.php?id=69

Hindu Women Look at Women's Suffrage in America: Vision of American Freedom http://www.oldmagazinearticles.com/eastern_women_view_of_america

http://en.wikipedia.org/wiki/Thomas_Lipton

http://afe.easia.columbia.edu/special/japan_1750_meiji.htm

http://www.carhistory4u.com/the-last-100-years/car-manufacturers-by-country/japan

http://en.wikipedia.org/wiki/Automotive_industry_in_Japan

INDEX

A Woman's World Tour in a Motor (book) 4, 200
Agabeg, Major F. S., 85-86
All India Congress Committee, 194
Ama-Terasu, (Goddess of the Sun), 144
American Express Company, 17, 32
American Federation of Labor, 192
Anand Bhavan (Abode of Freedom), 194
Anand Bjiawn (Abode of Happiness), 194
Andrew, Alfredo Silvano, 1, 3-4, 6, 177, 180-181, 197-198, 200
Andrew, Edgar Samuel, 3, 6, 179, 180-181, 197
Andrew, Harriet Fisher, 1
Antonio (translator), 38, 45, 50-51, 54, 58-59, 77-79, 81, 83, 86, 88, 113
Automobile Association of America (AAA), 1, 183
Automobile Blue Book, 170
Automobile Club of America (original AAA), 110, 177
Automobile Trading Company, 197
Batcheler, Albert E., 5, 7, 17, 19-20, 25, 33-35, 40-42, 44-45, 50, 59, 72, 7-78, 83-84, 88, 95, 97, 111, 115, 118, 121, 134, 137, 151, 153, 159, 162, 165, 167, 172, 181, 199, 324
Bella Vista Farm, 1-2, 45, 69, 87, 111, 175, 177, 180, 198, 200
Bennett, James Gordon, 95-96
Bennett, James Gordon, Sr., 95
Beulow, 105
Bhor Ghat, 37
Birnie, C.M., 107, 108, 111, 116, 123, 127
Blériot XI, 29
Blériot, Louis, 29
Bombay Harbor, 36
Borge, Maria, 17, 19, 25, 34, 41-42, 44, 54, 58-59, 62, 67, 75, 77, 80-81, 84, 86, 90, 97, 110, 133, 159, 164-165, 180-181, 199, 325
Bronson, Minnie, 192-193
Brooks, Harold Fisher, 3, 13-21, 23-25, 28-29, 32-39, 43-46, 50, 52-55, 57, 59, 62, 66, 70-73, 75-81, 83-86, 90-98, 105-115, 117-119, 123, 125-128, 131-138, 140-141, 143-144, 147, 152-153, 155, 158-160, 162-163, 165, 171-172, 175, 187, 198-199
Brown's Shipping Company, 107
Bryan, William Jennings, 140
Bullock, Edward C., 177
Burns, Ken, 187
Burton, Dick, 197
California
  Placerville, 154, 156
  Sacramento, 154
  San Diego, 192
  San Francisco, 100, 148, 151, 153-155, 157, 170, 188
  Stockton, 154
  Sugar Loaf, 154-155

Index

Carlotta (ship), 30
Catherine Apgar (ship), 108
Central Library of Baroda, 195
Ceylon (now Sri Lanka)
   Anuradhapura, 95
   Colombo, 88-89, 93- 94, 96, 98
   Dumbera, 96
   Kandy, 96
   Puttalam, 95
Chambal River, 50
Chateau de Fontainebleau, 17
China
   Peking, 102, 104
   Shanghai, 99-101, 103-104
Christmas Abroad (book), 200
Civil War, 10
Cliff House, 153
Coey, C.A., 187
Colorado
   Denver, 166, 168-169, 191
   Sterling, 169
Cowan, Josey, 180, 197
Curtiss, Glenn, 29, 95
The Daily Express (newspaper), 29
Daily Gazette (newspaper), 178
Daitokwan Hotel, 124
Dalai Lama, 90
de Reuter, Baroness Marguerite, 95
Delta (ship), 98-99
Democratic State Convention, 169
Devil's Bridge, 23, 116, 181
Devil's Gulch, 23, 25, 163
District of Colombia, 15
Eagle Anvil Works, 10
Egypt
   Cairo, 32-33
   Port Said, 32, 34
Elna Royal Yacht Club, 200
The Empress, 91
England
   London, 9, 14, 17, 196
Fetch, E. Thomas, 187
Fisher & Norris Anvil Works, 1, 6, 10-11, 13, 178, 200

Fisher, Bishop John, 14
Fisher, Carl, 183, 189-191
Fisher, Clark, 9-12, 91, 110, 176, 182
Fisher, Mark, 10
Flyer, Thomas, 187
France
   Bois de Boulogne (public park), 19
   Cherbourg, 17
   Contrexeville, 20-21, 23
   Marseille, 30, 32
   Paris, 17-19, 26, 38, 176
   Rheims, 95
Fujikawa River, 126
Galle Face Hotel, 93-94, 97
Gandhi, Indira, 194-195
Gandhi, Mohandas Karamchand, 195
Ganges River, 57, 62-64, 70-73, 184
Germany
   Hildesheim, 9
Gillette, Charles Howard, 171
Gilman, Charlotte Anna Perkins Stetson, 192
Godavari River, 43
Goodyear Tire & Rubber Company, 190
Grace Church, 180
Grand Hotel d'Establissement, 21
Great Northern Hotel, 58
Great Prize of Brescia, 29
Green River, 164
Gwalior Light Rail, 47
Gwalior State, 49-50
Hakone Pass, 129, 181
Hakone Range, 131, 135
Hanks, Tom, 187
Hansen, Hans, 187
Hendrickson, Franklin, 178
Henshaw Hotel, 170
Highway Association (Lincoln), 191
Himalayan Mountain Range, 89
Hoosier Tour, 190, 191
Horatio's Drive, 187
Hot Creek Ranch, 158
Illinois
   Chicago, 159, 170-171

INDEX

India
  Agra, 46, 50-51, 53
  Aligarh, 53
  Allahabad, 55, 57, 63, 70, 194
  Asenol, 85, 86
  Benares, 69-75, 193
  Bombay (Mumbai), 31-32, 34-39, 60, 87-88, 176
  Buhri, 85
  Burdwan, 86
  Calcutta, 6, 35, 37, 39, 75, 83- 89, 91-92, 176
  Darjeeling, 89-90, 199
  Dehri-on-Sone, 75, 81
  Delhi, 53-55, 60
  Dhulia, 43
  Goona, 46
  Gwalior State, 46, 70
  Gya, 80-81, 83
  Igatpuri, 43
  Indore, 44
  Karli, 37
  Khardi, 40- 42
  Madhya Pradesh, 50
  Maharshtra, 43
  Malabar Hill, 37
  Malegaon, 43
  Mhow, 44
  Munar, 43
  Nahsik, 43
  Sarangpur, 44
  Shapura, 40
  Tagpturi, 40
  Trimbak, 43
Indian Freedom Movement, 194
Indian Independence Movement, 57, 194- 195
Indian National Congress Party, 194
Indiana
  La Porte, 171
  Valparaiso, 171
  Waterloo, 171
Indianapolis 500-Mile Race, 189
Indianapolis Motor Speedway, 189

Iowa
  Davenport, 170
  Des Moines, 170
  Newton, 170
  Iowa Auto Supply Company, 170
Italy
  Brescia, 28-29, 170
  Cadenabbia, 30
  Genoa, 31-32, 35
  Magenta, 30
  Montichiari, 28
  Rome, 28
  Venice, 28
Ito, Prince Hirobumi, 138, 140
Izamage, Guardian of Japan, 144
Jackson, Horatio Nelson, 187
Japan
  Atami, 114, 126, 132-138
  Kobe, 107-110, 113-115, 123
  Kyoto, 112, 114, 118-120
  Nagasaki, 105-107
  Nagoya, 114, 120-121, 123
  Nara, 118-119
  Nikko, 114, 144
  Osaka, 109, 112-114, 118, 126
  Shizuoka, 124
  Tokyo, 1, 107, 114, 121, 125, 137, 140-143, 146, 160
  Yokohama, 114, 121, 123, 128, 138, 140-143, 147, 152
Jeanne d'Arc (Joan of Arc), 21
Jefferson, Thomas, 195
Jeffries, Jim, 155, 157
Johnson, Jack, 155
Johnson-Jeffries Fight, 155
Johnstown Flood (Great Flood of 1889), 200
Joy, Henry, 190
The Jungle Book - R. Kipling, 69
Kanaya Hotel, 144
Kelsey, Cadwallader "Karl" Washburn, 188
Kipling, Rudyard, 69
Knutsford Hotel, 163

207

INDEX

Kobe Herald, 110
Krarup, Marius C., 187
Kunisue Automobile Works, 197
Kyoto Hotel, 118
Laddey, Clara Schlee, 192
Lake Como, 12, 14, 17, 27-28, 30, 96, 140, 152
Lake Maggiore, 26
Lake Rhoda, 169
Lake Tahoe, 155-156
Lauries' Great Northern Hotel, 50
Laxmi Vilas Palace, 195
Library of Congress, 195
Lincoln Highway (Coast-to-Coast Rock Highway), 182-183, 190
Lincoln, President Abraham, 190
Lindenthal, Gustav, 2
Lipton Tea Company, 4
Lipton, Sir Thomas, 93, 97-98, 196
Locomobile Company (of America), 4, 151, 153
Lynch, Don, 197
Maharaja of Baroda (Sayajirao Gaekwad III), 67, 98, 143, 195
Maharini of Baroda, 106, 148, 195, 196
Mahaweli Ganga, 96
Malaysia
    Penang, 99
Mantua, 32
Maryland
    Baltimore, 15
    Havre de Grace, 15
    Perryville, 15
Massachusetts
    Boston, 31, 152, 170, 198
    Lowell, 13
Mathewson, E.L., 187
Maxwell-Briscoe Car Company, 188
Mayflower (ship), 14
Michelin Tire Corporation, 154
Mikado Emperor Meiji the Great, 145
Mikado Hotel, 109, 112, 114
Mikado Palace, 109, 112, 114, 120, 143-145, 196

Mikimoto, 143
Moana Hotel, 147
Monkey Temple, 70
Mount Fuji, 129
Mumtaz Mahal, 51
My Four Acre Farm (book), 200
Nagoya Hotel, 121
Namouna (yacht), 96
Nara Deer Park, 119
National Association of Manufacturers (NAM), 110, 200
National Authors' Club, 200
Nebraska
    Grand Island, 169
    North Platte, 169
    Ogallala, 169
    Omaha, 170
Nehru, Jawaharlal, 57, 194
Nehru, Judge Motilal, 55, 57-60, 62-67, 70, 193-194
Nevada
    Cherry Creek, 160
    Cobra, 160
    Currant Creek, 159
    Ely, 159
    Grangerville, 156
    Hawthorne, 156
    Hot Creek, 158-159
    Kingsbury, 156
    Lucin, 160
    Lucky Boy Camp, 156
    Mina, 156-157
    Montello, 160
    Tonopah, 157-159
    Wellington, 156
New Jersey
    Elizabeth, 14
    Ewing, 1
    Lakewood, 183-184
    Menlo Park, 11
    Trenton, 2, 10, 16, 152, 176-177, 184, 198
New Jersey Woman's Suffrage Association, 192

INDEX

New York (ship), 17
New York
  Buffalo, 16
  Catskills, 16
  Flushing, 2, 69, 177
  New York City, 1, 16-17, 176, 180, 187
  Rochester, 175-176
  Troy, 10
New York Herald, 95
New York Times, 2, 12, 103, 145, 184, 200
New York Women's Republican Club, 200
Norris, John, 10
Oceanic (RMS) (ship), 180, 197
Ohio
  Cleveland, 9, 15, 175
  Painesville, 175
  Sandusky, 171-173
  Toledo, 171
  Youngstown, 15
Ohio Daughters' Club of New York, 200
Oriental Place Hotel, 141
Osaka Daily News, 109
P & O Steamship Company, 88
Pacific Commercial Advertiser, 147
Pacific Mail Company, 152
Packard Motor Company, 190
Palace Hotel, 151, 154
Palace Ramnagar, 71
Panama Canal, 182
Panama-Pacific International Exposition, 190
Pennsylvania
  Erie, 16, 175
  Pittsburgh, 15
Persia (SS)(ship), 35
Prince Ito, 142
Professional Women's League of New York, 200
Public Broadcasting System (PBS), 187
Queen Hotel, 96

Queen Victoria, 91
Ramsey, Alice Huyler, 187-189
Reed, Joshua, 177
Reed, Judge Alfred, 177
Rensselaer Polytechnic Institute, 10
River Seine, 18
Roberts, Montague, 187
The Rochester Herald, 175
Rospinin, Brocca, 30
Rougier, Henri, 29, 30
Russo-Japanese War, 197
Saint Gotthard's Pass, 24
Sanford Motor Company, 169
Saraswati River, 57
School Life in Germany (book), 200
Schuster, George, 187
Scott, Melinda, 192
Seiberling, Frank, 190
Sha Jahan, 51
Siberia (steamship), 147-148, 152
Singh, Prabhu Narayan, 193
Snider, Austin B., 178
Solimney, Zucchini, 28
Soochow Creek, 100
Standard Motor Construction Company, 14
State Suffrage Association, 192
Strait of Malacca, 99
Suez Canal, 32
Suffragettes, 182, 192
Susquehanna River, 15
Swaraj Bhavan (Abode of Bliss), 58, 194
Swaraj Party (Indian political party), 57
Taj Mahal (Crown of Palaces), 35, 51
Taj Mahal Hotel, 35
Tapti River, 43
Titanic (RMS)(ship), 3, 6, 180-181, 197-198
Tokugawa Dynasty/Shogunate, 144
Tokyo Motor Vehicles, Ltd., 197
Trenton Evening Times (newspaper), 200
Trimbakeshwar Shiva Temple, 43
Trotti, Marquesa, 27, 30

INDEX

Troutt, Edwina Celia, 181, 198
Uchiami, Frank (Japanese translator), 112-118, 124, 128-129, 132-136, 138-142
Union Pacific Railroad, 160
United States Navy, 10, 110
Utah
   Kelton, 161, 163
   Ogden, 160, 163
   Salt Lake City, 163
   Terrace, 160
Vanderbilt Cup Race, 13
Verne, Jules, 147
Vickers, George T., 192
Vickers, Mrs. George T., 192
Villa Carlotta, 12, 17, 27, 30, 115, 177, 200
Villard, Fanny Garrison, 192
Villard, Henry, 192
Vuitton Rue Scribe, 19
Waterloo Hotel, 171
Westminster Abbey, 14
White City (Lakeside Amusement Park), 169
White, Peregrine, 14
Windsor Castle, 91
Woman Patriot, 193
Wright Brothers, 29
Wu Ting Fang, 103, 193
Wyman, George A., 187
Wyoming
   Bitter Creek, 164
   Cheyenne, 163, 165, 167, 191
   Evanston, 163-164
   Granger, 164
   Hanna, 165
   Laramie, 166-167
   Medicine Bow, 165-166
   Point of Rocks, 164
   Rawlins, 165
   Red Desert, 164
   Rock Springs, 164
Yamakawa, Yoshihiro, 109
Yamuna River, 50, 57
Young Ladies' Classical Seminary, 9

ABOUT THE AUTHOR

Lisa Begin-Kruysman resides and works from her waterfront community on the New Jersey coastline, with her husband Rich and foster-to-forever dog Teddy always nearby. Best known for her inspirational writing about the dog-human bond, her works of fiction and nonfiction have received positive reviews and continue to attract readers worldwide. She is the National Dog Week Blogger and serves on the board of Healing Companions, Inc.